Introducing Decision Support Systems

PAUL FINLAY

INTRODUCING DECISION SUPPORT SYSTEMS

 BLACKWELL

First published 1994
Reprinted 1995

NCC Blackwell Ltd.
108 Cowley Road
Oxford OX4 1JF
UK

Basil Publishers
238 Main Street
Cambridge, Massachusetts 02142
USA

British Library Cataloguing in Publication Data

British Library data is available

American Library of Congress Data

Library of Congress data is available

Typeset in 10 on 12pt Palatino by H&H Graphics, Blackburn.
Printed and bound in Great Britain by Hartnolls Limited, Bodmin, Cornwall.

ISBN 1-85554-314-1

This book is printed on acid-free paper

Contents

TO MY WIFE
ANN

Acknowledgements

My thanks are due to Mrs Barbara Clarke for assistance with formulating the types of Decision Support Systems that are described in Chapter 4, and which form the principal rationale for the structure of this book. Barbara also contributed to the sections concerned with Executive Information Systems in Chapters 5 and 11.

Other colleagues at Loughborough to whom I am indebted are David Coates, Neil Doherty, Chris Marples and John Wilson who very kindly provided details of computer software. For the same reason, I would also like to thank Valerie Belton, Robert Fildes, Simon French and Mike Pidd.

I am indebted to Mr John Hough, Operational Research manager of Rolls-Royce plc. who first brought to my attention the work of Alter on whose work the classification of Data Retrieval Systems builds.

Additionally, I would like to thank Professor Colin Eden for giving generous permission to use his numerous writings throughout Chapters 8, 9 and 14.

I am indebted to the following for allowing copyright material to be quoted:

Prentice Hall International, Englewood Cliffs, NJ, for allowing reproduction of Figure 4.2 from page 286 of 'Structuring of Organizations: A Synthesis of the Research' by H. Mintzberg, 1979.

The University of Pittsburg Press for allowing reproduction of Figure 4.3 from the chapter by Thompson and Tuden entitled 'Strategies, Structures and Processes' which appeared in the book 'Comparative Studies in Administration' edited by James D. Thompson et al., 1959.

The Chartered Institute of Management Accountants for allowing reproduction of Figures 4.4 and 4.5 from the article by Michael Earl in 'Management Accounting and Practice' edited by David Cooper and Robert Scapens.

MIS Quarterly for allowing reproduction of portions of three articles:

by P.G.W. Keen entitled 'Value Analysis: Justifying Decision Support Systems', March 1981, pp 1–15, which appears on page 173.

by J. Miller and B.A. Doyle entitled 'Measuring the Effectiveness of Computer-based Information Systems', March 1984, pp 17-25, which appears on page 172.

by R.T. Watson, G. DeSanctis and M.S. Poole entitled 'Using a GDSS to facilitate Group Consensus: Some Intended and some Unintended Consequences', September 1988, pp 463–478, which appears on pages 150 and 151.

The Addison-Wesley Publishing Company for allowing reproduction of portions of two texts:

by E.D. Carlson entitled 'An Approach for Designing Decision Support Systems' which is Chapter 2 of 'Building Decision Support Systems' edited by J.L. Bennett, 1982 which appears on pages 249 and 250.

by P.G.W. Keen and M.S. Scott Morton entitled 'Decision Support Systems: An Organizational Perspective', 1978, which appears on pages 36 and 37.

Information Resources for allowing reproduction of Figure 5.2.

Peter Bartram for allowing reproduction of Figure 5.4.

Ellis Horwood Ltd for allowing reproduction of Table 10.1

Lotus Developments (UK) for allowing reproduction of Figure 10.3

Microsoft$^{(R)}$ Ltd. for allowing reproduction of Figure 10.4.

Introduction

WHO SHOULD READ THIS BOOK

The advent of powerful yet user-friendly computer packages that contain at their core mathematical and logical models, enables many esoteric management tools to be made available much more widely than ever before. This book is an introduction to this area. It is aimed both at practitioners in the business community and at students studying in Higher Education establishments.

Although the terms 'Business' is used frequently throughout the book, the contents are equally applicable to managers operating in not-for-profit organisations. This book should appeal to anyone who is involved in creating or implementing Decision Support Systems. This would include accountants, managers in all business functions and computer professionals.

Few assumptions are made about the reader's prior knowledge: the one assumption is that the reader will have used a computer, and have a feel for what computer systems can do.

ABOUT THIS BOOK

In the 1970s a new view of how computers could be used to help managerial decision making emerged. This view has manifested itself in the form of Decision Support Systems. Decision Support Systems contain ideas from several schools associated with information technology and decision analysis, and hold much promise for improving both the efficiency and effectiveness of managerial decision making. Today, Decision Support Systems are well established in many organisations.

This book begins with a review of the nature of managerial work and of business problems, with particular emphasis on planning and control. The rationale for starting in this way is to establish the framework for the use of Decision Support Systems by managers in Business, and to introduce formally the terminology of the subject. Of particular concern are the definitions of information and intelligence, as these are used to define the major divisions of Decision Support Systems that structure the whole book.

A literature review in search of a definition of Decision Support Systems is undertaken in Chapter 3. The outcome is a simple definition that encompasses any computer-based system that helps managers to be better at tackling problems. This broad view enables all aspects of decision making to be covered, and thus includes systems that are often excluded from books on decision support, such as Management Information Systems and those to help group decision making processes. In Chapter 4 two broad classes of Decision Support System are identified. These are Management Information Systems and Management Intelligence Systems. Each of these classes is subdivided into two further sub-classes; Management Information Systems into Data Retrieval and Extrapolatory Systems, Management Intelligence Systems into Preference Determination and Scenario Development Systems. Further subdivisions follow. Concise definitions of all the systems are given. The rationale for the categorisation is the different objectives for the systems and the different ways in which they would be developed and implemented.

The tools, techniques and methodologies associated with each type of Decision Support System are considered in Chapters 5 through 8. Proprietary software to support each type of Decision Support System is given at the end of each section. The particular computer packages listed are those that the author has used and found valuable and those recommended by experienced practitioners in the field. The dominant criteria that have been used in the selection are that the packages should be good of their kind and should not be domain specific; i.e. they should have a wide applicability and not be restricted to use in one specialised functional area of Business. The emphasis is on microcomputer software, as the features of microcomputers generally make them better vehicles for Decision Support Systems than mainframe computers. A list of the software packages mentioned in this book is given in Appendix C, together with the relevant contact addresses and telephone numbers.

Data Retrieval Systems are discussed in Chapter 5. Particular emphasis is given to Executive Information Systems which are currently exciting great interest.

In Chapter 6 the tools for the creation of Extrapolatory Systems are categorised and described. The tools and techniques available for such systems are those of Management Science. The selection of the tools has been made on the grounds of popularity and use. However, the complexity of several of the techniques underlying these systems is such that it was not considered reasonable in this introductory text to burden the average reader with their intricacies. Consequently, only a simple treatment has been given. Readers interested in knowing more about the techniques will need to refer to other, suggested texts.

Chapters 7 and 8 deal with the two types of Management Intelligence System. In Chapter 7 Preference Determination Systems are described. Such systems differ from Extrapolatory Systems in that the modelling is not so closely structured, they do not rely on such esoteric techniques and there is more emphasis on the process of decision making. Scenario Development Systems, which place even less constraints on managerial thought processes, are described in Chapter 8.

The categorisation derived in Chapter 4 is in terms of Decision Support Systems for the individual manager. Chapter 9 looks at an additional area of growing interest, that of group decision support. The special requirements for systems to support group activity are considered. Of particular interest are the requirements for strategic decision support, and the discussion in this chapter complements the discussion of Executive Information Systems given in Chapter 5. The discussions also link to Chapter 14 in which metasystems are considered.

In Chapters 5 through 9 the emphasis is on two of the major elements of Decision Support Systems – on the data and logic models. The dearth of discussion about the third major element – of the human-computer interface is rectified in Chapter 10.

Decision Support Systems have had a chequered career as far as success is concerned. How success for Decision Support Systems can be defined is discussed in Chapter 11.

The leitmotiv of this book is that different types of Decision Support System require different methods of development and implementation. These requirements are explored in Chapter 12, with the associated considerations of validity and validation treated in Chapter 13. Quantitative scales of measurement are fully described, since the level of measurement has a significant impact on the way in which Decision Support Systems are implemented, and is a topic seldom addressed.

It is important to consider the wider, organisational context within which Decision Support Systems, both individual and group, are used. Providing the appropriate problem solving culture within an organisation lies in the realm of organisational development. Metasystems are now available that could provide part of this culture, and in Chapter 14 two such metasystems are described. The rationale for such a depth of discussion of the methodologies is that these systems are not widely known, yet are at such a stage of development that their use could provide substantial benefits. These systems place their emphasis very strongly on the process of decision making rather than on the tools and techniques employed, and on their concern for consensus and commitment to action.

Chapter 15 is concerned with a consideration of Expert Systems. The commonality between Expert Systems and more conventional decision support tools are explored, and Expert Systems are placed within the typology of Decision Support Systems.

In Chapter 16 a brief look is taken at the future of Decision Support Systems over the next decade. The prognosis is good.

This book is aimed at the practicing manager and at students in Higher Education. Without wishing to slight the many women in both categories, the male version of pronouns and possessives will be used throughout for simplicity.

1 The Nature of Managerial Work and of Business Problems

It would be inappropriate to begin a detailed exploration of Decision Support Systems (DSS) before considering the context in which they would be used. This context is important, because it defines both the potential for DSS and also the limits to their application. To focus discussion, it is necessary to have a definition of DSS. However, the arguments surrounding a considered definition are too complex to develop so early in this book and are deferred until Chapter 3. A definition sufficient for our immediate purposes is simply to consider a DSS to be a computer-based system that aids the process of decision making. With this definition, consideration will first be given to the nature of managerial work. This will be followed by a consideration of the nature of business problems and the ways open to managers to deal with them.

THE NATURE OF MANAGERIAL WORK

In the past, many systems designed to help management make decisions have had a great deal of time and effort spent on them yet have been little used. Partly this was because of the unrealistic expectations that managers had for the systems. Often, however, the systems were constructed by people with little appreciation of the context in which the systems would be used: consequently the systems were inappropriate to the problems facing the decision-maker – created too late, inflexible, demanding too much data input, too complex and demanding too much time from the manager. It will be appreciated from this that to guide the development of DSS it is very important to have an understanding of the managerial context in which DSS will be used.

Readers wishing to explore further the inappropriateness of many of the early DSS should read the classic articles by Ackoff (1967) and Dearden (1972). Although these articles are somewhat dated, they do highlight many

1

of the common fallacies in the assumptions underlying some of the approaches used in the design and implementation of DSS.

Managerial Roles

Planning and control are undoubtedly major managerial roles and ones demanding considerable information input and interpretation. The characteristics of these roles and their impact on the development and use of DSS will be discussed in Chapter 2.

However, whilst planning and control are fundamental activities for managers, it is important to realise that they are not the only activities in which managers are engaged. In a famous article, Mintzberg (1975) examined the activities of American chief executives and also quoted from similar British studies. He concluded that the classical view of a manager as almost totally occupied in organising, planning and controlling the operations of an enterprise just did not stand up to investigation: a large part of a manager's time was spent performing many other roles. In all, Mintzberg identified 10 roles for the manager. One such role is the figurehead role, in which the manager carries out ceremonial duties. Mintzberg cites the cases of the President of a US corporation greeting touring dignitaries, of a sales manager taking an important customer to lunch, of chief executives presiding at Christmas dinners and so on.

Another role is in liaison, with the manager making contacts outside of his vertical chain of command, and not limiting his contacts to people within his own organisation. Part of this process of liaison is concerned with a manager's role in monitoring and disseminating information. The manager, as head of a unit, is in a position to garner information not available to a subordinate, but which the subordinate needs in order to carry out his job efficiently. He is also in the position to act as spokesperson for the unit, passing information to people outside the unit – to his superiors and to other interested parties.

The theme of Mintzberg's study is the homogeneity of management work: that although the specifics will change from manager to manager, the broad patterns of work will remain the same. Stewart (1967) has looked closely at how British management spends its time. Whilst her work and that of Mintzberg are in agreement about the general nature of managerial activity, Stewart's emphasis is on the variability of the work patterns between individual managers. Her first study covered the activities of 160 British managers in a wide range of jobs. She found for example, that 28 managers in the sample spent less than 20% of their time on paperwork, while 10% spent over 60% of their time on it. The figures for time involved in telephoning, informal discussion and committee meetings show a similar variation.

The same holds for the interactive component of the manager's work. Stewart found that the average time a manager spent working alone varied greatly: four managers spent less than 10% of their time working alone at one extreme, with another four spending more than 70% working alone at the other. On average, a manager spent 26% of his time with immediate subordinates but again this sample figure masked a large variation: two managers apparently spent no time with subordinates while five spent over 50% of their working time in this way.

The Pressures of Managerial Work

Not only does Mintzberg's work show that a manager has many roles to play, it also highlights the fragmentary nature of management work. In his words, management activities are characterised by 'brevity, variety and discontinuity'. In support of this contention he cites his research findings in which half of the activities engaged in by the chief executives lasted less than nine minutes, and only 10% exceeded one hour. Stewart found that the managers in her study worked for half an hour or more without interruption only about once every two days.

This brevity and discontinuity suggests a hectic pace and Mintzberg's work confirms this: coffee breaks and lunches were inevitably work related and the chief executives in his study met a steady stream of callers and mail from the moment they arrived in the morning until they left in the evening.

Management work is thus characterised by many brief segments of action following one another at a hectic pace. These segments may be ad hoc, one-off activities, but more often than not, they will form part of a continuous thread of problem-solving actions. Mintzberg found that the chief executives he studied supervised as many as 50 projects at the same time and to quote Mintzberg again, the chief executive 'is like a juggler, he keeps a number of projects in the air: periodically, one comes down, is given a new burst of energy, and is sent back into orbit'.

An oft-quoted phrase is 'information is power'. Whilst a manager will get some of his information from written sources – computer print-outs, company statements and trade magazines for example – much comes to him verbally. There is very strong evidence that managers greatly favour obtaining information verbally, through meetings, one-to-one discussions and telephone calls. One reason for this is that managers like both the richness of the information available from informal sources and its timeliness, and very often this must come verbally from the web of contacts that any good manager cultivates. Usually this information is fragmented and "soft" (gossip and rumour), and as such is difficult to handle in a systematic way. A consequence of this is that decision-making that relies on such information is difficult to delegate.

A final point to come from the Mintzberg and Stewart studies is that management work is highly interactive, not reflective: in Mintzberg's study, scheduled meetings were the single, most time-consuming element. These studies are complemented by that of Lawrence (1984) who investigated how British middle management spent its time at work. His findings, although concerned only with production management, give credence to the reply often given by secretaries when one tries to phone a manager – HIAM – he's in a meeting. Lawrence found that approximately 50% of a manager's time is spent at meetings or in formal discussions, with only around 10% spent at 'desk work'.

The empirical studies of management work patterns by Mintzberg and Stewart illustrate the range of activities in which managers are involved. Whereas formal planning and control is an activity where DSS may be heavily used, most of the other activities of managers do not readily lend themselves to the use of DSS, or indeed to any form of information technology. Consequently, the scope of DSS in the totality of a manager's professional life is rather limited. Stewart's work indicates a high variation between individual managers, and it is suggested that this variation comes about in part by choices made by the managers themselves. The content of his work and the patterns of work activity of one manager may lend themselves more to the use of DSS than do those of another manager: in any event the approach is likely to differ from manager to manager and this should be taken into account when using and developing DSS.

THE NATURE OF BUSINESS PROBLEMS

Jackson (1975) considers a problem to exist if an objective has been defined and an obstacle exists to prevent its realisation. In his way of putting it:

PROBLEM = OBJECTIVE plus OBSTACLE

Examples of problems would be a person wishing to be healthy, with the obstacle to attaining this objective being an inadequate diet; or again, a company wishing to be profitable yet facing the obstacle of not being able to raise sufficient cash to finance the measures necessary to achieve profitability.

Problems as Jackson defines them include both difficulties and opportunities, since the objective need not be to avoid something (such as liquidation) but can be more positive – to attain something. For example, a company may see the opportunity to increase its market share and consider the obstacle to achieving this to be a lack of trained sales people or a limited production capacity. Thus, the term 'problem' is not restricted simply to threats, but would include any situation, actual or forecast, that is at variance with a preferred and attainable state.

A prerequisite for tackling problems is a model of the overall situation in which the problem shows itself. Without such knowledge, action may make the problem worse or, as often seems to be the case in medicine, the symptoms of a particular problem may be made to disappear, but the 'cure' causes other problems to surface. Ackoff (1977) has written about the analogous business case. He argues that managers are in a mess, in that they face a set of overlapping problems. The knack is for the manager to tackle an individual problem in the context of all the other problems and potential problems in such a way as not to make the overall picture worse.

Models of Decision Making

One well known model of decision making is the 4-phase model proposed by Simon (1977), involving Intelligence, Design, Choice and Review.

The Intelligence phase involves searching the environment for the conditions calling for a decision, i.e. searching for problems. Simon writes that the meaning of the term 'intelligence' is borrowed from military usage. In the author's view, the military meaning is wider than this: this difference of meaning will be returned to later. The Design phase involves inventing, developing and analysing possible courses of action: it is in this phase that models would be built with which to carry out these explorations. The Choice phase is when one particular course of action is selected from those investigated. Simon considers the review phase to be concerned with assessing the execution of a decision.

A slightly modified and extended version of Simon's model of decision making is considered more applicable to the main thrust of this book. This model consists of three phases and seven stages, and is set out in Figure 1.1. The Structuring phase is discussed below, whilst the Understanding phase is discussed in subsequent chapters. Note the stage of Decision Taking:

taking a decision is the culmination of all the other stages of decision making, and is generally quite straightforward, since all the supportive work has already been done.

The Understanding phase includes the implementation of the DSS to help in exploring courses of action. This is not the same as the implementation of change which takes place in the 'real world' (in the Action phase). The Action phase will not be considered further in this book.

Phases	Stages
Structuring	Problem detection Problem definition
Understanding	Detailed system design Exploring courses of action Decision taking
Action	Implementation of change Review

Figure 1.1   Phases and Stages in Tackling a Problem

It should not be construed from Figure 1.1 that tackling problems is a totally sequential process, starting with problem detection and moving continuously and without interruption through the seven stages to the implemention of the desired changes. Although there tends to be a general 'linear' direction in the decision making process, there is likely to be much backtracking and iteration amongst the stages. [This is explicitly acknowledged in the Soft Systems Approach discussed in detail in Chapter 14]. Furthermore, the time to move from the initial detection to implementation may be weeks or months: this in itself gives much latitude for second thoughts and the consequent backtracking between stages.

A point that will be taken up in the next chapter is that the Structuring phase shown in Figure 1.1 may have been made possible through the prior existence of systems to aid in the problem definition and detection.

Problem Detection

In Business, a manager's initial awareness that a problem exists may start simply as a 'gut feeling' that something is wrong. In many cases, this awareness develops during an 'incubation period' whilst further stimuli are sensed that support these initial feelings. Three sorts of signals can be recognised. First, there are the internal performance measures, such as those emanating from an organisation's budgetary control system. Second, there is 'client' reaction, either from the customers outside the firm or from those within the firm to whom the manager is supplying a product or service. Third, there are changes in the manager's environment.

A formal Management Information System could provide much of this alerting information, especially that related to the internal performance measures. Environmental scanning would be carried out to detect changes in the manager's environment: a good example is that described by El Sawy (1985) of a strategic scanning system that applies sophisticated classifications and pattern matching operations on incoming information to identify significant trends and events.

Linking back to what was written above, it is only possible to detect a problem if a manager has an appropriate overall view of the problem situation. For example, a person without any medical knowledge would be quite unable to detect that someone with a temperature of 38°C was likely to be ill or not. He was unable to detect the problem because he had no model of the workings of the human body to guide his thoughts. This need for an overall view, or scenario, is taken up in Chapter 2.

Eventually a point is reached when the general evidence shown by the signals appears so convincing that the problem is deemed to exist, and that something has to be done about it. It is at this point that the problem needs to be defined.

Problem Definition

A problem will have been defined once an objective and the associated obstacle have been defined. How a problem is defined determines how the problem will be tackled. An example from the annals of Management

Science will illustrate what is meant. In a tall office block, concern was expressed about the lift service. At peak times – in the morning when people arrived for work and in the evening when people went home – the office workers claimed that too much time was spent waiting for a lift to arrive. Experts were asked to look into the problem and to suggest answers. They saw a problem that had as its objective the minimising of the time people waited for a lift ('wasted' time), with the obstacle lying in the performance of the lifts. Answers were sought in terms of speeding up the lift, having the lifts stop only at alternate floors, etc. No answer was really satisfactory. All seemed lost until someone came up with the idea of putting mirrors next to the lifts. The reasoning behind this was that the female staff would look at themselves in the mirrors and the males would look at the females. Sexist stuff perhaps, but it worked, in the sense that complaints about delays reduced dramatically. What had happened was that the problem had now been defined in a different way to that of the experts – the objective was seen as one of preventing people feeling that they were wasting time and the obstacle was that there was nothing to do whilst waiting. A different definition, a different way of tackling the problem.

Problem Life Cycles

In the lift example described above, different definitions of the problem produced a different focus of attention and, if systems had been required to investigate how to proceed, these would almost certainly have been very different. However, it is not always necessary or advisable to proceed. In his book, Jackson (1975) describes problems as having life cycles. At some stages the problem is ill defined and one should wait until matters become clearer: at another stage the problem has passed and thus ceases to require attention (until the next time!). Thus it can be seen that the time context of the problem situation has an enormous impact on the form of DSS and on their implementation.

Solving, Resolving and Dissolving Problems

Problems are tackled by altering the relationship between objective and obstacle: most commonly, ways are sought to remove or mitigate the effects of obstacles. Ackoff (1981) has identified three broad ways of tackling a problem, which he terms solving, resolving and dissolving. Solving is where an optimum or best solution is sought, resolving is where the person with the problem seeks only to obtain an answer that is good enough, whilst dissolving occurs when conditions change to eliminate the problem. An example will make this clearer. At the time of writing this book I lectured in Loughborough and lived in Nottingham. I wished to keep doing this yet public transport between the two places was difficult and my old car had failed to get a new test certificate. Given my other commitments, another car seemed to be called for. The problem then became that my objective was to buy a new car, the obstacle was ignorance of the car market and restricted financial resources.

Using Ackoff's terminology, to solve this problem would necessitate my finding the optimum solution, and this in turn would require that I completely and precisely specified my requirements and those of my family, and also scoured the literature to determine all relevant particulars about all potentially suitable makes of car. Visits to showrooms and test drives would also be called for. This could be an extremely time consuming business, and even if an optimum match of car and requirements could have been found, it was very unlikely that the answer would remain optimum for long: my overall requirements might change, and certainly new cars (for which new claims would almost certainly be made) would come on the market.

Thus, although the quest for optimum answers has been one of the driving forces behind many academic initiatives over the last 20 years, very often it is a search that is not worth the effort. Most managers have realised that optimizing part of a problem is not necessarily a greater help in tackling the total problem than is an answer that is sensible and understandable and not grossly wrong: resolving or being 'good enough' is the stuff of a great deal of management problem tackling. In the car buying problem, to resolve the problem I would have sought a broad idea of key requirements – the car must be able to seat five people and do more than 30 miles per gallon for example – and then have selected a car from the half dozen I knew something about. This process would not be nearly so time consuming as that of optimising and would get me a reasonable car. This was, in fact, the way I tackled the problem.

Finally, to dissolve the problem the relationship between obstacle and objective has to be changed. This would be done by changing the situation within which the problem was embedded: either by chance events or by decisions of a higher level. The car buying problem would be dissolved if I taught in Nottingham or if I went to live in Loughborough. The need for a car would now no longer exist, or the problem so transformed as not to be the original one. Dissolving is a case where there would be no need to proceed to the development of a DSS.

SUMMARY

It may seem odd to begin a book on DSS with a chapter that plays down their role in a manager's working life, and it would be unfortunate if the reader were to infer from this that DSS have a negligible role to play in business operations. DSS do have a role to play, but it is important that this role is seen within the wider context of business life, and thus that any DSS be tailored to fit the realities of managerial activity.

These realities are that managerial work is typically fragmented and hectic, but that managers have considerable discretion about what they do and how they do it. Thus different managers act differently, and this should be recognised in the development of DSS. [This point is returned to in Chapter 12].

What the present situation happens to be should not be confused with what should be or could be. The fact that several observers found that US and UK managers led hectic, fragmented business lives does not necessarily mean that DSS must be developed to fit in with this turmoil of firefighting and dealing with unforseen problems. It could be that properly designed DSS would change the pattern of managerial work, and that the pace and form of managerial life is a symptom of a situation that DSS can help alleviate.

The chapter started with a working definition of DSS as 'a computer-based system that aids the process of decision making'. Strangely perhaps, the term 'decision making' was little in evidence during the second half of the chapter, where the discussion was about tackling problems. This was done deliberately to bring home the point that decision making defined as widely as that encapsulated in Figure 1.1 is the same thing as problem tackling. For the sake of brevity, the phrase 'problem tackling' will be used instead of the more cumbersome 'solving, resolving and dissolving problems' unless one specific way is to be explicitly treated. The terms 'decision making' and 'problem tackling' are taken to be synonymous, and will be used interchangeably throughout this book. The terms 'decision maker' and 'manager' will also be used interchangeably.

To support the whole range of activities involved with decision making, systems must be able to do one or more of the following:

- help managers detect existing or incipient problems;
- help managers model their problem situation in order to clarify it;
- provide the tools so that options can readily be considered;
- help with the implementation of change and its review.

REFERENCES

Ackoff R.L., (1967) *Management Misinformation Systems,* Management Science, Vol.14, No.4, December, pp 140–B156

Ackoff R.L., (1977) *Optimization + Objectivity = Optout,* European Journal of Operational Research, 1, pp 1–7

Ackoff R.L., (1981) *The Art and Science of Mess Management,* Interfaces 11, 1, pp 20–25

Dearden J., (1972) *MIS is a mirage,* Harvard Business Review, Jan–February, pp 90–99

El Sawy O.A., (1985) *Personal Information Systems for Strategic Scanning in Turbulent Environments: Can the CEO go On-line?,* MIS Quarterly, Vol.9, No.1, pp 53–60

Jackson K.F., (1975) *The Art of Solving Problems,* Heinemann, London.

Lawrence P.A., (1984) *Management in Action,* Routledge and Kegan Paul, London.

Mintzberg H., (1975) *The manager's Job: folklore and fact,* Harvard Business Review, July–August, pp 49–61

Simon H.A., (1977) *The New Science of Management Decision,* Harper and Row, New York, 3rd edition

Stewart R., (1967) *Managers and their Jobs,* MacMillan, London.

2 Planning and Control: Models and Systems

Managers are constantly engaged in the intertwined processes of planning and control, in which they are primarily concerned with matching the capabilities of a unit with its environment. To do this they need to monitor both their own organisation and its environment, looking for opportunities and threats, and examining these in the light of their own unit's strengths and weaknesses.

Monitoring will produce triggers, indicating that the match of the unit to its environment is not as it should be, or that a mismatch is likely to occur in the near future. An action associated with a trigger may be autonomous – relying on recipes according to Johnson and Scholes (1993). In these cases there is little in the way of planning and decision making, and the monitoring-action nexus is akin to that in process control. An example of this might occur with someone wanting to read in the evening when the light begins to fade. The reader would go and switch on the light without any (conscious) planning or decision taking.

However, from time to time the monitoring process will throw up a new situation for which there is no available recipe. There is then a need to assess formally the options available and to decide between them. When this occurs, the planning and control cycle is as shown in Figure 2.1.

In the previous chapter problems were taken to include both opportunities and threats. Problem tackling thus involves dealing with opportunities and threats, strengths and weaknesses. Given that planning and control are primarily concerned with matching a unit's capabilities with its environment, then it can be seen that the process of planning and control encompasses problem tackling as set out in Figure 1.1 of the previous chapter. This basic model of planning and control illustrates the continuous nature of the process of identifying problems and searching out ways of dealing with them. Planning and control is problem tackling involving a whole set of apparently independent problems.

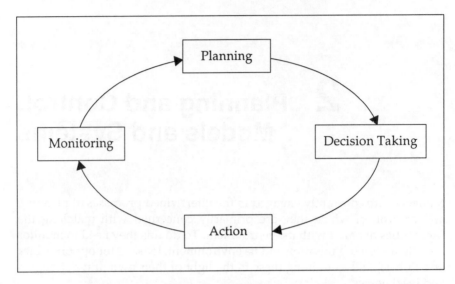

Figure 2.1   **A Basic Model of Planning and Control**

Comparing Figure 2.1 with Figure 1.1, Monitoring would correspond to the Problem Detection phase; the Planning phase would correspond to Problem Understanding, with Decision Taking the last stage within this phase. Action in Figure 2.1 corresponds to the Action phase in Figure 1.1.

LEVELS OF PLANNING AND CONTROL: STRUCTURED AND UNSTRUCTURED SITUATIONS

The problems encountered and the associated planning and control processes are not the same for all levels within an organisation. Davis (1974) describes transaction processing, operational control, management control and strategic planning. Anthony's (1965) three levels are operational control, management control and strategic planning. For the purposes of this discussion, it is convenient to take a 3-level approach, operational, tactical and strategic.

The operational level is concerned with carrying out day-to-day, well established procedures. Decisions at this level are what Dermer (1977) has called 'structured' and Simon (1977) has calls 'programmed'. Simon deliberately borrowed this term from the computer world, because he wanted to use it in the same sense in which it is used there: a program is a complete specification that states the exact sequence a process should take in response to some prespecified type of input. The terms 'structured' and 'ill-structured' are preferred to 'programmed' and 'non-programmed' because they link to the problem situation rather than to the computer method employed.

In general, operational decision making bases its decisions on what has already occurred in the recent past. The tactical level is concerned with activities that have a longer time span than do the operational activities. Decisions at this level are reasonably structured but are influenced by some ill-structured inputs. Stabell (1979) has defined a task to be ill-structured when:

- Objectives are ambiguous and nonoperational, or objectives are relatively operational but numerous and conflicting.

- It is difficult to determine the cause of changes in decision outcomes and to predict the effect on decision outcomes of the actions taken by the decision maker.

- It is uncertain what actions taken by the decision maker might affect decision outcomes.

Note that in ill-structured situations, the cause-effect relations are only poorly recognised and are unlikely to be easily articulated. As Murray (1974) puts it, tactical decisions are routine decisions that are affected by non-routine inputs. The calculation of economic order quantities and of the most appropriate routing schedules for deliveries are examples of the sort of problem to be tackled at this level.

Planning at the stategic level is concerned with the long term relationships between the organisation and its environment: much of the concern is with events outside of the control of the organisation. A broad distinction between tactical and strategic planning is that tactical problems are primarily concerned with the most appropriate use of the resources already available – with efficiency – whereas strategy tends to be concerned with the levels of resource needed to achieve organisational goals – with effectiveness. In military terms, 'tactical' refers to actions in the face of the enemy (competition in the business world), whilst strategic refers to actions taken away from the hurly-burly of the action. Note however, that much of the monitoring activity carried out by senior executives is of a tactical nature, and thus has much of the nature of tactical decision making.

Gorry and Scott-Morton (1971) have combined the concept of levels of decision making in hierarchical organisations with the concept of problem structure to form a matrix of decision making situations. This matrix, with examples, is shown in Figure 2.2. This matrix suggests that the procedures for successful system development might well be different for each situation, and that these procedures may not necessarily be generalised.

	Operational	Tactical	Strategic planning
Structured	Invoicing	Production scheduling	Financial planning
Ill-structured		Factory location	Acquisition

Figure 2.2   Types of Decision-making Situations

SCENARIOS

Ackoff (1981) describes managers in a "mess", as being confronted by a set of interacting and overlapping problems. Apart from the most structured of situations, this applies at all levels in an organisation, but more so the more ill-structured the situation. With this view, it can be seen that it would be unwise for a manager to concentrate solely on a single problem: he needs to take account of the interaction of any particular problem with the other problem areas. To do this he needs a broad model. This broad model or world view is termed a scenario: in the methodology he has developed for soft systems Checkland (1981) uses the term 'Weltanschauung'.

In Figure 2.3 the manager's scenario is shown open to prompting by an alerting mechanism. In the light of this prompting, the problem area within the scenario will be defined and if no recipe will suffice, this portion of the scenario is then focused on in a search for a resolution of the problem. This problem area will be called a local scenario. It would be wider than an initial consideration of the problem would suggest, but narrower than the whole scenario. In practice, there would not be a clear distinction between the local scenario and the rest of the scenario; a gradual weakening of the influence of factors in the scenario would be expected to occur as one moves away from the centre of the local scenario.

The model shown in Figure 2.3 is applicable both to individual and group planning and decision making. For an individual working on his own, the clear split between scenario and the focusing activity is unlikely to occur. Where more than one person is involved, the focussing activity might involve a clear-cut separation, with staff personnel heavily involved in the focused activity, yet with frequent links back to the scenario to establish and maintain the context and to ensure the viability of any proposed action. [The problems associated with the use of staff analysts is considered in Chapters 12 and 13].

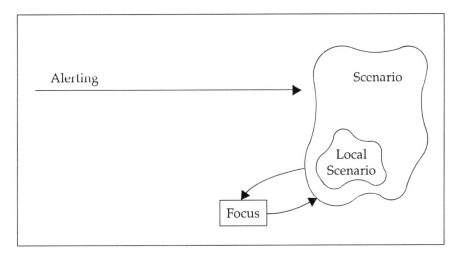

Figure 2.3   Monitoring and Planning

DATA, INFORMATION AND INTELLIGENCE

Data can be considered to be those stimuli from outside the system that pass the rules embedded in the interface between the system and its surroundings. For example, parts of a computerised order entry system might be constructed so that only numerical values are accepted: non-numeric stimuli would be rejected at the interface.

According to information theorists, information is used to shift the probabilities associated with the options facing a decision maker. Often, this shifting of probabilities will rule out some options. In a business context, information may be defined as data that is perceived by an employee to be of use or potential use to him in his job. For data to become information, it is almost always necessary that the data be combined in some way. For example, an information system for sales management might be designed to provide monthly summaries of aggregated sales for the preceding month and nothing at a finer detail. Here, a model of information requirements (viz. that only aggregated monthly sales figures are required) has been used with the data to provide information. The alerting stimulus shown in Figure 2.3 is information that is likely to have been derived from a Management Information System (MIS). MIS will be considered in more detail in Chapter 4.

Without an efficient means of filtering and aggregating data, a manager could easily be in the situation of being data rich, yet information poor. As Drucker (1974) has put it, anything beyond what is truly necessary is noise. It does not enrich but impoverishes.

Murray (1979) rather felicitously defines intelligence as 'the outcome of the meshing and reconciliation of a set of information carrying inferences'. Note that this usage,which will be adopted in this book, differs considerably from that used by Simon (1977). With Murray's definition, it can be seen that the focusing activity shown in Figure 2.2 is producing intelligence. Systems to do this will be termed Management Intelligence Systems (MINTS): they are systems for helping with the interpretation of information. For example, it may be that a sales manager has a computer-based system to help him decide his preferences for fleet car purchase for his salesforce. MINTS will be discussed in more detail in Chapter 4.

This concept of intelligence is important: the position is taken in this book that the biggest difference between types of DSS is between systems that provide information and those that provide intelligence. Information is only a means to enable a manager to form a better scenario than he had previously. The scenario is the sum of all the intelligence that he possesses, with intelligence about a particular problem situation equivalent to a local scenario. It is with building and updating this local scenario where a manager wants help: simply providing him with information is not providing him with all that he really needs. Information is the raw material for intelligence, but a manager may need help to interpret it and include it into his scenario.

Where a manager uses resources outside his own capabilities to help in providing focus, the situation is akin to operational military intelligence. Here, intelligence officers gather information and present the commander with an overview of the situation together with a list of options that they see as open to him. After questioning and digesting what the intelligence officers have to tell him, the commander is then in a better position to take a decision.

Figure 2.3 can be extended to encompass these terms and concepts and to include the links between decisions and the consequent actions affecting the task environment. A fuller model of planning and control is shown in Figure 2.4.

This model is termed a knowledge model since it incorporates data, information, intelligence and the process whereby these are formed – all aspects of knowledge. This model is applicable to any type of cognitive system, not solely to computer-based ones such as a DSS.

DIMENSIONS OF INFORMATION

Earlier in this chapter, the different levels of planning and control in organisations were described, and in particular the differences concerning the degree of structure in the problems encountered were noted. It would be expected that this would lead to different information requirements and this is indeed the case. Figure 2.5 illustrates the different requirements at the different levels.

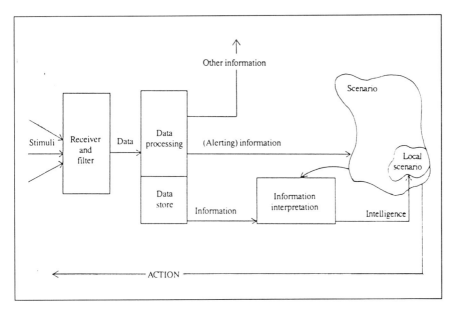

Figure 2.4   A Knowledge Model of Planning and Control

Dimension	Operational	Tactical	Strategic
Problem type	Structured	$----\!\!>$	Ill-structured
Time frame	Immediate past	$----\!\!>$	Future
Source	Largely internal	$----\!\!>$	Largely external
Organisation	Tight	$----\!\!>$	Loose
Scope	Detailed	$----\!\!>$	Wide-ranging
Age	Current	$----\!\!>$	Old
Hardness	Hard	$----\!\!>$	Soft
Exactitude	Accurate and precise	$----\!\!>$	Accurate
Expectation	Prescribed	$----\!\!>$	Surprise
Freqency of usage	Often	$----\!\!>$	Infrequent

Figure 2.5   Levels of Information Requirement

The split of problem type into structured and ill-structured has already been explained, as has the concern of operational decision making with the immediate past, in contrast with strategic planning where the focus is very much on the future.

Operational activities are predominantly those buffered from the direct influences of an organisation's environment, and thus the sources of the information that they need are internal to the organisation. In planning at the strategic level, the need is very much to look outwards, since the matching of the organisation with its environment is the primary consideration.

The organisational dimension of information is concerned with the form in which the needed information reaches those who require it. An example of tightly organised information is a report with a pre-defined categorisation of the information, e.g. a report itemising the reasons for machine downtime. Loosely organised information would be where information would come in many forms from many diverse sources, i.e. the raw material for the production of intelligence. An example of loosely organised information would be that associated with strategic planning, where inputs would be from a variety of sources – formal internal reports, informal discussions, external databases and external rumours. Closely allied to this concept of tight/loose is that of Scope. Scope is concerned with the level of detail provided.

Because of the concern with monitoring operational activities over very short time intervals, information has to be fed back very quickly for it to be of use. Speed of feedback is generally not so critical in strategic planning.

The hardness of information relates to the objectivity associated with its source. Consequently, it is often the case that hard data is quantitative and soft data is qualitative. As Mintzberg's (1975) classic study showed, managers prefer verbal and soft information rather than harder and written information. The reason seems to be that managers prefer the richness of the information conveyed verbally, and the control they have to further question the source.

The concept of the softness of data is discussed directly and more fully in Chapter 9 where group and strategic decision support is considered, and obliquely in Chapter 14 where soft systems are discussed.

The concept of Exactitude involves two further concepts: that of a systematic deviation from 'reality' and that of a random deviation. Accuracy is a measure of the systematic deviation, whilst precision is a measure of the random deviation. Figure 2.6 should make this clear. Consider the case of forecasting the level of sales of some product, say cigarettes, where the total sales is composed of the sales of many individual brands. If there were no systematic error in the forecasts, then one would expect an accurate prediction, following either of the two patterns a) or b) shown in Figure 2.6, depending on the random errors associated with the individual brand forecasts. On the other hand, if the forecasts were all affected by the same error-producing feature, then patterns c) or d) would be expected: again which one would depend on the errors of the individual brand estimates. For example, if all the forecasts were based to some extent on the general economic situation, and this were predicted to be overly good, then one would expect pattern c) or d).

At the operational level high levels of both accuracy and precision are required. At the strategic level, concerned as it is with an uncertain future, high precision of data is generally unobtainable: the concern is with accuracy.

At the operational level the whole organisation thrust is to remove surprise, and to convert all procedures into routine. Information is unlikely to surprise at this level, though it could well do at the strategic level. It is for this reason that every well managed organisation has broad strategic contingency plans to put into practice should the unexpected happen.

Given the nature of strategic planning and operational activities, it would be expected that information would be required almost continuously in operational tasks, but rather infrequently in strategic planning, especially as strategic planning tends to be periodic with a periodicity seldom less than 3 months.

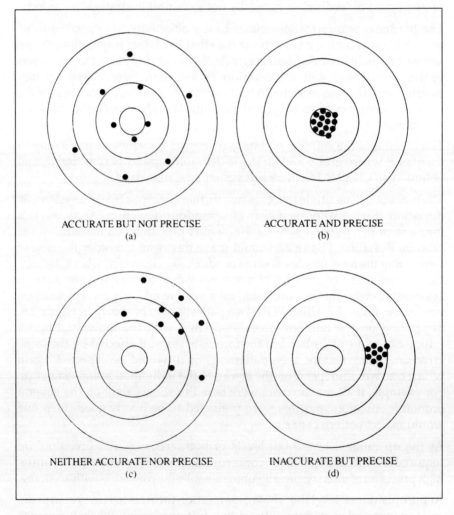

ACCURATE BUT NOT PRECISE
(a)

ACCURATE AND PRECISE
(b)

NEITHER ACCURATE NOR PRECISE
(c)

INACCURATE BUT PRECISE
(d)

Figure 2.6   Exactitude – Accuracy and Precision

MODELS AND SYSTEMS

So far, the terms 'model' and 'system' have been used without their meaning being defined, and with no explanation of the interaction between the two. Since these two terms will be used extensively throughout this book, it is important that the reader has a solid grasp of what is meant by them.

A succinct definition of the term model is 'a representation of reality'. However, this definition is rather limited if 'reality' is taken to mean only that which presently exists. Many exploratory tools have been constructed to explore situations that do not yet exist – for example, models for new cars, and financial plans for an organistion covering the next five years. To encompass such tools under the term modelling, reality must be taken to include that which could come about in the future as well as what presently exists.

Until the last few years, mathematical modelling formed the core of almost all DSS. Now there are many applications that use logical relationships other than mathematical ones as the basis of the DSS, although mathematically-based DSS still constitute the majority of applications. Finlay (1985) fully describes mathematical modelling in his book.

It is worth building models to aid decision making for the following reasons:

- Models make the structure of a problem explicit.

- Models can usually be analysed more readily than the original problem.

- It is possible to experiment with models, and thus answer 'What if?' type questions.

- The process of model building leads to a deeper understanding of the problem.

A simple example from budgeting will make the concept of modelling clear. This area of organisational activity has been chosen because most readers will have had some exposure to the budgetary process, and because financial modelling is the area in which DSS have been most extensively used.

Virtually every organisation uses budgets in which its activities are represented as a set of cash flows – of incomes and expenditures.

Figure 2.7 shows a very simple example of part of a budget. Two things have had to be done to obtain these figures. First, the rules of calculation have had to be defined and second, the input data required to 'start the model off' have had to be selected. The rules of calculation constitute a logic

	January	February	March
Sales	10,000	11,000	10,000
Price (£)	11	11	12
Revenue (£)	110,000	121,000	120,000

Figure 2.7   A Simple Budgeting Example

model whilst the input data make up a data model. Together, the data and logic models make up the complete model, which is what will be meant when the term 'model' is used.

The result of applying the input data to the rules (or put another way, of linking the data and logic models) is the budget shown in Figure 2.7. Creating the data and logic models is the process of modelling. The modelling 'lying behind' the budget figures is shown in Figure 2.8. Note that the budget (i.e. the output from the model of Figure 2.7) is itself a model, since it is a financial representation of the expected operations of the organisation.

Both the logic and data models used in the budgeting example are extremely simple. In particular, it should be noted that the data model hardly does justice to the very large data models holding vast amounts of corporate data that are found in many large organisations today.

Budgeting is only one area in which financial modelling occurs: similar modelling is involved in capital investment decisions and in long range planning. However, it must be stressed that modelling goes far beyond financial modelling, into such areas as scheduling, resource allocation, preference determination, ideas management and many more.

The logic models do not necessarily consist of equations – they may consist of ideas captured by English phrases (described in Chapter 8), and systems where all that is required of the data model are simple categorisations of

Logic Model	Data Model
Revenue = Sales x Price	Sales = 10,000 : 11,000 : 10,000
	Price = 11 : 11 : 12

	OUTPUT		
	January	**February**	**March**
Sales	10,000	11,000	10,000
Price (£)	11	11	12
Revenue (£)	110,000	121,000	120,000

Figure 2.8   Logic and Data Models and Their Relation to Output

attributes into one of two or three classes – such as 'good, bad' and 'high, medium, low' (*see* Chapter 7). In all these areas computer assistance only becomes possible if a formal model is created and is available for use.

Whilst a model will form the core of a computer application it does not constitute the whole of it. In using the simple budgeting application described above, the way in which the user selects the information he wishes to view is important: for example, can the chosen set of figures be obtained by a few keystrokes or is a lengthy routine required? Again, is the user helped in what he is doing by useful prompts on the screen or does he have to look in a manual? The help messages on the screen, the manual and the way in which instructions are handled are all part of the system, as indeed are the computer itself and the people involved in its use. Although the word 'system' is a much overused one, there seems no good alternative to cover the totality described above.

PLANNING AND CONTROL SYSTEMS

This book is concerned with computer systems produced specifically to aid problem tackling by managers, which has been shown to be the same as the planning and control of the activities within an organisation. The systems will have at their heart a computer model, and will themselves form a part of the whole planning and control system used by a manager or set of managers, as described in stylised form in Figure 2.1. This linkage between systems and models is shown in Figure 2.9.

What is not shown in Figure 2.9 is the Information Technology 'platform' upon and within which the DSS resides. This platform provides the infrastructure and would include the computer itself, its operating system, the programming language used and any network to which the computer is attached. The existence of an appropriate platform is assumed and will not be considered further apart from listings being provided of suitable computer software for specific DSS applications.

PHYSICAL SYSTEMS AND ENVIRONMENTS

System has been contrasted with model in the previous section, and defined implicitly as all the things necessary for a computer to provide decision

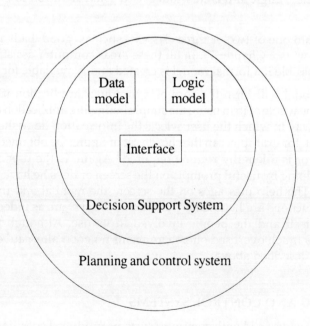

Figure 2.9   The Relationship Between Models and Systems

support or, in the wider context, to plan and control the operations of a unit. In formal terms and in the context of computer systems, a system will be considered any combination of logic and data models and user interface used to provide information and/or intelligence.

A manager's physical system (as opposed to his information/intelligence system) can simply be considered to be those 'things' over which he has direct control, with the environment being everything else. It is useful to split a manager's environment into two; into a local environment over which he has no direct control, but upon which he can have significant influence, and an external environment over which he has no significant influence. An example of an element in the local environment of a middle ranking manager in the production function might be the organisation's personnel policy; he can influence it but he is not responsible for it and cannot control it. Examples of elements from the external environment of this same manager would be governmental minimum wage legislation, and diktats from the parent company concerning capital investments. This second example indicates that environments need not be physically outside the manager's organisation: it is the level of control and influence that determine what is in his system and what is in his environment.

SUMMARY

This chapter has been concerned with the terminology of DSS. The terms 'information' and 'intelligence' have been defined, with information seen as the raw material for the creation of intelligence. The terms 'model' and 'system' have been discussed, with models providing the heart of DSS. In management terms, the managerial environment can be considered anything that is not under the direct control of the manager.

MIS are the formal means whereby information is provided to alert managers to the presence of problems and to provide information to MINTS. MINTS are systems for helping managers to interpret information, helping managers develop a scenario of their system and its environment.

The information needed by managers operating at different levels within organisations are not of the same form, and any successful DSS implementation must bear this in mind.

REFERENCES

Ackoff R.L., (1981) *The Art and Science of Mess Management*, Interfaces, 11, 1, pp 20–25

Anthony R.N., (1965) *Planning and Control Systems: A Framework for Analysis,* Harvard Business School, Boston

Checkland P., (1981) *Systems Thinking, Systems Practice,* John Wiley and Sons

Davis G.B., (1974) *Management Information Systems: Conceptual Foundations, Structure and Development,* McGraw Hill, New York

Dermer J., (1977) *Management Planning and Control Systems: Advanced Concepts and Cases,* Irwin

Drucker P.F., (1974) *Management, tasks, responsibilities and practice,* Heinemann, London

Finlay P.N., (1985) *Mathematical Modelling in Business Decision-Making,* Croom Helm, London

Gorry G.A. and Scott-Morton M.S., (1971) *A Framework for Management Information Systems,* Sloan Management Review, Fall, pp 55-70

Johnson G. and Scholes K., (1993) *Exploring Corporate Strategy,* 3rd edition, Prentice Hall International

Mintzberg H, (1975) *The manager's job: folklore and fact,* Harvard Business Review, July-August, pp.49–61

Murray T.J., (1979) *Data, Information and Intelligence in a Computer Based Management Information System,* Journal of Applied Systems Analysis, Vol 6, pp 101–105

Simon H.A., (1977) *The New Science of Management Decision,* Harper and Row, New York, 3rd edition

Stabell C.B., (1979) *Decision Research: A Description and Diagnosis of Decision Making in Organizations,* Norwegian School of Economics and Business Administration, Bergen, Norway, Working Paper A79.006, June

3 Towards a Definition of Decision Support Systems

In Chapter 1 a working definition of DSS was given as 'a computer-based system that aids the process of decision making'. This was a sufficient definition for the discussions of Chapters 1 and 2 where the context within which DSS would be used was discussed. However, many people working in the area of DSS will find this simple definition too all-embracing to be acceptable. Thus it is necessary to argue the case for such a definition. The argumentation is provided in this chapter.

Definitions and classificatory systems can be neither right nor wrong; they can only be more or less useful. Usefulness implies appropriateness and this in turn implies purpose. The major purpose for seeking a definition of DSS and the subsequent classification of the next chapter, is to better identify the most appropriate approach in their development and implementation. A further important reason is to focus research effort.

Before advancing the arguments for and against what are and what are not DSS, it is useful to look at the origins of DSS, and to see what they have contributed. This will not only help the reader get a richer picture of what constitutes a DSS but will also counter the view that there is no 'theoretical framework' underpining DSS. In a strict academic sense there is no theory, since there is no set of tried and tested laws that can be applied to define the route DSS developments should take. There are however conceptual frameworks that provide 'cognitive coathangers' to help DSS developers and users. These frameworks have their origins in five schools: these are the schools of Management Science, Computer Science, Ergonomics, Decision Analysis and Decision Research. As would be expected, these schools are associated with the three major elements of DSS identified in the previous chapter. Management Science and Decision Analysis with the logic model, Computer Science with the data model, and Ergonomics and Decision Research with the human-machine interface. With the advent of Group DSS there is a need to consider a sixth conceptual framework that of Group Dynamics and Organisational Behaviour.

THE THEORETICAL UNDERPINING OF DECISION SUPPORT SYSTEMS

Management Science

Management Science began during the second World War when scientists and mathematicians were engaged in the analysis of military operations. Following the undoubted success in this field, Management Science groups were founded in many of the larger organisations in the UK and abroad; for example, in what is now British Coal, in ICI and in the oil companies.

Put simply, Management Science is the application of the scientific method and the techniques of mathematics to business decision-making. The goal for Management Science models is better decisions through better models of the decision situation.

The focus of Management Science lies in the Understanding phase of problem tackling (*see* Figure 1.1), particularly with detailed system building and exploring courses of action. Little emphasis is placed on the problem finding phase. Monitoring and evaluation of decision outcomes is primarily a means to follow up and adjust model parameters and model structure.

At the core of the Management Science methodology is the creation of a mathematical model that allows the problem situation to be explored. In Chapter 2 it was shown that this model would contain both a logic and data model. Management Science has traditionally been concerned overwhelmingly with the logic model, with both the methodology by which such logic models can be produced and the associated mathematical techniques, with very little emphasis on the data model. The lack of importance of the data model has been due to the emphasis with the future rather than the present situation. In an uncertain world, high precision in data values pertaining to the future is unobtainable, and this tends to lead to use of (a small number of) aggregated and averaged values. In this situation there is little need to be concerned with the problems associated with storing and accessing large volumes of data.

The process in the building of logic (Management Science) models is described in Chapter 12.

Computer Science

Whilst management scientists have been primarily responsible for developing logic modelling, it is the computer scientists who have been mainly responsible for the development of data modelling.

One of the most far-reaching developments in Computer Science has been the capability of managing large volumes of data. This has made it possible to store these large volumes of data and provide suitable access paths to them. To a large extent this has been made available through the development of Database Management Systems.

Database Management Systems allow for the separation of data and the programs that use them. This permits the data to be considered a corporate resource, not a resource owned by one particular individual or department in an organisation. The coupling of this database facility with a flexible report generator for hard copy and an 'English-like' query language to allow for ad hoc requests, produces a facility that can be used easily by non-programmers almost anywhere within an organisation. The process of building data models (databases) is described in Chapter 12.

A further area where Computer Science has contributed to DSS is in electronic communications, particularly with networking. Electronic communications allow decision makers to make use of data at other locations, and to communicate with one another. Most importantly, without networking some forms of Group DSS would be severely restricted.

Ergonomics

Ergonomics is the study of the interaction of humans with their physical environment. In the UK, ergonomics had its beginnings in the scientific study of human problems in ordnance factories during World War I. This work enjoyed a further impetus during World War II where operators of military equipment were often working at the limits of their capabilities. In 1949 the Ergonomics Research Society was formed in the UK, with the Human Factors Society formed in the USA in 1954.

Ergonomics uses the findings in three, more basic, disciplines as part of its intellectual underpinning – anatomy, physiology and psychology. Anatomy provides the ergonomist with an understanding of the physical features of the human body. Physiology contributes a background on how the body functions and how humans react to their physical environment. Psychology contributes in several very important ways. First, it enables ergonomists to understand how humans process information, tackle, solve and resolve problems and make decisions. Second, it provides information on the human motor abilities – for example how well humans can employ a joystick when interacting with a computer. Third, it provides basic information on the speed of human response to stimuli or the lack of it – for example, how quickly must a response be generated by a computer to prevent human irritation. Finally, psychology has an important, wider role in guiding the designer of information systems in that it provides information on how humans behave at work (for example, how they respond to training, how they are motivated, the circumstances in which they work best as a team).

One particular area of ergonomics that has been extensively researched is that of human-machine interactions. Human-computer interactions are a further subdivision of the field, and warrant special study (considered in detail in Chapter 10). The central human factors issue in information technology is the problem of 'usability'. The general approach is not simply one of good technical design, but of devising a human-computer interface that a non-expert user will find acceptable. The non-expert is likely to be using the system intermittently, and this poses arduous demands on the design of the interface. These demands arise because interaction with a computer requires a conceptual effort on the part of the computer user, while generally it is simply physical effort that is required of a machine user. Furthermore, the level of involvement between humans and computers is generally deeper than that between humans and machines. For example, a computer operator's involvement with a word processor is much deeper than a typist's involvement with a typewriter, since the facilities available are so much greater in the word processor.

Decision Analysis

Decision analysis is concerned with decisions under uncertainty and where there are multiple objectives. It provides a framework whereby decision situations can be structured and 'rational' choices made. In common with all analytical methods, Decision Analysis tackles a problem by decomposing it into more manageable parts. A unique feature of Decision Analysis is how this decomposition is carried out.

A decision is viewed as a sequence of choices, that are dependent on the outcomes from earlier choices. The decision situation is frequently summarised in a decision tree. Decision Analysis and the use of decision trees is covered in more detail in Chapters 4 and 7. The decision maker is the key, and often the only, source of input, reflecting the method's focus on the decision maker's subjective estimates and preferences.

The method is general and independent of the content of the decision situation. It focuses on the choice phase of the decision process: problems are assumed to exist and to have been identified and defined before Decision Analysis is used. It does not support the phase of the decision making process following the taking of a decision.

Research into the human ability to provide good estimates of probabilities and preferences (such as that of Tversky and Kahneman (1974)) suggest that humans are poor at providing such estimates and frequently resort to rules-of-thumb to overcome their limited abilities to deal with and process information. In Stabell's (1986) phrase we are all 'cognitive cripples'. Computer-based applications are used to ease the cognitive load associated with Decision Analysis.

Decision Research

The Decision Research school is concerned with the cognitive processes involved in decision-making, and in particular how these can be improved, so that decision making can be enhanced. This calls for both a descriptive and a prescriptive model of how decisions are made. First, there is a need to understand and describe how decisions are made. Second, there is a need to prescribe the most appropriate environment within which enhanced decision making can be encouraged.

A key principle of the Decision Research approach is that any DSS should be designed to support the current mode of decision making; ie. it should be designed to achieve efficiency of the current decision making mode rather than aim to improve decision making through an increase in effectiveness (through a shift to a better form of decision making). This is the view of Eden et al. (1983) whose approach is described in Chapters 8 and 14.

Group Dynamics and Organisational Behaviour

Group DSS are a development of DSS whereby the support is given to a group *working as a group* – generally, though not always, in face-to-face meetings. Huber appears to have been the first person to coin the term Group DSS in 1984 when he was undertaking pioneering work in this area: thus the development of such systems has been ongoing for less than a decade. However, research into the workings of groups has a much longer history.

In contrast to single-user DSS, it is not simply the informational and cognitive aspects of decision making that are to be supported through the use of a Group DSS. What is occurring in the group situation is that change is being negotiated and it is change which the participants themselves will have to implement and for which they will be held organisationally accountable. Thus it is important to integrate what is known of group dynamics and organisational behaviour into the design and use of Group DSS. For example, in some cases it may be very useful to use a Group DSS to enforce anonymity within the group, in order to prevent one person or a subgroup from dominating proceedings.

The Integration of the Contributions

Figure 3.1 shows how the contributions from these various schools merge to support the development of DSS and Group DSS. The base disciplines that feed into the schools are also shown. This Figure has its origins in the paper by Jarke (1986).

What is not explicitly included in Figure 3.1 is the discipline of artificial intelligence and the derived fields of knowledge-based or Expert Systems. The rationale for this apparent omission is examined and explained in Chapter 15.

A DEFINITION OF DECISION SUPPORT SYSTEMS

In Chapter 2 it was argued that managerial decision making involves the need for both information and intelligence. Systems that provide these were termed Management Information Systems (MIS) and Management Intelligence Systems (MINTS). Whilst MINTS are what are often referred to in the literature as DSS, it will be argued here that both MIS and MINTS are DSS, and in Chapter 4 both will be taken into a general taxonomy of DSS.

Impact/Payoff/Relevance Criteria

According to Elam et al. (1986), the concept of DSS was introduced by Gorry and Scott Morton (1971) in their classic article 'A Framework for Information Systems Design'. The term DSS seems to have been first coined by Keen [see Freyenfeld (1984)]. In 1978, Keen and Scott Morton wrote their book that became the standard text on the subject of DSS for several years. In this book, they make a distinction between MIS, Management Science and DSS, and in this way attempt a definition of DSS. Of these three areas they write (pages 1–2)

Management Information Systems

a)   The main impact has been on structured tasks where standard operating procedures, decision rules, and information flows can be reliably predefined.

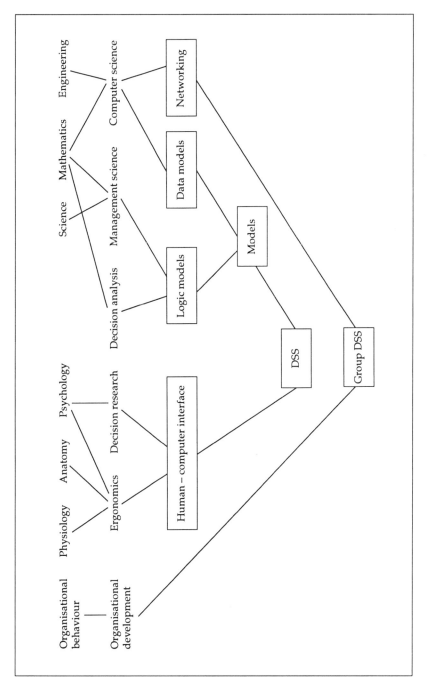

Figure 3.1   Contributions to Decision Support Systems Development

b)   The main payoff has been in improving efficiency by reducing costs, turnround time, and so on, and by replacing clerical personnel.

c)   The relevance for managers' decision making has mainly been indirect, for example, by providing reports and access to data.

Management Science

a)   The impact has mostly been on structured problems (rather than tasks) where the objective, data, and constraints can be prespecified.

b)   The payoff has been in generating better solutions for given types of problem.

c)   The relevance for managers has been the provision of detailed recommendations and new methodologies for handling complex problems.

Decision Support Systems

a)   The impact is on decisions in which there is sufficient structure for computer and analytic aids to be of value but where managers' judgement is essential.

b)   The payoff is in extending the range and capability of managers' decision processes to help them improve their effectiveness.

c)   The relevance for managers is the creation of a supportive tool, under their own control, which does not attempt to automate the decision process, predefine objectives, or impose solutions.

Of particular interest is the point that MIS is concerned with structured tasks, that Management Science is concerned with structured problems and that DSS is concerned with ill-structured problems. It is also important to note that in both the MIS and Management Science domains, the output from the systems is almost totally prescribed – in the terms used in the next chapter an answer is produced – and the need for post-output judgement is limited. This links MIS and Management Science tools with common characteristics: they do seem different from those ascribed to DSS as this term is used by Keen and Scott Morton.

There is much in Keen and Scott Morton's categorisation with which to agree, but also some points that are more contentious. Within MIS, the impact ascribed to MIS seems to be more relevant to the Data Processing associated with routine operational tasks such as order entry and invoicing than to MIS. The payoffs from MIS are more likely to reside in the provision of more timely and correct information with which to inform managers rather than in reducing costs and replacing clerical personnel. The main limitation of Keen and Scott Morton's definition of DSS is that it does not explicitly address the different requirements associated with the different phases of decision making, such as the need for a sound base of data for budgetary variance reporting for example, which might help with the detection of problems. It is also deficient in that it doesn't address the case of ill-structured situations that become structured through the extension of the decision aid and through the insights gained by the use of the DSS. For example, years ago discounted cash flow techniques were considered esoteric management tools and computer systems that provided Net Present Values or Internal Rates of Return would have been considered to be DSS, supporting the decision maker through the handling of what were considered ill-structured problem situations. However, with the spread of knowledge about the principles of discounting, the simple financial side of capital investment decisions has become well-structured. Would anyone have been able to say when the aid ceased being a DSS?

Further Approaches to a Definition of Decision Support Systems

Keen and Scott Morton used the dimensions of impact, payoff and managerial relevance to define DSS. Others have taken a different view. Some have attempted to encapsulate what DSS are in terms of a short definition. Sprague and Watson (1986, page 8)) sum up these definitions of DSS as 'interactive computer-based systems, which help decision makers utilise data and models to solve unstructured problems'.

In 1984, Freyenfeld (1984) proposed the following empirical definition of DSS based on discussions with some 30 supplier, user and academic organisations.

A Decision Support System is an interactive data processing and display system which is used to assist in a concurrent decision-making process, and which also conforms to the following characteristics:

i)   It is sufficiently user-friendly to be used by the decision maker(s) in person.

ii) It displays its information in a format and terminology which is familiar to the user(s).

iii) It is selective in its provision of information and avoids its user(s) in information overload.

It is difficult to agree with the requirement that DSS be solely concerned with concurrent decision making: many decisions take time to be made, their 'incubation period' may span weeks or months. Many decisions are aided by staff who feed the decision makers with information and intelligence, sometimes generated by the use of computers. Again, the use of the term 'data processing' is also rather restrictive, in that Preference Determination, Cognitive Mapping and Expert Systems (see later chapters) are concerned with the processing of logic and ideas rather than simply data. Even in the mid 1990s, the requirement that a computer system can only be classed as a DSS if it is used by the decision maker in person means that there will be difficulty in finding many cases of DSS apart from those based on the use of spreadsheets. His other two characteristics would seem to be advantages enjoyed by any successful information system rather than uniquely by DSS.

Characteristics of Decision Support Systems

Freyenfeld (1984) has done more than simply define DSS, since his definition includes the characteristics that he has found in the examples of DSS he has used in reaching his definition. Thus Freyenfeld straddles two camps who have attempted to separate what are and what are not DSS. He is half a 'definer' and half in the camp of those who believe that the common characteristics of systems that 'everyone' agrees to be DSS can be used to define DSS. This is hardly a purist approach!! Keen (1981) has looked at about 30 examples of what he feels are DSS and Alter (1983) has done similar work. From such pragmatic approaches Sprague and Watson (1986 page 8) sum up the characteristics that define DSS as:

–   they tend to be aimed at the less well structured, underspecified problems that upper level management face;

–   they attempt to combine the use of models or analytic techniques with traditional data access and retrieval functions;

–   they specifically focus on features which make them easy to use by non-computer people in an interactive mode; and

–   they emphasize flexibility and adaptability to accommodate changes in the environment and the decision making approach of the user.

There would appear to be some agreement about what a DSS is. The common elements would seem to be that they are computer-based and are usable by non-computer people. Additionally, the major difference between

MIS and DSS is *almost* universally seen as caused by the amount of structure in the problem.

Almost universally! Moore and Chang (1983) disagree quite violently with the view that problem structure or the lack of it, can usefully be used to define DSS. They argue that the concept of structure in a problem is not meaningful, because it depends on the user's perception of the structure. To quote Moore and Chang:

> ". . . a problem can only be considered more or less structured with regard to a particular decision maker, or group of similar decision makers, and at a particular point in time. In our experience there is simply no structure that can be identified with any decision making problem independent of the decision maker."

Without using the concept of structure in their definition of DSS, they define a DSS as a system that can be extended, capable of dealing with ad hoc data analysis and decision modelling, where the time horizon is future and the usage is irregular and at unplanned intervals.

It is important to note the phrase 'at a particular point in time' in the quote from Moore and Chang. This fits with the view expressed earlier in this chapter and exemplified by the discussion of Discounted Cash Flow techniques: that what may have been seen as an ill-structured problem at one time can change to be seen as structured, as use and education lead to greater understanding.

In Moore and Chang's definition, a computer system must be able to support ad hoc data analyses. It could be argued that the divide between MIS and DSS is that MIS is institutionalised – dealing with recurrent problems (i.e. tantamount to being structured), whilst DSS deals with ad hoc problems. What is lost in this view is that problems can be viewed as being similar to cherries in a mixed fruit cake: the cherries may be readily discernible but the surroundings can be quite different. The cherries correspond to the structured parts of a problem for which well established techniques may be available; the rest of the cake corresponds to the problem situation in which the techniques are to be used, and this is likely to differ markedly from one situation to another. In managerial terms this is repeating the view that each manager has a unique and time-dependent scenario within which problems surface and have to be dealt with.

There are those who disagree with making any distinction between MIS and DSS. Naylor (1982), for example, argues that there is nothing new about DSS that does not already exist in Management Science and MIS and disputes the need for a new term DSS.

There do not appear to be any significant differences about what constitutes the combined area of MIS and DSS: where the argument occurs is about where one ends and the other begins. There are several views on this, summarised in Figure 3.2.

SUMMARY

DSS are complex systems that have evolved from the coming together of developments in several research areas The diverse backgrounds of those active in the field have lead to problems of definition. There are some who consider that the term DSS applies only to a very limited type of computerised management support. Others take the view that DSS are simply one form of MIS.

The view taken here and followed throughout the rest of this book, is that the term DSS should encompass both systems that provide management information (MIS) and those that provide intelligence (and which will be termed Management Intelligence Systems (MINTS)). This enables the simple definition with which this book started, viz. 'a Decision Support System is a computer-based system that aids the process of decision making' to be retained. Specifically, DSS will not be restricted to systems used in person by the decision maker, interactively and/or concurrently. From the discussions of Chapter 2, this means that all aspects of managerial problem tackling that are helped by the use of computers will be covered by the term DSS.

The argument that the concept of problem structure is meaningless without taking the perceptions of the manager into account is a powerful one. This means that the term 'structure' cannot be used in any absolute sense, but is context specific.

REFERENCES

Alter S., (1977) *A Taxonomy of Decision Support Systems*, Sloan Management Review, No. 1, Fall, pp 39–56 12.

Eden C., Jones S. and Sims D., (1983) *Messing About in Problems: An Informal Structured Approach to their Identification and Management, Frontiers of Operational Research and Applied Systems Analysis*, Volume 1, Pergamon Press

Elam J.J, Huber G.P. and Hurt M.E., (1986) *An Examination of the DSS Literature* (1975–1985), in the Proceedings of the IFIP WG 8.3 *Working*

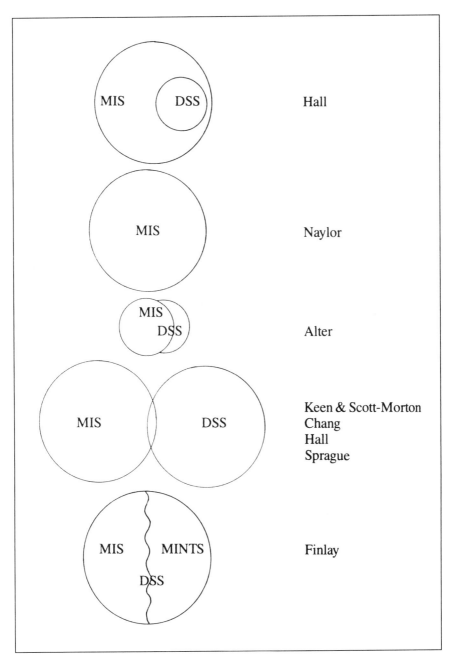

Figure 3.2   The Relationships between MIS and DSS

Conference on Decision Support Systems: A Decade in Perspective, (eds. E.McLean and H.G.Sol), Noordwijkerhout, The Netherlands, 16–18 June, pp 1–17.

Freyenfeld W.A., (1984) *Decision Support Systems*, NCC Publications, Manchester, UK.

Gorry A. and Scott Morton M.S., (1971) *A Framework for Information Systems Design*, Sloan Management Review, Vol.13, No.1, pp 55–70.

Hall J.A., (1983) *Management Information Systems*, Management Accounting, July, pp 10,23

Jarke M., (1986) Group Decision Support Through Office Systems: *Developments in Distributed DSS Technology*, in the Proceedings of the IFIP WG 8.3 Working Conference on Decision Support Systems: *A Decade in Perspective*, (eds. E.McLean and H.G.Sol), Noordwijkerhout, The Netherlands, 16–18 June, pp 145–156.

Keen P.G.W and Scott Morton M.S. (1978) *Decision Support Systems: An Organisational Perspective*, Addison-Wesley.

Keen P.G.W., (1981) *Decision Support Systems: A Research Perspective, in Decision Support Systems:* Issues and Challenges, Pergamon Press.

Moore J.H. and Chang M.G., (1983) *Meta-Design Considerations in Building DSS, in Building Decision Support Systems* ed. Bennett J.L.,Addison-Wesley Series on Decision Support, pp 173–204.

Naylor T.H., (1982) *Decision Support Systems or Whatever Happened to MIS?*, Interfaces, Vol.12, No.4, pp 92–94.

Sprague R.H Jr and Watson H.J., (1986) *Decision Support Systems. Putting Theory into Practice*, Prentice-Hall International.

Stabell C.B., (1986) *Decision Support Systems: Alternative perspectives and Schools*, in the Proceedings of the IFIP WG 8.3 Working Conference on Decision Support Systems: *A Decade in Perspective*, (eds. E.McLean and H.G.Sol), Noordwijkerhout, The Netherlands, 16–18 June pp 173–182.

Tversky A.and Kahnemann D., (1974) *Judgement under uncertainty: Heuristics and Biases*, Science 185, pp 1124–1131.

4 Types of Decision Support Systems

This chapter is devoted to the classification of DSS into types, and the reader deserves to know why this is necessary. The reason is that the ways in which DSS are developed and implemented differ markedly depending on type. For example, as described in the last chapter, the emphasis placed on logic modelling within Management Science contrasts with the emphasis on the data modelling of Computer Science. A DSS where the major component is the logic model, is likely to be developed by people with different skills and for different types of people and for a different purpose than a DSS where the major component is the data model: most significantly, the interaction of developer and user is likely to differ markedly. Thus to achieve successful development and implementation, it is vital to determine which type of DSS is sought. The development and implementation of DSS will be dealt with in detail in Chapter 12.

A further reason for classifying DSS is to provide a framework for research: without such a framework the results of findings about such disparate types of system cannot be communicated effectively, and without such communication, progress in understanding the factors of importance in the development of DSS will be inhibited.

PREVIOUS CLASSIFICATIONS OF DECISION SUPPORT SYSTEMS

One well-known classification is that of Alter (1977). This classification is reproduced in Figure 4.1.

The major split made by Alter is between data-oriented and model-oriented systems, following the traditional split between Computer Science and Management Science. Alter has little to say about systems outside of these two areas. The data oriented systems are similar to those that are classified as Data Retrieval Systems in the classification given later in this chapter. The model-oriented systems cover similar ground to the Extrapolatory Systems, again as described later.

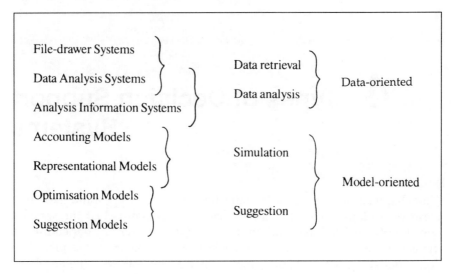

Figure 4.1   Alter's Classification of Decision Support Systems

Freyenfeld (1984) takes a very different and very pragmatic approach in his classification. He classifies by what was currently available and with a mix of location in an organisation in which a system will be used (the level in the hierarchy and to some extent function) and on the predominant decision making method employed. He identifies six types of DSS, viz:.

- Chief Executive Information Systems

- Commercial Operational Analysis and Planning Systems

- Industrial Operational Analysis and Planning Systems

- Preference Determination Systems

- Cognitive Mapping Systems

- Expert Advisory Systems

Neither of the classifications given above is adequate. Alter's classification does not include the newer types of DSS, and Freyenfeld's is confusing in that different criteria for classification are used at different points in the classification. As will be argued below, the emphasis on development and implementation calls for a classification based on the degree of difficulty likely to be experienced by the manager in use of a DSS; this in turn is dependent on the degree of complexity and uncertainty the manager perceives.

ENVIRONMENTAL COMPLEXITY AND DYNAMISM

The structure within organisations defines and is defined by the centres of responsibility and the hierarchies of control. In his review of the link between the way in which organisations are structured and the organisational environment, Mintzberg (1979) identified two factors as major determinants of organisational structure. These two factors are environmental complexity and environmental dynamism. Complexity is a measure of the diversity of environmental influences, the amount of knowledge, information needed to successfully tackle the problem situation, and the interconnectivity of factors. Dynamism is the rate of change of the environment

The matrix devised by Mintzberg is reproduced in Figure 4.2.

A centralised organisation is one in which all major decisions are taken by a central unit, whereas in a decentralised organisation, many decisions are devolved to local units. An example of a centralised organisation would be that associated with car assembly. A bureaucratic organisation would be one where the policies under which the subordinate units/personnel must act are very tightly defined. Traditionally, the Civil Service has been organised bureaucratically.

Under Mintzberg's model, as the environment becomes more complex, the appropriate move is to decentralise: as the environment becomes more dynamic, the appropriate organisation is an organic one. An organisation takes the structure that it does, because that is the structure which allows it to react to environmental changes in the most appropriate fashion: ie. the

	Dynamism	
	Stable	**Dynamic**
High Complexity	Decentralised *Bureaucratic*	Decentralised *Organic*
Low Complexity	Centralised *Bureaucratic*	Centralised *Organic*

Figure 4.2   Structure and Environmental Influences
(after Mintzberg)

structure allows members of the organisation to tackle problems in a more suitable way.

The importance of this view for classifying DSS is that, just as the most appropriate structure changes with the dynamism and complexity of the situation, then so too should the type of DSS used in the organisation. With this view, the major factor determining the characteristics of a DSS is the manager's perception of the uncertainty of his situation. This uncertainty is a combination of the dynamism of the environment and of its complexity. The consequences of this uncertainty will now be explored.

UNCERTAINTY AND ITS INFLUENCE ON DECISION SUPPORT SYSTEMS

Thompson and Tuden (1959) take the view that the way in which organisations make decisions differs depending on the level of agreement surrounding a decision issue. Each decision is seen as involving an objective to be attained and the means of achieving this end. Agreement within a decision unit can exist in either the objective (in Thompson and Tuden's words, the preference about possible outcomes) or in the means (again, in Thompson and Tuden's words, beliefs about causation) or both. [By decision unit is meant the group of people who are a party to the decision, who 'own' the problem and the subsequent decision: the unit could be one person or it could be a well-defined group such as the Board of Directors of a company]

Thompson and Tuden's matrix is reproduced in Figure 4.3. Earl (1983) has placed DSS into this framework. When what is sought is simply computation, then all that is required from a DSS is that it provides answers. When there is no uncertainty whatsoever, then an answer generating system will produce the one and only answer. Examples in this class are accountancy models for control and executive information systems. When there is uncertainty about cause and effect – about the rules governing the way the world operates – yet little uncertainty about the objectives of the enterprise, judgement is needed. DSS can only assist in this area if they provide the means whereby judgement can be enhanced and this calls for learning. Examples of DSS that are useful in this area are those for financial planning and for simulation.

Where there is uncertainty about the objectives of the parts of a business unit concerned with a decision but little uncertainty about cause and effect, the role of a DSS is either to act as a framework within which debate can take place or help focus debate. An example of the use of a financial planning model to do just this is described by Finlay (1983). Compromise is necessary

		Preferences about possible outcomes	
		Agreement	Disagreement
Beliefs about causation	Agreement	Computation	Compromise
	Disagreement	Judgement	Inspiration

Figure 4.3   Thompson and Tuden's Matrix of Decision Issues

in such a situation and a DSS can assist, by helping each 'side' see the other's point of view and the consequences to each side of departing from their initial positions.

Finally, in the area of inspiration, Earl dubs DSS as 'ideas systems' – systems to help generate ideas and stimulate creativity. There may seem to be little possibility of a role for DSS in this area, but as described in Chapter 8, systems have been developed and successfully used.

A matrix representation following Earl's view of how an ideal organisation would behave is reproduced in Figure 4.4. This view of the role of DSS is rather idealistic; in reality, managers will use the system to further their own causes, as long as these are not seen to be too different from those of the organisation. The second matrix of Earl's that is reproduced in Figure 4.5 is

		Uncertainty about outcomes	
		Low	High
Uncertainty about Cause and effect	Low	Answer generating system	Dialogue system
	High	Learning system	Ideas system

Figure 4.4   Uses for Decision Support Systems (after Earl, 1983)

a more cynical view than that of Figure 4.4, but certainly more realistic. This shows that where managers should be exercising judgement and learning, they expect the system to produce answers: where they should be seeking compromise and engaging in dialogue and debate they seek to use the systems to produce information to gain an advantage over the opposition: and where inspiration is needed, systems are not used to generate ideas but to justify decisions already taken – purely for political purposes. The uses cited by Earl are all ways of using DSS, and are likely to require different forms of system.

Although these matrix pictures illustrate important conceptual perspectives, a major difficulty remains with using them to classify DSS. This arises because the dimensions that are used lay emphasis on a distinction that is hard to maintain in practice. The problem is that there is rarely a sharp distinction between means and ends: (almost) every means is an end and vice-versa. For example, cutting costs may be considered as an end in itself, but also as a means to increasing margins: increasing margins could be a means to the end of increased profits: increased profits a means to acquiring another company: this acquisition as a means to organisational growth and so on. Before leaving Figures 4.4 and 4.5 it is interesting to reflect that the left-hand side of these figures contain quantitative systems for focused problems, and as such their use would augment the left half of the brain. On the other hand, the right-hand side of these figures is concerned with systems to aid the more creative activities of management, corresponding to right-brained activities.

Looking at the matrix, one can see that insights would be needed where there was a high uncertainty about outcomes (where dialogue systems are

		Uncertainty about outcomes	
		Low	High
Uncertainty about	Low	Answer generating system	Ammunition system
Cause and effect	High	Answer generating system	Rationalisation system

Figure 4.5   Uses for Decision Support Systems (after Earl, 1983)

called for), and dialogue would be needed where uncertainty about cause and effect exists. Although the right-hand side of the matrix in Figure 4.4 is concerned far more with group decision making than is the left-hand side, there is a merging of the attributes required of the systems in the lower left-hand quadrant, and the upper right-hand quadrant. Thus a more applicable view of DSS can be obtained from a 'linear' model. Such a picture can be derived by placing the right hand side of the matrix of Figure 4.4 under the left-hand side and thus forming Figure 4.6. Whilst the general form of Figure 4.6 better mirrors reality, the terms used by Earl are no longer appropriate in this model. The names of system types used in Figure 4.6 will be replaced for reasons that will be explained in the following discussion.

CONTRASTS BETWEEN MANAGEMENT INFORMATION AND MANAGEMENT INTELLIGENCE SYSTEMS

As one moves down Figure 4.6, the uncertainty increases. Additionally, there is a shift in emphasis in the type of output – from systems producing information to systems that produce intelligence.

The distinction between information and intelligence has been defined in Chapter 2 and is important, since the emphases within DSS change depending on whether one is dealing with information (and using a MIS) or with

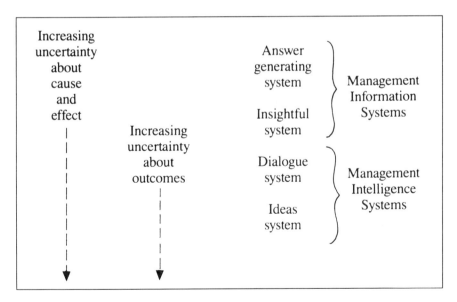

Figure 4.6   Relationships Between Decision Support Systems

intelligence, where a MINTS would be employed. A comparative view of the emphases within MIS and MINTS has been developed by Finlay and Forghani (1987). An augmented version of this view is reproduced in Table 4.1. A detailed discussion of the terms used in this table is given in Chapter 12, where the design of DSS is discussed.

Most of the items in Table 4.1 are self explanatory; those that are not will be described later where most appropriate. What is important to recognise at this stage is that MIS are generally context independent whereas the form and use of a MINTS relies very heavily on the context. What is meant by this is that MIS will be used in essentially the same way whatever ups and downs the organisation goes through: for example, weekly variance reports will still be needed, managers will still be using forecasting techniques and so on. This is certainly not the case with MINTS: for example, the factors to be taken into account in considering whether to go ahead with a capital investment, and the weight to place on these factors, will depend on the specific situation. If new government legislation covering minimum wage rates were in the offing, this would create a different situation.

With this view of MIS and MINTS, it is seen that the top portion of the Figure 4.6 corresponds to MIS, the lower portion to MINTS. As anticipated in the summary of the preceding chapter, the term DSS is used to encompass both MIS and MINTS. MIS are concerned with efficiency (doing the thing right) whilst MINTS are concerned with effectiveness (doing the right thing).

MIS may be viewed as being of two broad types. First, there are those that purely provide information about the past ('facts'): these are termed Data Retrieval Systems. Second, there are those that provide information about the future through extrapolation from past data or using relationships based on past data. These are termed Extrapolatory Systems.

MINTS may also be considered to be of two broad types. First, there are what are termed the Preference Determination Systems, where decision makers have to choose between options without formally considering cause and effect, or at the very least not being called upon to formally articulate it. Second, in the situation where there is great uncertainty in both the preferred outcomes and in the perceived cause and effect relations, the required systems have been termed Scenario Development Systems. With such systems, the decision maker is using a DSS to develop his overall view of the world, i.e. of his scenario.

Fitting these types of DSS into Figure 4.6 produces Figure 4.7.

Table 4.1 The Emphases Associated with Types of IT System

	Management Information System	Management Intelligence System
Type of system	Internal control/budgeting	Planning
Focus	On efficient, structured information flows and data structures Efficiency	On effective decisions, flexibility, adaptability and quick response Effectiveness
Objectives	Prespecified	Ad hoc/contingent
Type of situation	Within fixed policies	Within a given scenario
Created by	IT specialists/business analysts	Users/business analysts
Design perspective	Organisational	Individual/small group
Design methodology used	'Classical' systems approach and prototyping of inputs and outputs	'Breadboarding'
Hardware/software orientation	Hardware and software	Software
Models i) ii) iii) iv) v)	Fixed logic Mainly deterministic relations Mainly arithmetic and mathematical Mainly deterministic data Ratio and interval scales	Evolutionary logic Judgemental relations Mainly logical Probabilistic data Nominal and ordinal scales
Output i) ii) iii) iv)	General format Standardised/interrogative reports An answer Management information	User created Iterative/interactive ill-structured reports Insight, learning, dialogue Intelligence
Time scale	Past, present and future	Present and future
Context	Context independent Structured	Context dependent Ill-structured
Exactitude	Precision and accuracy	Accuracy
Validation	'Classical' systems methodology	Appropriateness
Usage	Largely mandatory	Discretionary

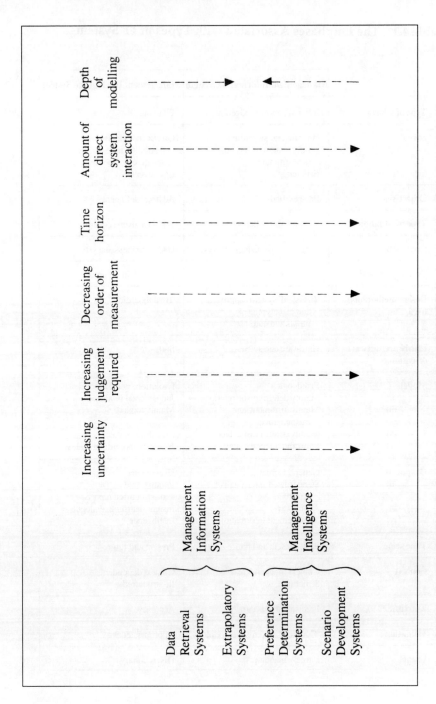

Figure 4.7   Types of Decision Support Systems

DSS are not used in isolation within an organisation: they are used within what might be termed a decision making or problem tackling 'infrastructure'. Systems to enhance this infrastructure, although not DSS in themselves, are significant in the successful use of DSS. These systems are termed Metasystems and are discussed in Chapter 14.

TYPES OF MANAGEMENT INFORMATION SYSTEM

Data Retrieval Systems

The crucial attribute that distinguishes Data Retrieval Systems from other DSS is that they are limited to the analysis of past data and the reporting of the current situation. Data Retrieval Systems can usefully be divided into three subclasses.

File-Drawer Systems

These systems provide rapid, ad-hoc access to a set of pre-structured data in support of a regular operational task. A system consisting of personnel records would be a good and common example of file drawer systems.

Data Analysis Systems

Data Analysis Systems provide straightforward analyses, reports and graphical output of predefined situations. Predefined variance reporting is a good example of data analysis systems.

Executive Information Systems

These systems are a recently evolved type of data retrieval system that provides selected and summarised information and trend forecasts in a form suitable for senior executives.

Extrapolatory Systems.

The term 'Extrapolatory System' is used to cover those DSS that are concerned with looking to the future and which rely on extending a present situation in a formalised manner. Many of these systems employ Management Science techniques. A practical approach is to classify Extrapolatory Systems into three categories.

Definitional Systems

These systems are such that definitional relations form the totality of the logic model. Definitional relations are relations between variables that are as they are because they have been defined to be so. Accounting is an area in which such systems abound. The budgetary system discussed in Chapter 2 is an example of this genre.

Causal Systems

Here the approach is to identify cause and effect relationships that have been found to apply in the past, and to use these with putative future data values to obtain a result. The cause and effect relations used may be derived from statistical data, and may contain considerable judgement in their derivation. The techniques involved in such systems are such as to require considerable mathematical modelling expertise on the part of the systems builder, who may not be the end user. A simple example of this class of system might involve algebraic equations and a spreadsheet package. A more complex example would be a system incorporating linear programming techniques (*see* Chapter 6).

Probabilistic Systems

These systems differ from other Extrapolatory Systems in that they explicitly include probabilistic features within themselves. This means that probabilities and/or statistical distributions need to be explicitly included in the data models of such systems. Examples of common probabilistic techniques are those to carry out simulation and statistical forecasting as described in Chapter 6. As with Causal Systems, considerable mathematical and statistical expertise is required by the systems builder.

TYPES OF MANAGEMENT INTELLIGENCE SYSTEMS

Preference Determination Systems

The distinctive approach in Preference Determination Systems is that an exhaustive list of feasible options is needed, often with an exhaustive list of associated criteria. It is convenient to classify the Preference Determination Systems presently available into two types, based on the predominant decision making methodology employed. The types are those based on decision trees and on multi-attribute utility theory.

Decision Tree Systems

Some types of decision are characterised by a series of either/or decisions and the play of an uncertain environment. The decision tree technique is a way of graphically illustrating such a series of decisions in a clear and convenient way. Decision Trees span the boundary between Extrapolatory Systems and the other Preference Determination Systems, in that they combine probabilistic features with a exhaustive list of possible options and outcomes.

Multi-Attribute Decision Systems

When using such systems, the specific problem or issue must first be named, and the options open to the problem owners listed. For example, if the decision concerned the choice of a new car, the options would be the feasible types of new car. Associated with the decision would be several criteria which would also have to be specified. In the car example, criteria for selection might be the purchase price, fuel consumption figures and seating capacity. The interaction of options and criteria will produce a matrix.

Judgement alone is required to produce these lists, and judgement is the sole means of obtaining responses. The systems rely for their efficacy on the way in which the options are displayed to the participants, the form of questioning adopted, and the way in which the (often many) responses are combined.

This preference methodology exposes the structure of the problem situation and hence systematically identifies the options available for selection. Both dimensions of uncertainty can be incorporated, typically requiring a large amount of subjective input from the decision makers. Group decision making is explicitly supported with several of the tools currently available.

Scenario Development Systems

The emphasis in most DSS lies with the technology of the support – with the tools. Scenario Development Systems shift the emphasis, so that the system acts as a tool (or set of tools) that assist and enhance human cognitive and interactive processes rather than constraining or inhibiting them.

Two types of Scenario Development Systems have been identified. Cognitive Mapping Systems are suitable to codify and expose the ideas that people already have and can articulate: Ideas Generation Systems are used to unearth and examine novel ideas.

Cognitive Mapping Systems

These systems are such as to impose little or no formal structure on the decision-making processes on the individual or group of managers who 'own' the problem situation. In operation, a facilitator extracts significant ideas and linkages of concepts from the free flowing discussion taking place. These linked concepts form a cognitive map for the group, allowing each member of the group to see how his concepts are viewed by the other members and vice-versa. Analysis of these maps identifies where disagreement lies, and where resolution needs to be sought.

Ideas Generation Systems

Ideas Generation Systems support processes to unearth novel ways of tackling problems. Since such sessions (including so-called brainstorming) call for relatively uninhibited responses from the participant(s), Ideas Generation Systems must in turn impose very little in the way of formality on the creative process.

SUMMARY

DSS have been broadly classified into MIS and MINTS. MIS have been further subdivided into Data Retrieval Systems where the logic model is extremely simple but often with extensive data models, and Extrapolatory Systems, where the reverse is often the case. MINTS have been subdivided into Preference Determination Systems where generally the user has little need to articulate the reasons for his responses and his logic remains obscure, and Scenario Development Systems, where the emphasis is on unearthing and structuring ideas.

In MIS, the support to the manager is through improving the efficiency of the system for which he is responsible, whilst MINTS seek to affect system effectiveness. Ironically, MIS seek this improvement in system efficiency by attempting to change the effectiveness of problem tackling (this is especially true of Extrapolatory Systems), whilst MINTS seek to improve system effectiveness through an improvement in the efficiency of problem tackling: there is little or no attempt to move managers away from problem tackling procedures with which they are familiar and comfortable, to procedures that might appear to be more 'rational' and more appropriate.

In Chapter 3 the need to classify DSS was proposed because of the different forms of development and implementation routes and skills required. This was stated with little evidence apart from a link back to the origins of DSS. Whilst it is in Chapter 12 where the development and implementation of DSS are considered in detail, this chapter should have given the reader a good feel for the widely differing types of DSS, and his/her imagination should have led him/her to realise intuitively that no single prescription is sufficient to cover the development and implementation of all forms of DSS.

Short definitions of all the types of DSS discussed above are given in Appendix A.

REFERENCES

Alter S., (1977) *A Taxonomy of Decision Support Systems*, Sloan Management Review, No.1, Fall, pp 39–56

Earl M.J., (1983) in *Management Accounting and Practice* by David Cooper and Robert Scapens, ICMA, London

Eden C., (1986) *Managing strategic ideas: the role of the computer*, ICL Technical Journal November, pp 173–183

Finlay P.N., (1983) *How to Manage Non-Financially with Packages*, Management Today, May, pp 39–44

Freyenfeld W.A., (1984) *Decision Support Systems*, NCC Publications, Manchester, UK.

Mintzberg H., (1979) *The Structure of Organizations: A Synthesis of Research*, Prentice Hall, 1979, p268

Thompson J.D. and Tuden A., (1959) *Strategies, Structures and Processes of Organisational Decision, in Comparative Studies in Administration*, ed. J.D.Thompson et al., University of Pittsburg Press

5 Data Retrieval Systems

The crucial attribute that distinguishes Data Retrieval Systems from other DSS is that they are almost completely limited to the analysis of past data or the reporting of the current situation. They enable the 'What is . . ?' type of question to be answered. Thus their contribution to decision making is mostly restricted to providing the base information on which decisions will be made.

Data Retrieval Systems can be subdivided into three subclasses: File-Drawer Systems, Data Analysis Systems and Executive Information Systems. Referring to the matrix of Figure 4.7, it will be seen that there will be some Data Retrieval Systems that are operating in areas with effectively no uncertainty.

FILE-DRAWER SYSTEMS

The simplest level of Data Retrieval System are 'File-Drawer Systems'. These give rapid, ad-hoc access to a set of pre-structured data in support of a regular operational task. They are really mechanised versions of manual filing systems and are primarily designed for line personnel: at their most complex, they hold data on major aspects of organisational activities.

The emphasis in such systems is on data modelling, with little in the way of logic modelling. Examples of this type of Data Retrieval System are personnel records systems and inventory recording systems.

Computer Software for File-Drawer Systems

Database and database management systems are the tools that are nowadays most often used to support file-drawer systems. The clear industry standard for microcomputers has been DBase. Although not a full relational database, this package will allow the vast majority of data handling jobs to be performed very adequately. It has its own programming language which allows easy extension to non-standard applications. Currently, the fastest-selling microcomputer packages appear to be Paradox and DataEase, both offering a fully relational database. DataEase is particularly easy to use.

A forceful development is that of distributed databases in which the totality of the corporate data is held on many different computers at many locations. The location of any set of data is hidden from the users, who have easy access to the whole of the database. The market leaders appear to be Ingres, INFORMIX and ORACLE.

DATA ANALYSIS SYSTEMS

Data Analysis Systems provide straightforward analyses, reports and graphical output of predefined situations. They will tend to be designed to accept formatted input data. They generally possess report generators and thus although they may be inflexible per se, they can be simple to redesign. Examples of this genre of DSS are Budget Variance Reporting and Staff Attendance Reporting Systems and systems for the statistical analysis of market research data and marketing analyses.

Computer Software for Data Analysis Systems

There are a very large number of packages available to support Data Retrieval types of DSS. Many are specific to a particular application. This specificity, and the rather marginal contribution Data Retrieval Systems make to managerial decision making result in individual data retrieval packages not being described here. However, it is worth mentioning those packages that are constructed on database principles, and thus offer powerful data analysis features, yet also have some facilities to allow planning to be undertaken. These packages overlap the Data Retrieval and Extrapolatory System categories, and act as a bridge between data from the past and extrapolations into the future. These packages might be termed 'Database Planning Packages'.

Packages of this type are Express (and its micro offspring pcExpress), FCS-MULTI and System-W. These packages are such that the analyst does not have to specify the form of the output he requires at the outset, but is simply called upon to specify the basic features of the data model: its dimensions, elements and the logic that links the variables – plus of course the input data. Contrast this with a spreadsheet in which the form of the output is intimately linked with the form of the input.

For example, a company selling several products (bolts, screws, etc.) in several regions might create a model with the dimensions of product, cost, region and time. Elements for each dimension would be specified (for example, London, Leeds and Glasgow for the dimension 'Region'; January, February, March, etc. for the dimension 'Time'). It is then possible to report on any two dimensions – costs against time for bolts for London say, or products against costs for the London region for the whole year. In the marketing world this sort of data retrieval is known as 'slice and dice'. This is illustrated in Figure 5.1.

Logically, planners seldom need to have absolutely up-to-date information on the current situation in the organisation in order to plan for the future. For example, in order to plan the purchase of raw materials for three future years, it is not necessary to know the precise current stock position when plans are being made: and the further into the future the planning takes the organisation, the less should the current position matter. However, it is the author's experience that managers find it compulsive to have exact figures about the organisation available when planning, and the database financial modelling packages can provide these fairly readily.

Finally, a mention of packages for statistical analyses. There are around 100 packages that might be described as appropriate for use in general statistical analyses. Many of these programs were written by individuals, and do not have a good commercial base. Others come as micro versions of mainframe packages. The best known of the latter are SPSS and Minitab (with the micro versions known as SPSS PC and Microtab respectively). Statgraphics has exceptional graphics and provides many analytical techniques.

EXECUTIVE INFORMATION SYSTEMS

The term 'Executive Information System' first appears to have been coined by Rockart and Treacy (1982). These systems, sometimes marketed as boardroom systems, are a type of Data Retrieval System that provides selected and summarised information in a form suitable for senior executives. They assist in the assessment of the impact of changes in the business environment or of strategic policy by providing top managers with information on critical areas of the organisation's activities, drawn from both internal and external databases. The importance of having access external sources of information is reflected in the 5,000+ databases that are available on-line in 1994. A great many of these are business databases offering, inter alia, such information as individual company statistics, financial exchange rates, stock market prices and financial indicators such as Dow Jones.

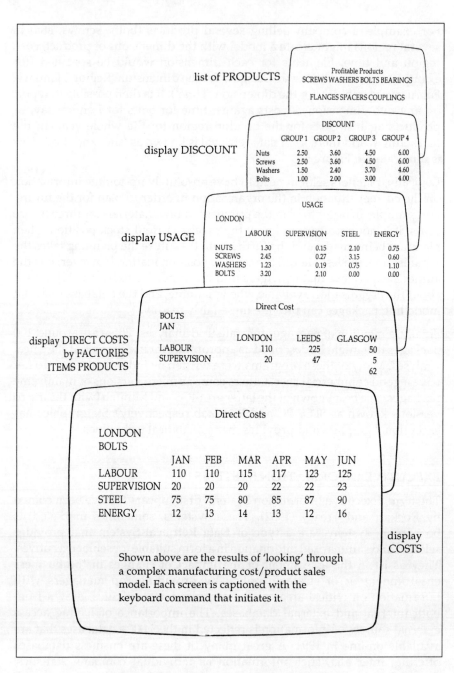

list of PRODUCTS

Profitable Products
SCREWS WASHERS BOLTS BEARINGS

FLANGES SPACERS COUPLINGS

display DISCOUNT

DISCOUNT

	GROUP 1	GROUP 2	GROUP 3	GROUP 4
Nuts	2.50	3.60	4.50	6.00
Screws	2.50	3.60	4.50	6.00
Washers	1.50	2.40	3.70	4.60
Bolts	1.00	2.00	3.00	4.00

display USAGE

USAGE

LONDON

	LABOUR	SUPERVISION	STEEL	ENERGY
NUTS	1.30	0.15	2.10	0.75
SCREWS	2.45	0.27	3.15	0.60
WASHERS	1.23	0.19	0.75	1.10
BOLTS	3.20	2.10	0.00	0.00

display DIRECT COSTS
by FACTORIES
ITEMS PRODUCTS

Direct Cost

BOLTS
JAN

	LONDON	LEEDS	GLASGOW
LABOUR	110	225	50
SUPERVISION	20	47	5
			62

Direct Costs

LONDON
BOLTS

	JAN	FEB	MAR	APR	MAY	JUN
LABOUR	110	110	115	117	123	125
SUPERVISION	20	20	20	22	22	23
STEEL	75	75	80	85	87	90
ENERGY	12	13	14	13	12	16

display
COSTS

Shown above are the results of 'looking' through
a complex manufacturing cost/product sales
model. Each screen is captioned with the
keyboard command that initiates it.

Figure 5.1   Different Views of the Data

The formal and easy linking of external databases into Executive Information Systems has finally meant the passing of the era when the preoccupation of top management information systems was with providing internal information – when the managers they were supposed to be supporting often had much more need of external information. Harvey-Jones (1988), when he was in charge of ICI, was loud in the praise of Executive Information Systems; in his view, the one in use in ICI contributed significantly to strategic decision making. His successor, Sir Denys Henderson, continues to use the system to review the company's operating performance in relation to its competitors. Sir Brian Nicholson, chairman of the Post Office, and Sir Colin Marshall, chairman of British Airways are also reported users of Executive Information Systems (Rolph and Bartram (1992). However, it must not be thought that only top executives should be allowed to use such systems: the view seems to be gaining ground that their use should be encouraged further down organisations: for example, Rolph and Bartram (1992) describe how about 40 executives in Rank Xerox make use of its Executive Information System.

The growing success of Executive Systems can largely be attributed to their use of menu selection instead of command languages, and by the use of a touch screen or easy point-and-click technology as alternatives to keyboard operation (see Chapter 10 for further details). The presentation of information is predominantly through the use of computer screens. By meeting the stringent 'ease of use' requirements of senior managers, these systems are breaking down their resistance to the use of computer-generated information. An example of the main menu of an EIS (rechristened an Enterprise Intelligence System!!) is given in Figure 5.2.

Executive Information Systems are geared to doing three principal tasks, exception reporting, 'drilling down' and trend determination. Exception reporting is facilitated by allowing users to set tolerance limits for the values of key variables. Should these limits be exceeded then the area on-screen will be highlighted – by flashing, the use of a different colour or through some other alerting means. For example, an Executive Information System might be used to alert a finance director that a particular cost centre is well over budget in the latest reporting period.

Drill-down permits managers to examine information in more and more levels of detail in a logical progression. The first screen provides the most summarised version of a set of information – at corporate level perhaps – whilst the last screen provides the most detailed information – at the business unit or cost centre level perhaps. To investigate an identified problem at the corporate level the executive would move progressively

Figure 5.2   An Example of an EIS main menu
(reproduced by kind permission of Information Resources)

through the screens down the organisation until the source of the problem became clear. In the example, the finance director might track an adverse variance through to a specific cost centre. An alternative route to the source of problems is through a 'hot-spot' capability whereby an executive can leapfrog the sequence of menus and move directly to the troubled area. In the example given, the finance director could use the Executive Information System to find out who is responsible for a cost centre that is over budget (by accessing a personnel chart) and to read the more detailed reports that would normally be read only by lower level managers.

Trend analysis enables current and historical data to be compared, trends to be determined and for these to be extrapolated into the future. In this respect they are encompassing a little of the capabilities of Extrapolatory Systems.

One problem with the development of Executive Information Systems is the amount of work needed to integrate the software with existing computer systems, to allow information to flow automatically. The full cost of developing an Executive Information System is high. Users who select a system based on a mainframe can expect to pay between £25–150,000 for the use of a proprietary package: users of PC-based systems with a licence for use on several workstations can expect to pay in the region of £5–20,000. In addition, there are the costs of development and maintenance. In a large organisation, a team of between 3–6 analysts might typically be required to develop the first prototype Executive Information System working over perhaps three months, and nine months to develop an EIS suitable for executive use. Rolph and Bartram (1992) give as an example the timetable for the introduction and continuous development of ICI's Executive Information System. This is reproduced below:

How ICI's Executive Information System Continues to Grow	
1986 April	Prototype
1986 September	5 users; 4 modules
1987 September	Chairman becomes the 10th user
1988 April	18 users including 4 directors
1989 March	60 users including 7 directors
1991 October	140 users including 7/9 directors: 60 modules

A team of 1–3 analysts would typically be required to enhance and maintain an Executive Information System of the size of ICI's.

Rolph and Bartram (1992) provide many further examples of the development and use of EIS. Two further, short articles are those by Wilson (1993) and Cavanagh (1993).

Computer Software for Executive Information Systems

Although it is possible to build an Executive Information System without buying a package specifically designed for this purpose, (and the Airline Management Information System (AIMS) used by British Airways for approaching 10 years and developed in-house, is an example of a successful implementation), it is becoming more common to purchase such software. There are now several Executive Information System packages marketed in the UK. The main ones appear to be Commander EIS, EMPOWER, Epic,

Express/EIS, Forest & Trees, Holos and Lightship. Other products from other suppliers are entering the field (*see*, for example, Reference 1 and Bird (1991)).

If an Executive Information System is to provide executives with the capability of drilling down through a hierarchy of data and to move horizontally within the data, it must have access to very large volumes of data. The freedom of executives will be severely limited if only a summary of the corporate database is available to them. The likely 'explosion' of data as one moves down the data hierarchy is shown in Figure 5.3.

Second and third tier information is critical to the overall value of an Executive Information System and generally means that several thousand potential screens will need to be accommodated. These should not be prescribed in detail, and this means that the system should be able to access the full corporate database. This means that the microcomputer used for display must be able to link in with the database held on a mainframe and use its powerful data processing capabilities.

Two distinct technological approaches towards EIS have been taken. One approach is what its designers term 'seamless micro – mainframe integration'. Software is distributed between PC and mainframe. When a manager arrives in his office in the morning, he turns on his PC: this starts the PC portion of his software running. This software in turn connects the PC to the mainframe, logs the user on, and starts the mainframe portion of the software. The PC and mainframe then run checks to make sure they are both running the same release of the software. The user, meanwhile, sees a series of menus on his PC and he makes selections from them. The PC and mainframe talk to each other send data and commands back and forth in order to fulfil the manager's request. The database resides on the mainframe and data is served up to the PCs on an as-needed basis: in practice this may be difficult to do in a time-scale acceptable to the executive user. The PCs handle all the user interface, including graphics. This architecture provides the speed of access and data processing of the mainframe, with the ease of use and presentational capabilities of the PC.

In a second approach organisational databases such as that maintained by a transaction processing system and external databases such as that offered by the Stock Exchange on share price movements allow key data to be extracted and stored in a database dedicated to the EIS. Whilst this approach guarantees a fast response to executive queries it generally requires constant maintenance by IT professionals to service changing executive demands. Products such as Lightship and Forest & Trees on the other hand offer users tools by which they can query data held on the organisation's databases such as those in a company's general ledger system.

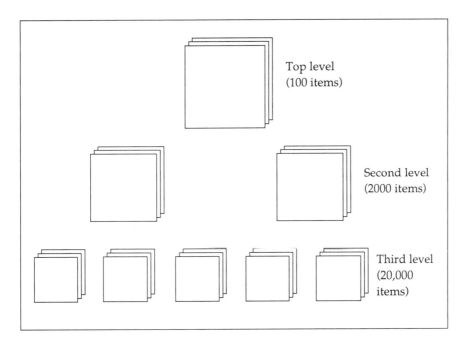

Figure 5.3   The Explosion of Information Requirements

Rolph and Bartram (1992) put forward an approach that they term 'co-operative processing' for a distributed environment: their view is reproduced in Figure 5.4.

The executive PCs are linked via a network that contains a server PC. A request for information from any executive PC will be handled by the server which will retrieve the required data from whichever PC(s) is holding the data. This approach takes advantage of the move to open systems, whereby hardware from different manufacturers can be easily linked together and provides the technical advantage that only needed data is downloaded to the executive PCs. The political and organisational advantage of this approach is that it follows the general business trend towards decentralisation.

SUMMARY

The contribution of Data Retrieval Systems to managerial decision making is in providing, through the use of databases and database management

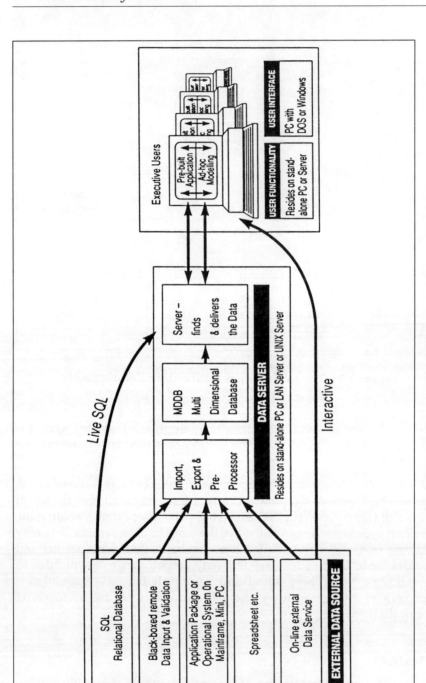

Figure 5.4   Example of a Cooperation Processing Approach

systems, ready access to the data that is the raw material for most DSS. Executive Information Systems extend this contribution by providing a powerful and 'senior executive-friendly' means for organisations to obtain quantitative information on organisational activities and access to external databases. The development and maintenance costs are likely to be high.

REFERENCES

1. *Executive Information Systems*, (1992) Computing, 3rd September, pp 21–22.

Bird J., (1991) *Executive Information Systems, Management Handbook*, NCC Blackwell.

Cavanagh E., (1993) *The Best Fit for Figures*, Retail Week, 12th February.

Harvey-Jones J., (1988) *Making it Happen: Reflections on Leadership*, Collins, p 187.

Rockart J. and Treacy M., (1982) *The CEO goes on-line*, Harvard Business Review.

Rolph P and Bartram P., (1992) *How to Choose and Use an Executive Information System*, Mercury Books.

Wilson K., (1993) *Brent cleans up its act*, The Guardian, May 6th.

6 Extrapolatory Systems

The term 'Extrapolatory System' is used to refer to a DSS that helps see the consequences of extending current practice into alternative (future) situations. Many of these systems employ Management Science techniques and hence fall into categories that follow traditional classifications of Management Science problems. This type of classification deals with well-known types of problem and the abstract models of operational situations. However, a classification such as this does not suit the approach taken in this book, which is directed towards the different routes to the development and implementation appropriate to different forms of DSS.

Three broad types of Extrapolatory System have been identified. These are Definitional Systems, Causal Systems and Probabilistic Systems. Significantly, there is no category for optimising systems (as was the case in Alter's classification which was introduced in Chapter 4). Although optimisation forms the basic driving force for some Management Science techniques (for example, Linear Programming, which is described in this present chapter), it is now uncommon for optima to be considered as answers to be acted upon without managerial judgement being used to interpret the outputs. Indeed, where an optimised output led straight to implementation, it is difficult to see the system as being one giving support, and thus it wouldn't be classified as a DSS.

It is important for readers to note that the techniques given as examples of Causal and Probabilistic Systems are a sample of those available. The choice of the sample has been governed by the need to express the range of techniques available, and the popularity of the techniques. It should also be noted that although the use of computer packages tailored to specific techniques is widespread, Extrapolatory Systems can and are developed using general purpose software tools such as BASIC, FORTRAN and C.

The scale of measurement used in Extrapolatory Systems is interval or ratio, and thus the full range of the mathematical and statistical modelling methodologies can be deployed.

DEFINITIONAL SYSTEMS

It is in financial planning that the most widespread use of Definitional Systems are found. This is because accountants have been clever enough to restrict their modelling activities almost exclusively to definitional systems. These are systems in which the logic model consists solely of equations that have been defined to be as they are. [In this respect they are identical to Data Retrieval Systems]. One example of a definitional relation was given in Chapter 2, viz:

$$Revenue = Sales \times Price$$

In definitional systems, there is no dispute about the relationships used in the logic model. There may, however, be dispute about the values the variables should take, and indeed about what constitutes a component of a variable – for example, what constitutes a sale.

There have been very many financial planning systems created: almost all would use either a spreadsheet software package or a financial modeller for their implementation.

Computer Software for Definitional Systems

Spreadsheets

The most popular decision support tool by far is the spreadsheet with a great many offerings to choose from. The market leaders seem to be Excel, Lotus 1-2-3, Quattro Pro and to a lesser extent CA-SuperCalc. Even though a fairly mature product, worthwhile enhancements continue to be made to Lotus 1-2-3 and it now offers true 3-dimensionality, with sheets stacked one behind the other. This facility will find many applications as the sheets allow data on separate markets or products to be 'filed away' in an easily controllable and accessible form.

The use of Lotus 1-2-3, the spreadsheet industry leader, has been increased by the emergence of products from independent developers that augment the product. This augmentation takes two forms. First, through 'add-ons' to the basic package, and here 4-5-6 World is the UK leading distributor. It offers many enhancements, such as 3-D Graphics, and Sideways which allows wide spreadsheet output to be printed down a page. The second form of augmentation is through the sale of ready-to-run applications, and here SystemBuild are in the van of development. SystemBuild offer several prewritten application 'templates' for use with Lotus 1-2-3 covering such areas as sales management, financial management and vehicle costing.

The use of spreadsheets is likely to continue to grow strongly, not only as new users come to use these packages as calculators, but as they are used as an easy interface to more sophisticated packages.

[Note: Risk Analysis is a facility that the recent improvements in processing speeds have made feasible on micros. Predict! allows probability distributions for input variables to be included in a spreadsheet, and thus for the distribution of the values of related outputs to be calculated and displayed. This allows spreadsheets to be used to build probabilistic models].

Financial Modellers

One of the problems of many spreadsheets is that their 'cell-specific' logic makes documentation and validation difficult. [Interestingly, Lotus Improv – fundamentally a spreadsheet – now allows formula to be expressed in natural language rather than relying on the rather restrictive cell-specific logic]. Financial modellers allow programming in structured English (to write, for example, the relation Revenue = Sales x Price) and thus mitigate these problems. The most significant area of development for financial modelling software is the full emergence of packages based on database principles, yet capable of supporting planning activities. Examples of such products are Express and pcExpress, FCS-MULTI and System-W. These packages cut the tight links between input and output inherent in spreadsheets, allowing the components of the models to be specified independently of any detailed knowledge of the outputs required. Any specific output can easily be specified and displayed.

CAUSAL SYSTEMS

Causal Systems are those systems that go beyond the definitional relations that are used in Definitional Systems and include cause and effect relations. For example, the Definitional System cited above takes values for the variables Sales and Price as input. It might be that a causal relation linking Sales and Price could be determined and incorporated within the system. If this were done, then the system would cease being simply a definitional one and become a causal one. The relations might become something like:

$$Sales = Revenue \times Price$$

$$Sales = \frac{20 \times Competitors' \ Price}{Price}$$

Two of the techniques most commonly used in creating Causal Systems will now be described – Network Analysis and Linear Programming. Popularity is one reason for selecting these two techniques: the second reason is that Network Analysis illustrates judgemental relations between activities, whereas Linear Programming illustrates judgemental relations between variables.

Network Analysis

Network Analysis (otherwise known as Project Scheduling and Critical Path Analysis) is a management tool designed to help managers plan projects composed of a number of identifiable parts, and which have to be completed within a specific time. It allows the logical progression of the activities making up a project to be identified, and will highlight limitations of resources and suggest how these might be mitigated. Once a project is underway, actual dates and the actual expenses incurred can be monitored against the plan.

Although a very simple project, it is instructive to consider the making of a cup of tea: although very simple, this example can be used to illustrate all the major aspects of the technique. The first thing that needs doing when carrying out a Network Analysis is to list all of the activities that make up the project. All the activities involved in the making of a cup of tea are listed in the table below, together with the time each activity takes (its duration).

Table 6.1 Activities and Durations

Activity	Duration (secs)
Fill kettle	15
Get cup	10
Get milk	12
Get pot	13
Put tea in pot	20
Boil water	40
Fill teapot	10
Pour milk	5
Pour tea	5
Get tea	17

The carrying out of these activities follows a logical sequence. For example, the teapot can't be filled until the water has been boiled. One way of showing the sequence of activities is to use the 'Activity-on-Arrow' convention. In this convention, activities are represented by an arrow, with the start and finish of each activity ending with a circle. These circles denote events. Using this convention, the activity 'Put tea in pot' would be as drawn as in Figure 6.1.

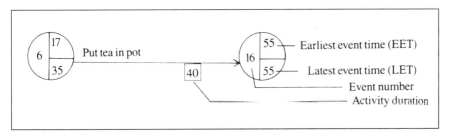

Figure 6.1   The Activity-on-arrow Representation

The following points about Figure 6.1 should be noted.

a)   The length of an arrow bears no relation to the time taken to complete the activity represented by it.

b)   It is the convention that an activity proceeds from a lower numbered event to a higher one.

(The terms 'earliest event time' and 'latest event time' will be defined later.)

Sometimes an event cannot occur until more than one activity has been completed. In the case of making a cup of tea, the activity 'Fill pot' cannot begin until both the activities 'Boil water' and 'Put tea in pot' have been completed. This situation is shown in Figure 6.2.

The full logical network of the tea making project can now be drawn. This is done in Figure 6.3.

Note: An activity can't begin until all activities leading to its preceding event have been completed.

Figure 6.3 is logically correct, but with computers being used in network analysis, it has become necessary that each activity be uniquely defined by its start and finish events. In Figure 6.3, both the activities 'get milk' and 'get cup' are defined by the events 2 and 14, and thus are not uniquely defined by their head and tail events. To ensure the required uniqueness, dummy

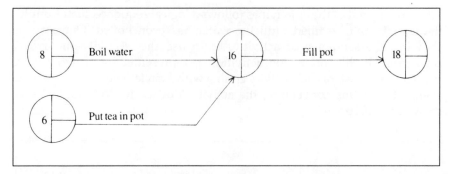

Figure 6.2   Putting Activities Together

activities are inserted into the network. Dummy activities have no activity label and have no duration associated with them. Figure 6.4 shows how a dummy activity can be incorporated into the network of Figure 6.3 to ensure the required uniqueness.

The Critical Path

One important piece of information that can be drawn from this diagram is the total project time, i.e. the shortest time in which the tea can be made. The set of activities that determine this shortest time is called the critical path.

To find the total project time a forward pass of the arrow diagram must be carried out. This pass will determine the earliest event time for each event.

The Forward Pass and Earliest Event Times

The earliest event time is defined as: the earliest possible time at which all the activities leading to a certain event can finish, or conversely, as the earliest time at which activities beginning at a certain event can start. The earliest event time of event 20 is equal to the total project time.

To carry out a forward pass, a zero is put into the top right hand quadrant of event circle 2. Following each activity that starts at this event and adding its duration to the time in the top right hand quadrant the earliest time that this activity can finish is determined. This will certainly be the earliest event time if only one activity precedes the event. If an event has two or more preceding activities, the time required for the last activity to be completed is the earliest event time, since an activity cannot begin until all preceding activities have been completed.

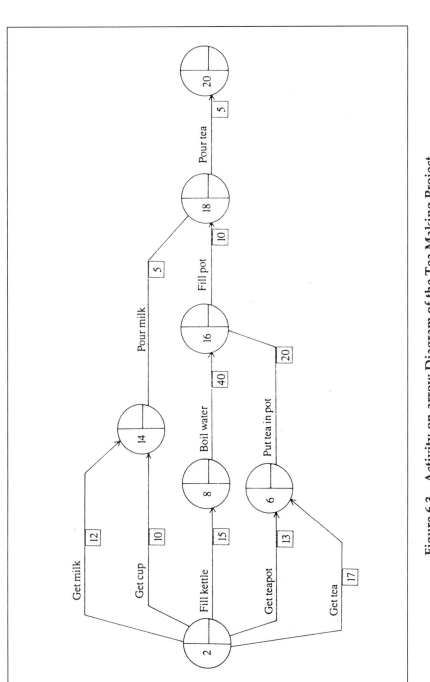

Figure 6.3 Activity-on-arrow Diagram of the Tea Making Project

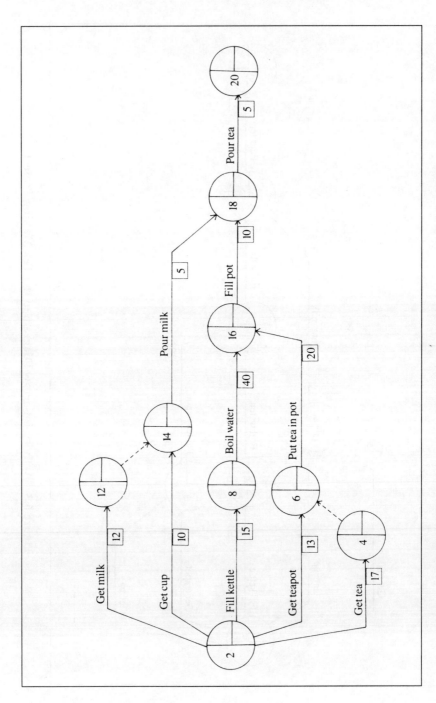

Figure 6.4 Activity-on-arrow Diagram of the Tea Making Project Incorporating Dummy Activities

For example, the earliest start time for the activity 'Fill pot' is determined by the chain of events 2–8–16 and 2–4–6–16. The chain 2–8–16 takes a minimum of (15+40) = 55 seconds and the chain 2-4-6-16 takes (17+20) = 37 seconds. Therefore, the earliest start time for the activity 'fill pot' is 55 seconds.

Looking at the whole diagram, the earliest start time of event 20 is dependent upon the three chains 2-8-16-18-20, 2-4-6–16–18–20, and 2–12–14–18–20. The longest of these chains takes a total of (15+40+10+5) = 70 seconds. It is important to note that the total project time depends upon the longest chain. This is the critical path.

All the earliest event times and the critical path are shown in Figure 6.5.

The Backwards Pass and Latest Event Times

The latest event time is defined as the latest possible time by which all the activities leading to an event must be completed (or again, the latest possible times at which activities from an event can begin) while leaving the total project time unchanged. The latest event times are determined by carrying out a backward pass of the network.

Starting at the final event, each activity is followed back. By subtracting the duration of an activity from the latest end time of the event, a candidate for the latest event time for the head event of the activity is found. This time will be the latest event time if the activity under consideration is the only one exiting from the event. If it is not then the smallest of all the calculated candidate latest event times is the actual latest event time.

For example, the latest starting time for the activity 'Pour tea' will be equal to the total project time minus the time required for the activity 'Pour tea' (70–5) = 65 seconds and the latest time to start the activity 'Pour milk' will be equal to the total project time minus the time required to pour the tea minus the time required to pour the milk (70–5–5) = 60 seconds.

The Complete Network

The complete network of the tea making project is drawn as Figure 6.5. This network diagram incorporates all of the conventions and all event times.

Identifying the Critical Path and Float

The critical path is defined as the longest path through the network. In general, a better term would be 'potentially critical path', since the longest path will not be critical if there is a lot of spare time to complete the project.

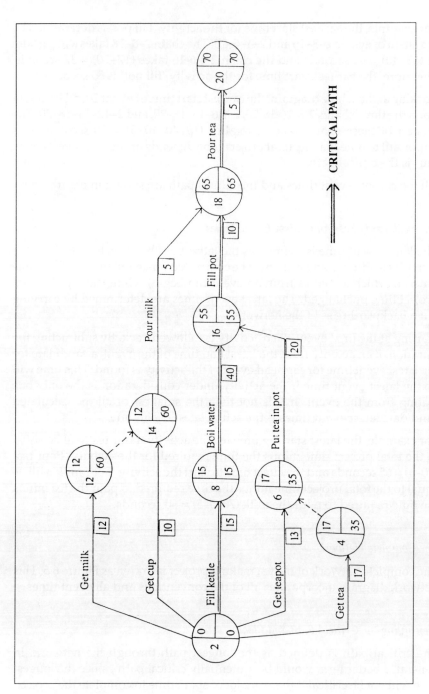

Figure 6.5 The Complete Network

Often a project must be completed in a specific time. Then the latest event time of the last event would be set equal to the time by which the project must be completed. If this time is equal to the earliest event time for the last event, then the earliest and latest event times for each event along the critical path will be equal. This property helps to identify the critical path. This has been done in Figure 6.5.

With the earliest and latest event times for the last event the same, events not on the critical path have different earliest and latest event times. The difference between these two times is the float time that each activity has, i.e. an activity can begin at any time between the earliest and latest event times without affecting the critical path, and thus the overall project time. It is important to note that if the project has to be completed in a time less than the earliest event time of the last event, then the latest event times on the critical path will be less than the earliest event times. When this occurs, events are said to have a negative float time, ie. the float time represents the time that each event exceeds the time at which the project would be completed as required.

For further information on the technique of project scheduling, the reader is referred to any of the many texts available.

Computer Software for Network Analysis

The development of network analysis tools on micros has widened the application of the technique. The software developments have been much more rapid in terms of the ease of use by the relatively unsophisticated user than that of many other forms of Extrapolatory Systems software. This is probably due to the fact that the technique itself is much simpler than with the other techniques, and so can be offered more widely.

Many networking packages are available offering considerable sophistication. Very user-friendly products are Pertmaster Advance, Project Managers' Workbench and CA-SuperProject. Both Project Managers' Workbench and Pertmaster Advance allow the network to be drawn for the user from the minimum of input elicited in a user-friendly way. Larger packages with very extensive facilities are needed by the Engineering industry and are extensively used. One of the industry leaders here is Trackstar, which also has many other features of value in the scheduling of large projects.

For more information on microcomputer project scheduling packages, the reader is referred to Smith (1987) and the computer press.

Linear Programming

Linear programming is a technique for the allocation of resources in the presence of constraints. The range of situations in which linear programming has been used successfully is very great, covering such diverse areas as portfolio selection, investment appraisal, production scheduling and personnel planning. One example of the use of Linear Programming in a large project is that described by Sullivan (1988).

For the linear programming technique to be used it is necessary that an objective be formally and explicitly quantified: if this cannot be done then linear programming is an inappropriate technique. Also the technique is an optimising one, searching for the 'best' solution. Thus it must be possible to specify an objective in the manner of 'to find the mix of products that gives an organisation the greatest profit', 'to select the set of investment opportunities that produce the best return', or 'to minimise production costs'.

The technique gets its name 'linear' from the fact that all the relations between variables used in the technique must be linear: put simply, this means, for example, that a 10% rise in the value of one variable causes a 10% change in the value of a related variable. Thus the relation:

$$\text{Material Usage} = 1.2 \times \text{Quantity Produced}$$

is linear, in that a doubling of the output will double the material usage. However, the relation:

$$\text{Material usage} = 1.2 \times \text{Quantity Produced}^2$$

is not linear, for here a doubling of the value of the quantity produced will not double the material usage: the change in material usage will depend on the base value of the quantity produced.

The term 'Programming' is merely a synonym for 'Planning'.

Thus linear programming is a technique that involves the planning of activities in the presence of constraints in order to produce some optimum result, and which requires that all the relations in the model be linear. Linear programming is a very large subject and it is not appropriate to do more than introduce it here. The way it will be introduced is to take a very simple resource allocation problem and initially to treat it using graphs.

Graphical Approach to Linear Programming

The problem that will be used is a very simplified form of a blending problem. To simplify the arithmetic, all the numbers have been kept artificially small.

Mr Jim Smith is a manufacturer who produces two products, alpha and beta. The situation is:

> One tonne of alpha requires 1/6 tonne of material thian and 1/2 tonne of material doxin together with a quantity of cheap and plentiful filler.

> One tonne of beta requires 1/2 tonne of thian and 1/3 tonne of Y, again mixed with the filler.

> In any one month, Mr. Smith is restricted to buying only 2 tonnes of thian and 3 tonnes of Y.

> The cost of thian is 2.31/tonne and that of doxin is 1.03/tonne.

> Alpha is sold at 2.00/tonne giving a contribution of 1.10/tonne.

> Beta is sold at 3.00/tonne giving a contribution of 1.50/tonne.

Mr. Smith wonders how he should arrange his production so as to maximise the Contribution (Contribution = Revenue − Variable Costs).

The first requirement if this problem is to be tackled using linear programming is that an objective has to be explicitly stated. This is easy in this case − the objective here is to maximise the Contribution. A second requirement is that a relation termed the Objective Function can be explicitly defined. By this is meant that the variable to be optimised can be specified in terms of the manager's decision variables, which are how much of alpha and beta to produce. In Mr. Smith's case, this would be:

> Overall Contribution = Contribution/tonne from alpha x tonnes of alpha produced + Contribution/tonne from beta x tonnes of beta produced

Putting this in symbols, if £Z is the contribution, A is the number of tonnes of alpha he produces and B is the number of tonnes of beta he produces then the Objective Function would be:

$$Z = 1.1 \times A + 1.5 \times B \qquad [6.1]$$

since the contribution on one tonne of alpha is 1.10 and on one tonne of beta it is 1.50.

Mr. Smith has not got complete freedom as to how many tonnes of alpha and beta to produce, since he is constrained by the amount of thian and doxin that are available to him.

The first constraint is the amount of thian available. Since A tonnes of alpha require $A/6$ tonnes of thian and B tonnes of beta require $B/2$ tonnes of X, then the quantities of alpha and beta that could be produced are restricted by the relation:

$$\frac{A}{6} + \frac{B}{2} \leq 2 \tag{6.2}$$

The symbol $\leq$ means that the left-hand side of this relation can be equal to 2, less than 2, but it cannot be more than 2. Relation 6.2 is not an equation but an inequality.

Proceeding in a similar manner for the constraint on the quantity of doxin available gives:

$$\frac{A}{2} + \frac{B}{3} \leq 3 \tag{6.3}$$

Plotting Inequalities and Defining the Feasible Region

Plotting inequalities on a graph is little different from plotting equations since to begin with the inequality sign is ignored and the relation is treated simply as an equation: in the case of relation 6.2

$$\frac{A}{2} + \frac{B}{3} = 2 \tag{6.4}$$

Equation 6.4 represents the maximum value that a combination of A and B can take. Plotted as a graph, equation 6.4 looks like Figure 6.6.

The easiest way of drawing this graph is to find two points that satisfy equation 6.4 and to join them with a straight line. Any two points will do, but the ones for which A=0 and B=0 are obvious choices. From equation 6.4, when A=0, B=4; when B=0, A=12. These two points allow the line to be drawn.

Equation 6.4 defines the maximum values that the combination of A and B can take; any values of A or B lying to the right of the line are not possible. For example, the limitation on the quantity of material thian available prevents more than 4 tonnes of beta being made, or of 8 tonnes of alpha and 2 tonnes of beta being produced. Thus it is only in the portion of Figure 6.6 that lies to the left of the line that feasible solutions exist. Since it is not possible to produce negative quantities of either alpha or beta, feasible solutions only exist within the unshaded triangle of Figure 6.7

The constraint on the quantity of doxin available has not been included in

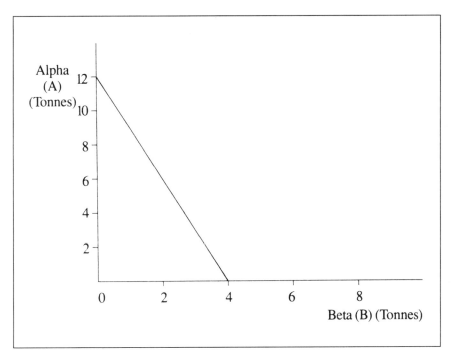

Figure 6.6   Plotting the Constraint on Thian

Figure 6.7. Including it produces Figure 6.8. It is only in the region of the quadrilateral PQRS that feasible solutions can exist. This region is termed the feasible region.

From the graph it is not possible to determine exactly the values of A and B at the point R. Point R is the (one and only) point at which the two equations defining the limits of the resource constraints cross. So at the point R, the values of A and B simultaneously fit both the equations.

$$\frac{A}{6} + \frac{B}{2} = 2$$

$$\frac{A}{2} + \frac{B}{3} = 3 \qquad\qquad [6.5]$$

The values of A and B that simultaneously fit both equations can be found quite easily. The point R has the values A = 4.29, B = 2.57.

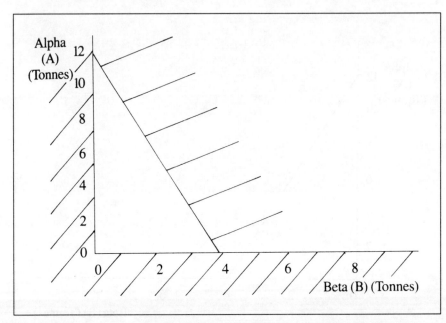

Figure 6.7   The Feasible Region Formed by Three Constraints

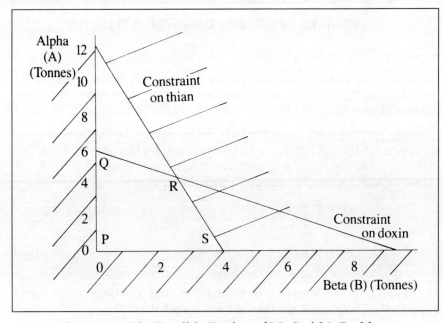

Figure 6.8   The Feasible Region of Mr Smith's Problem

Finding the Optimum Operating Point

Having defined the region within which solutions are feasible, it is now possible to move forward and find the combination of alpha and beta that maximises Jim Smith's contribution.

First it is instructive to look again at the Objective Function, equation 6.1, viz:

$$Z = 1.1 \times A + 1.5 \times B$$

Consider one specific value for the contribution – 1 say. This value could be attained by producing roughly 0.9 tonnes of alpha and none of beta, or roughly 0.7 tonnes of beta and none of alpha, or by producing any combination of alpha and beta that lie on the line 1 drawn in Figure 6.9, which is the line corresponding to the equation

$$1 = 1.1 \times A + 1.5 \times B \tag{6.6}$$

Consider a second value for the contribution – say 2. Line 2 in Figure 6.9 is the corresponding line. For a contribution of 3, line 3 is the appropriate line of the objective function.

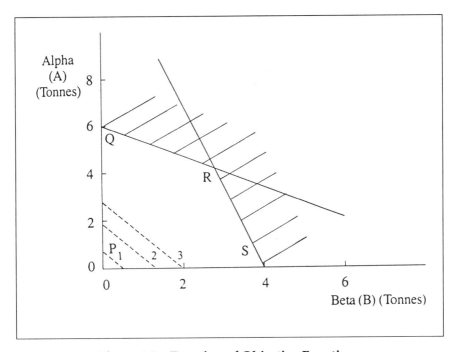

Figure 6.9   Drawing of Objective Functions

From Figure 6.9 it can be seen that all the objective function lines are parallel, and that a line drawn close to the origin has a smaller contribution associated with it than does a line drawn further from the origin. From this it should be intuitively obvious that the maximum objective function will be the one corresponding to the line that lies furthest from the origin and still remain in the feasible region. From Figure 6.9, in the case of Jim Smith's operation, the objective functions corresponding to the maximum contribution will pass through the point R.

From this it should also be evident that the optimum will always lie at the edge of the feasible region, and not somewhere inside it. Thus the search in linear programming problems is for the extreme point in the feasible region that provides the optimum value for the objective function.

Since the optimum value lies at an apex to the feasible region, it is possible to find the optimum through enumeration of the contribution at all extreme points. These points are where at least two constraints intersect. The enumeration is summarised in Table 6.2.

Table 6.2   Enumeration of Contribution at the Extreme Points

Point	Alpha (tonnes)	Beta (tonnes)	Contribution (£)
P	0.00	0.00	0.00
Q	6.00	0.00	6.60
R	4.29	2.57	8.57
S	0.00	4.00	6.00

From Table 6.2, R is seen to be the optimum point producing the maximum contribution of £8.57. This has been achieved by producing 4.29 tonnes of alpha and 2.57 tonnes of beta.

Shadow Prices and Reduced Costs

The graphical treatment given to Jim Smith's problem produced the operating point that gives him the maximum contribution. However, this piece of information is not the only significant piece of information that can be derived.

Suppose Mr. Smith were offered 1 further tonne of material doxin at £2 a tonne. Should he buy it? Figure 6.8, reproduced and augmented as figure 6.10 can show what he should do.

With 1 more tonne of doxin the constraining relation for doxin becomes:

$$\frac{A}{2} + \frac{B}{3} = 4 \qquad\qquad [6.7]$$

The limiting equation is drawn as a dashed line in Figure 6.10. The point R now moves to R' which has the values A = 6.86, B = 1.71. This level of production of alpha and beta will give a contribution of 10.11. At point R, the contribution was £8.57, and so the extra tonne of doxin has increased the contribution by £1.54. As at point R, all of thian and doxin are used in the making of alpha and beta. Since the extra tonne of doxin would cost Mr. Smith £2, it is worth his while to buy it, since he could pay up to £1.54 per tonne more for the extra tonne of doxin than he had paid originally (1.03) and still gain financially: i.e. he could pay up to £2.57 a tonne and not be out of pocket.

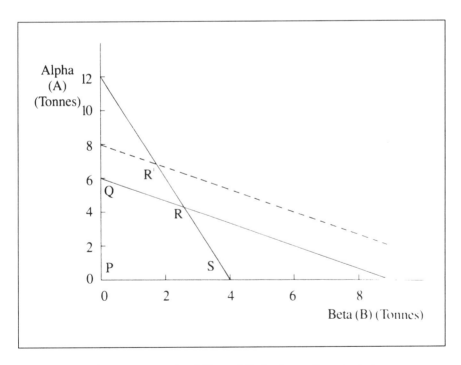

Figure 6.10   The Effect of Relaxing a Constraint

The potential increase in contribution that could occur from easing one of the constraints by a single unit is termed the Shadow Price of the resource. Here the shadow price for doxin is £1.54 per tonne. The rule could be to acquire extra resource so long as the increase in the value of the objective function is greater than the extra cost of acquisition, i.e. the cost over and above that incurred per unit of resource at the initial operating point.

It is also possible to determine the change in contribution that would make it not worthwhile to manufacture one of the products or, if a third product were possible, to determine how much its individual contribution would need to be raised to make production of it economically acceptable. The change in a contribution in Mr. Smith's problem that would just make it economically acceptable to start producing another product is, rather unfortunately, called the Reduced Cost. In general a reduced cost is the change in a coefficient in the objective function that just makes it worthwhile to produce the associated product.

Consideration of shadow prices and reduced costs are forms of sensitivity analysis. It can be seen that an optimising system can allow the problem situation to be explored, allowing other estimates to be considered.

For an introductory text on linear programming the reader is referred to the book by Finlay (1985) where, incidentally, Mr. Smith's problem is covered in greater detail. A much fuller exposition is given in many texts; for example, that by Hiller and Lieberman (1967).

Computer Software for Linear Programming

A number of micro based linear programming packages are available that take advantage of the interactive environment and processing power of micros. Input can be made in several ways, including the use of a spreadsheet. Indeed, small scale problems can be solved within the What's Best! package for use with the Lotus 1-2-3 spreadsheet.

It is now possible to buy linear programming packages that can cope with over 500 variables and around a thousand constraints, and thus deal fully with many large-scale commercial problems. The PC version of the very powerful Sciconic package and XPRESS-MP appear to be the UK leaders in linear and integer programming software: in the USA, LINDO and LINDO/ PC hold this position.

Whilst the micro versions of linear programming software are powerful and becoming ever more so, tests have shown that as the number of variables increases, the performance degradation is very apparent: mainframes are still needed to solve very large linear programming problems.

With linear programming software, the mainframe antecedents of many of the packages is still in evidence. The same antecedents were visible in financial modelling software until the early 1980s, but have since disappeared. Possibly the fact that the remnants of mainframe limitations still remain is due to the fact that a more expert and less fussy clientele uses linear programming software than is the case with financial modelling software. The sheer size of the latter market is also likely to be a cause.

PROBABILISTIC SYSTEMS

Probabilistic Systems are systems that explicitly have within themselves probabilistic or statistical features. This is in contradistinction to other forms of MIS, where uncertainty is taken into account outside of the computer systems, by the decision maker carrying out sensitivity analyses.

Two techniques that are commonly used as the basis for Probabilistic Systems will be looked at. These are the techniques of Simulation and Statistical Forecasting.

Simulation

The term 'simulation' has two meanings when used in the context of DSS. First, in the general sense of experimenting on a model of the real world, in playing and thinking through real world operations. This is exemplified in the use of sensitivity analysis. Second, in the narrower sense of experimenting specifically with models that represent the internal workings of a system. It is in this second, narrower sense that the term 'simulation' will be used here.

Simulation models would typically be developed where the operation of each individual part of a system is understood, with the difficulty coming in working out how these individual parts will interact with each other, especially when they do so in a complex way. The main concern with such systems is with the queues that form for the use of resources.

Examples where the use of simulation has been helpful are in decisions concerning the layout of steel plants, of supermarkets, dispatch areas and of harbours (reference 1). A large scale simulation that has helped in determining the operation of a national gas transmission system has been described by Clark (1985). With such decision making, simulation provides the only feasible quantitative decision aid.

Continuous and Discrete Simulation

There are a large number of types of simulation and there are many ways of classifying them. One very important distinction is between continuous and discrete simulation – the broad classes of simulation used for continuous systems and discrete systems respectively.

In general, the state of the system will change over time. Each change of state is termed an event. Continuous systems are those where the effect of an individual event and the time intervals between events are infinitesimally small. Physical and chemical processes, and systems where flows are important – of water and of traffic for example – are illustrations of continuous systems that have been modelled using continuous simulation.

In contrast, discrete systems are those where the effects of individual events are not infinitesimally small: the state of the system changes by a recognisable amount at an event. For example, the length of a queue at a supermarket checkout will be incremented at the moment customers join the queue and reduced the moment they leave the queue.

Discrete simulation has been used far more extensively in business than has continuous simulation, and it is discrete simulation that will now be discussed. Thus for the remainder of this section any mention of simulation should be taken to mean discrete event simulation – the development and use of a model that represents the internal workings of a system and is concerned with discrete events.

Simulation of a Supermarket

To illustrate the technique of simulation, the operation of a supermarket checkout will be investigated. The problem is to decide on the number of checkouts to have open at any one time. The decision must take into account the arrival pattern of the customers, their buying habits and the queue discipline they adopt. The overriding considerations are the overall costs and benefits of having any given number of checkouts open.

A system may be viewed as a set of components (often referred to as entities), with each component having one or more attributes – characteristics that describe the entities. In the supermarket, two entities of concern are likely to be customers and checkout operators. Important attributes of the customers might be the time they take to select their purchases and the amount they spend. The full set of entities and attributes (and their interactions) define what is termed 'the state of the system'.

All entities that have the same characteristics are considered to belong to the same class. Because all the entities of a class have the same characteristics, only the activities of the class as a whole need be considered when considering the logic of the model (though not in the operation of the model). An entity is engaged in an activity when it is doing something or when something is being done to it: examples are the customer 'selecting goods' and 'being checked out'. When not engaged in activities, entities are in passive states which are called queues.

There are several ways of representing models in simulation terms. Described below is one common way which is based on the cycles of activities undertaken and undergone in the system under investigation. Another common approach is to make the distinction between active entities (termed 'machines') that perform operations, and passive entities (termed 'materials') on which operations are performed. The simulation is then constructed around the events that machines undergo.

In the supermarket case, the model might initially have just two classes of entity – customers and checkout operators (checkout tills, supervisors etc. being of secondary importance).

Having decided on the entities, the next stage is to enumerate the logical sequence of activities of the entities. In the supermarket case these are:

checkout operators: are involved in the activity 'checking out', otherwise they are free, waiting for a customer requiring service.

customers: are involved in the activities 'selecting goods' and 'checking out'.

The activity 'selecting' goods is completely finished before the activity of 'checking out' starts. After 'selecting goods' the customer waits in a queue for service unless a checkout operator is free. The queue is serviced on a first-in, first out basis.

The symbols in common use are a square to represent an activity, a circle to represent a queue and an arrow to show the sequence of activity and queue: for example, see Figure 6.11.

In most formal simulations, especially where computer simulation languages are used, it is necessary to abide by two conventions:-

- that a queue lies between each activity, even when this is not really required by the 'real' logic

- that each entity follows an activity cycle: a cycle or closed loop of activity-queue-activity-queue, etc.

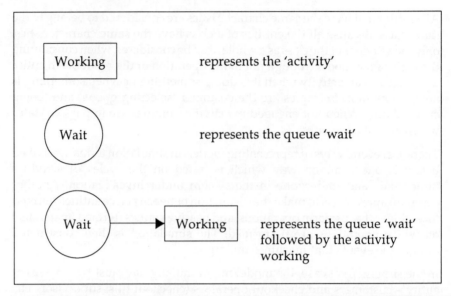

Figure 6.11   A Common Representation of Activities and Queues

The activity cycle diagrams for the checkout operators and customers as shown in Figure 6.12 conform to these conventions, with the queue 'outside' (outside the supermarket) included in the diagram.

From this diagram it can be seen that 'checking out' is a co-operative activity: it requires both a checkout operator and a customer for it to take place.

In the logic, entities in queues are passive things waiting upon events – upon the starting or stopping of activities. Although it is data about the state of the queues that is important (and this is the data the simulation has been built to generate), it is data for the activities that are needed in order to run the simulation model.

The data for the activities that are needed is:

– the number of checkout operators

– the number of customers

– the time spent on each activity

Suppose that the time a customer takes in 'entering', 'selecting goods' and 'checking out' is as indicated in figures 6.13, 6.14 and 6.15.

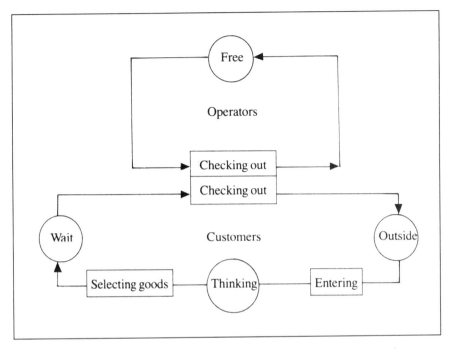

**Figure 6.12   The logical Sequence of Activities and Queues
for Operators and Customers**

To have obtained histograms like these, the time taken by each of 100
customers to complete each activity would need to have been sampled.
These times would then be grouped into time bands and the results shown
by drawing a rectangle of height corresponding to the recorded frequencies
on top of the associated time band. In this way the area of the rectangle
reflects the frequency of occurrence – for example, in Figure 6.14, of 100
customers, 15 took between 10 and 12 minutes to select goods (an average of
11 minutes), whilst the much smaller rectangle lying on the time interval 20–
22 minutes shows that only 2 in 100 customers took around 21 minutes to
select goods.

Using the Simulation Model

Suppose the supermarket simulation is started with three customers (R, S
and T) in the queue 'outside' and two checkout operators (X and Y) in the
queue 'free'. Together with the duration of the simulation (which, if a whole

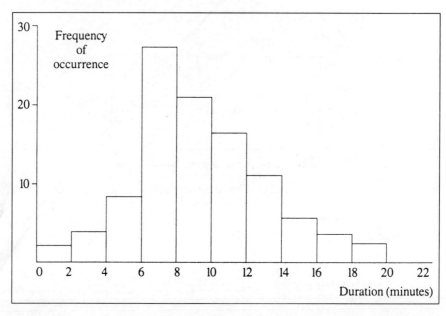

Figure 6.13   Time Spent by a Customer in 'Entering' the Supermarket

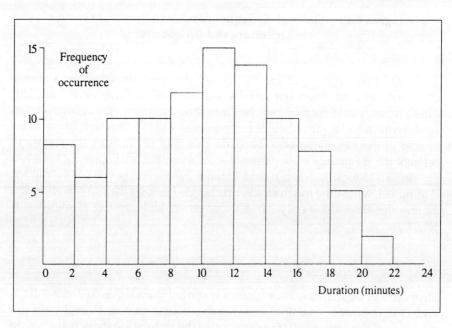

Figure 6.14   Time Taken by a Customer to 'Select Goods'

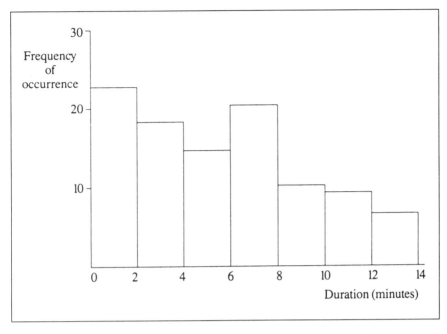

Figure 6.15   Time Taken to Serve One Customer at a Checkout

day's operation of the supermarket were to be simulated, would correspond to about 450 minutes), most of the initial conditions to start the simulation have been set up. To complete the initiation of the simulation the clock time needs to be set to zero and any of the starting activities must be got underway. The only possible activity that could be started is that of 'entering'. For customers R, S and T the times they will take for this activity need to be determined. This would be done by sampling from the histogram in Figure 6.13, selecting at random, but recognising that there is a greater chance of selecting a duration that occurs frequently and is associated with a big rectangle (as though one were rather inexpertly throwing darts and had a greater chance of hitting a large rectangle than a small one).

Suppose the sampling had produced times of 5, 11 and 7 minutes for the time taken by R, S and T respectively to enter the supermarket. The counters representing the customers would then be moved into the activity 'entering' in Figure 6.12 and these events would be entered as R(5), S(11) and T(7) in an event recording chart of the sort shown in Table 6.3.

After this initiation, the simulation is run in the fixed sequence of phases shown and described in Figure 6.16.

Table 6.3   Event Recording of the Supermarket Simulation

Line no.	Clock time (mins)	Start 'enter'	Finish 'enter'	Start 'selecting goods'	Finish 'selecting goods'	Start 'check out'	Finish 'check out'
1	0	R(5) S(11) T(7)					
2	5		R	R(16)			
3	7		T	T(16)			
4	11		S	S(14)			
5	14				S	S(21) X(21)	
6	16				R T	R(19) Y(19)	
7	19	R(26)				T(24) Y(24)	R Y

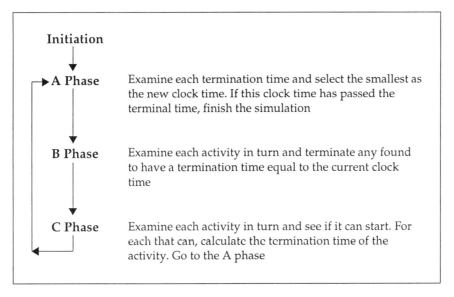

Figure 6.16   The Simulation Phase

In the A phase, examination of the termination times in Table 6.3 shows 5 to be the smallest (the next time when an event occurs – so the times of 1, 2, 3 and 4 minutes are of no interest): the clock time is advanced to 5 minutes. Moving on to the B phase, the only activity which terminates is that of 'entering' by customer R: consequently the counter representing R is moved into the queue 'thinking'. In the C phase, the only activity that can start is 'selecting goods' as it is the only activity with an entity in every queue immediately preceding it. In sampling from Figure 6.14, suppose a value of ll minutes has been obtained for the time R will take 'selecting goods': this will mean that R will finish selecting goods at clock time 16 minutes (the current clock time of 5 minutes plus the 11 minutes the activity of 'selecting goods' will take). The state of the simulation at time 5 minutes is recorded in the first and second lines of Table 6.3. The counter representing customer R is moved into the activity 'selecting goods'.

Returning to the A phase, the smallest clock time shown in table 6.3 that is greater than the current clock time (5 minutes) is 7 minutes, the time at which customer T finishes 'entering': 7 minutes now becomes the new clock time.

In the B phase, the activity that can be terminated is the activity 'entering' by customer B. This is done and T moves into the queue 'thinking'. In the C phase, the only activity that can start is 'selecting goods' by customer T. This is thus started.

Suppose that from Figure 6.14 a duration of 9 minutes for T is derived for the activity 'selecting goods'. Then the time that T would cease this activity would be at clock time 16 minutes (the current clock time of 7 minutes plus the activity duration of 9 minutes). The state of the system at 7 minutes would be as shown in the first three lines of table 6.3.

Returning to the A phase, the next termination time is that of customer S entering the supermarket. The new clock time becomes 11 minutes. At 11 minutes this is the only activity that can be terminated. This is done, and S moves into the queue 'thinking'. Since this is a dummy queue, S can begin to start the activity 'selecting goods'.

Suppose that a duration of 3 minutes were chosen from Figure 6.14 as the time S spends selecting goods. Thus S would finish selecting goods at clock time 14 minutes (the current clock time of 11 minutes and the duration of the activity 'selecting goods' which is 3 minutes). At time 11 minutes, the state of the system is described by lines 2,3 and 4 of Table 6.3.

Returning to the A phase, the new clock time would be 14 minutes. At that time S finishes selecting goods and moves into the queue 'wait'. Because the checkout operator X is in the queue 'free', the customer S can begin checking out. If a duration of 7 minutes were selected from Figure 6.15, then the state of the system at 14 minutes would be that shown in lines 2, 3 and 5 of Table 6.3.

At clock time 16 minutes, both R and T would cease to select goods and would move into the queue 'wait'. Since checkout operator Y is free at time 16 minutes, one of R and T can be checked out, but not both. Thus a queue forms in the queue 'wait'. If R starts checking out with a duration of 3 minutes, the state of the system is as shown in lines 5 and 6 of table 6.3.

At clock time 19 minutes operator Y becomes free and can immediately start serving customer T who has been waiting 3 minutes in the queue 'wait'. Via the queue 'outside', R can also start 'entering' again. If durations of 5 minutes for T checking out and one of 7 minutes for R entering were selected, the position at clock time 19 minutes would be as shown in table 6.3.

The simulation would continue in this way and at the end of the simulation a complete set of data would be available on the times for which customers had to wait for service, and on the numbers of customers in the queues. Just the data that the manager needs to help him decide on the number of checkouts to have open.

For a further introduction to the technique of simulation the reader is referred to the book by Finlay (1985) where, incidently, the supermarket case is covered in more detail. A deeper and more wide-ranging exposition of the simulation technique is given by Mitrani (1982).

Computer Software for Discrete Event Simulation

Until quite recently, the demanding processing requirements associated with the simulation of probabilistic real world systems meant that mainframes had to be used for all but the smallest simulations. Recent developments in hardware have changed this, and now there is a wide range of simulation software available for the micro, to deal with both discrete and continuous types of simulation. Excluding very specialist packages, there are about 20 companies offering micro simulation packages, varying from general purpose simulators to special systems geared to one type of environment: manufacturing and distribution are two areas in which simulation has found application.

GPSS/H, GPSS/PC Minuteman, Slam and Simscript are probably the most popular general-purpose simulation languages and over the last few years all have been implemented on widely available micros. All implementations appear technically sound, which is a particular concern when considering the way in which random numbers are generated.

As well as these general purpose languages, more specific and more immediately usable packages are on offer. Banks et al. (1991) term these Simulators. These packages allow the user very easily to enter the structure of his simulation – of the activity cycle diagrams, the probability distributions and the form of output required and often provide visual animation to provide on-screen display of the progression of the simulation.

The leading simulation packages appear to be Witness and ProModelPC. PC-Model is a programming language specifically designed for developing queueing systems.

Developments in simulation software will undoubtedly continue to be towards more interactive systems, with users being able to alter dynamically the way in which a simulation is proceeding. Fuller use of graphics are under development, both to present the simulation problem to the user and to show results.

For more information on microcomputer simulation packages, the reader is referred to the article by Banks et al. (1991) and to the tutorial papers of the Winter Simulation Conference held each year in the USA (see, for example, reference 2).

Statistical Forecasting Systems

Every manager forecasts, since every considered decision he takes will involve making an assessment about the future. There are three generic forecasting methods: statistical forecasting, where past data is the basis for the forecast: causal forecasting, where cause and effect relationships are derived and used to predict the future: and judgemental forecasting, where the forecaster simply uses his and other peoples subjective views to arrive at the prediction. This section is concerned with statistical forecasting. Causal forecasting falls in the area of Causal Systems. Judgemental forecasting will not be considered.

The fundamental assumption underpining statistical forecasting models is that future patterns will be extensions of past patterns and that these patterns are completely encapsulated in a set of past data values. One common approach to statistical forecasting is to use the technique of Time Series Analysis

Time Series Analysis

Time Series analysis is a technique whereby a set of data forming a series over time (such as the monthly sales of soft drinks), are broken down into components. Subsequently these components are used to build up a forecast for the future.

The specific choice of components to look for must be guided by a knowledge of the situation. However, there is a 'standard set' of components to be considered and these are:

 − a secular trend

 − seasonal variations

 − cyclical variations

 − random fluctuations

These components are sketched in Figure 6.17.

A secular trend exists if there is an underlying constant increase or decrease in the variable of concern. Three examples of trends are shown in Figure 6.18. In forecasting the word 'secular' is not used in the sense of 'non-ecclesiastical', but in the sense of 'noncyclical': with a secular trend there is no pattern that repeats itself in the time frame of concern. For the sake of brevity, the secular trend will subsequently be referred to simply as the trend.

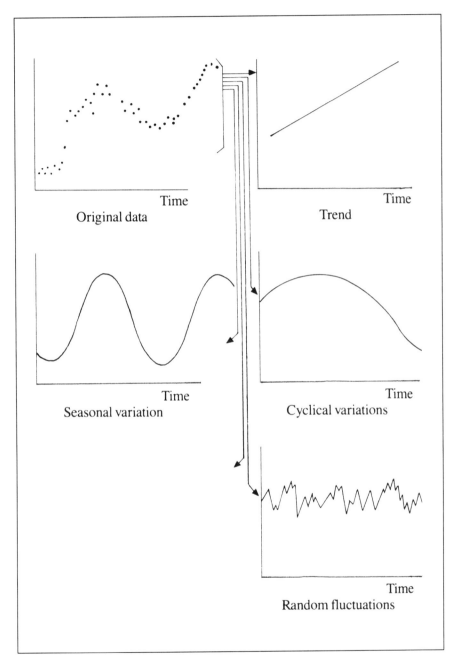

Figure 6.17   A Time Series Analysis

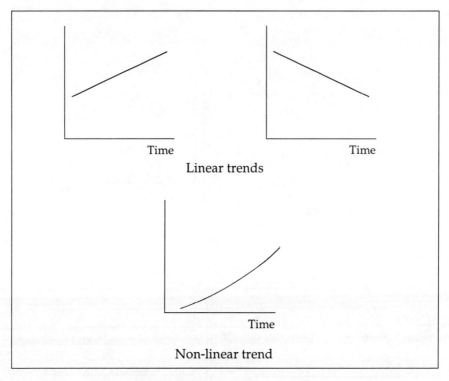

Figure 6.18   Types of Trend

As their name suggests, cyclical and seasonal variations are components of the time series that do repeat themselves. Seasonal variations are a special case of cyclical variations where the periodicity of the cycle is one year. Even in our rather artificial lives, the seasons of the year still play a major role, and this is reflected in the annual variability of many things, particularly the sale of consumer goods and the choice of leisure activities. For this reason the seasonal component is picked out and given a greater emphasis than are the other cyclical components, which have periodicities other than a year.

It is very unlikely that the trend, the seasonal and cyclical variations will completely describe the past data. Some unexplained contribution will remain. This residual is the random fluctuation. As long as the random fluctuations are small compared to the explained variations, then time series analysis will be a reasonable technique for forecasting.

The Time Series Analysis Technique

There are basically two ways in which the components of a time series can be assembled. These give rise to two types of model, the additive model and the multiplicative model.

The additive model assumes that the value of a variable can be forecast by adding together the contribution from each component. Thus in general, and again assuming that sales is the variable being forecast:

SALES = TREND + SEASONAL VARIATION + CYCLICAL VARIATIONS + RANDOM FLUCTUATIONS

In this additive model, the size of the seasonal variation is assumed to be independent of the size of the trend. So in the soft drinks case for example, the size of the summer peak in demand is not linked to average annual sales.

The multiplicative model assumes that the relation between the original data and its components (and subsequently that between the forecast data and the components) is as follows:

SALES = TREND x SEASONAL VARIATION x CYCLICAL VARIATIONS x RANDOM FLUCTUATIONS

This model assumes that the changes in one variable are linked to changes in the others. For example, a general change in national income or the rate of population growth may affect all components, the trend, the seasonal and cyclical variations and the random fluctuation.

A simple explanation of statistical forecasting techniques is given in the book by Finlay (1985).

Computer Software for Statistical Forecasting

There has not been much development in forecasting techniques over the last few years, but the amount of micro software is impressive. A number of packages are available that offer a multitude of forecasting methods. SmartForecasts uses the data that is offered to it to test out various forecasting methods and chooses the one that best fits the data.

In contrast to this package offering a smorgasbord of techniques, some packages offer only a restricted range of applications. FORECALC, for example, only offers exponential smoothing (*see*, for example, reference 3). AUTOBOX, whilst a very sophisticated and flexible package, only deals with various forms of time series analysis. Other packages of note are FORECAST! and FORECAST/DSS.

1,2,3 Forecast! is a menu-driven forecasting template that works with Lotus 1-2-3, enabling the user to import named ranges from a worksheet as data, and to use all the power of this standard package. The package's major limitation is its scope: it can handle only 10 independent variables and a maximum of 150 observations.

The International Journal of Forecasting (*see*, for example, references 3 and 4) publishes regular reviews and surveys of forecasting software including 'add-ons' to spreadsheet packages. The reader is referred to this source for up-to-date information on the power and merits of package software.

SUMMARY

Extrapolatory Systems are systems that generally use mathematical models to allow future possible situations to be examined. Definitional Systems find widespread application in financial planning systems that are generally developed by accountants.

Causal and Probabilistic Systems are very often used to tackle problems that are of a standard form (or can be 'bent' to be so). Consequently they often involve the use a standard techniques. The most commonly used techniques are those developed by management scientists.

It can be seen from the examples chosen to exemplify Causal and Probabilistic Systems that the scope of such systems is wide. The development of much more powerful microcomputer software allied to much greater user-friendliness has led to a wider use of the techniques than previously was feasible.

REFERENCES

1. *Systems Behaviour Course T241 Module 1* Deep-Sea Container Ports (Systems Appraisal and Simulation Modelling, Open University, 1982

2. *Proceedings of the 24th Winter Simulation Conference, WSC92*, edited by the IEEE Computer Society Staff and IEEE Systems, Management and Cybernetics Society Staff, IEEE, February 1993.

3. *Software reviews, International Journal of Forecasting, Vol.6, pp 395–398,* 1991.

4. *Software reviews, International Journal of Forecasting, Vol.7, pp 543–553,* 1992.

Banks J., Aviles E., McLaughlin J.R. and Yuan R.C., (1991) *The Simulator: New Member of the Simulation Family, INTERFACES Vol.21, No.2*, March–April, pp 76–86

Clark M., (1985) *The Development of a Simulation Model for the Operation of the National Gas Transmission System*, Journal of the Operational Research Society, Vol.36, No.4, pp 275–283

Finlay P.N., (1985) *Mathematical Modelling in Business Decision-Making*, Croom Helm, London

Hillier F. S. and Lieberman G.J., (1967) *Introduction to OPERATIONS RESEARCH*, Holden-Day, Inc., San Francisco, U.S.A.

Mitrani I., (1982) *Simulation techniques for discrete event systems.* Cambridge Computer Science Texts 14, Cambridge University Press,U.K.

Smith D.K., (1987) *Project Management Software*, Journal of the Operational Research Society, Vol. 37 No.12, pp 1201–1204

Sullivan J., (1988) *The Application of Mathematical Programming Methods to Oil and Gas Field Development Planning*, Mathematical Programming, Vol.42, pp 189–200

7 Preference Determination System

Preference Determination Systems form the class of MINTS that has the greatest affinity with MIS. The principal feature that distinguishes them from MIS is that an exhaustive set of decision 'points' has to be determined from the outset. In this sense, the use of Preference Determination Systems is more restricting than some MIS. Another feature of Preference Determination Systems that distinguishes them from MIS and may make them more acceptable to managers is that, apart from some aspects of Decision Trees (*see* below), there is little in the way of mathematics involved, with the scale of measurement used being largely ordinal. The disadvantage of using such a scale is the consequent limited amount of mathematical modelling and manipulation that is possible.

Although not a water-tight classification, it is convenient to classify the Preference Determination packages presently available into two types, based on the predominant decision making methodology employed. These types are those that adopt the decision tree approach and those that are based on multiple attribute decision making.

DECISION TREE SYSTEMS

The Decision Tree Technique

Some types of decision are characterised by a series of either/or decisions and the play of an uncertain environment. The decision tree technique is a way of graphically illustrating such a series of decisions in a clear and convenient way. Each branch of the tree represents one particular set of policy decisions, and the whole tree allows the consequences of all possible decisions to be assessed.

An example will help to show the method. It is conventional in decision tree analysis to represent decision points (or forks) by a square and the possible options emanating from the decision by lines.

Consider the case of JR Ewing of Ewing Oil. He holds a lease that he must either a) sell now, b) hold for a year or c) drill now. Drilling costs $150,000. This decision would be represented as shown on the left side of Figure 7.1.

Chance forks are represented by circles, as shown in Figure 7.1 (b). Here the probability that the drilling will produce a dry well is 0.5 (with a payoff of nothing), of producing a wet well is 0.4 (with a payoff of $400,000) and of producing a gusher 0.1 (with a payoff of $1,500,000).

If JR decides to sell the lease now he can get $200,000 for it. If he decides to sell later, gambling on a rise in oil prices, he is taking a risk. He estimates that there is a 15% chance that the oil price will rise, and if so he can sell for $500,000. On the other hand, if the oil price falls (an 85% chance) he would have to sell the lease for $145,000 (a loss over the option of selling now).

The full decision tree of this situation is reproduced in Figure 7.2.

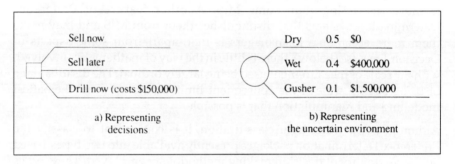

Figure 7.1   The Representation of Decisions and of an
Uncertain Environment

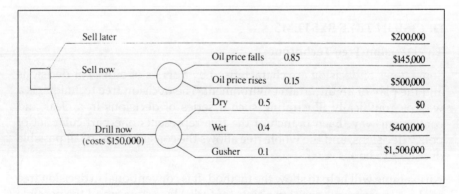

Figure 7.2   JR's Decision Tree

The terminal values of each decision and, where appropriate, each chance event, are shown in Figure 7.2. The expected monetary value for each branch of the tree can be calculated by working backwards from the righthand side. For example, the expected monetary values for the branches affected by the oil price changes would be calculated as: (0.85 x $145,000) + (0.15 x $500,000) = $198,250

This means that if JR were at the beginning of his set of decisions (at the left hand side of Figure 7.2), he would 'expect' to realise $198,250 if he were to sell later. From this example it can be seen what the expected monetary value is: it is the net amount of money that JR would get 'on average'. The expected monetary value would be calculated by taking each monetary outcome, weighting it by the chance of it occurring, and then adding together all the weighted monetary outcomes.

Working backwards in a similar way produces a net expected monetary value for drilling. This is calculated as the payoff minus the drilling costs. The payoff is calculated as:

$$(0.5 \times \$0) + (0.4 \times \$400,000) + (0.1 \times \$1,500,000) = \$310,000$$

With drilling costs of $150,000, the drill option has an expected monetary value of $160,000. Thus if JR were not a gambler he would go for the option with the highest expected monetary value, i.e. sell now. Being a gambler however, he might go for the option that has the highest possible return i.e. drill – hoping for a gusher!

One way of representing the possible outcomes is in the form of a table. This is done in Table 7.1 in which the net revenue for the sell later and drill options are set out for different values of the probabilities that the well will be dry, and that the oil price will fall. In this table, the probability that the well will be a gusher has been fixed at 0.1: thus if the probability that the well will be dry is 0.5, then the probability that it will be wet will correspondingly be 0.4.

Table 7.1 shows that when the probability that the oil price will fall is 0.85 and the probability that the well will be dry is 0.5, then the sell later option would be expected to yield $198,000, and the drill option would be expected to yield $160,000. [These values are those calculated above].

It can also be seen that the expected monetary values of the options at these probabilities are close: $200,000 for the sell now option, $198,000 for the sell later option, and $160,000 for the drill option. If the probability that the well will be dry were any less than 0.4, then the drill option would be superior in terms of expected monetary value. To sell later would be preferable, if the probability of the oil price falling were not 0.85 but was 0.8. Thus it can be

Table 7.1 Probabilities and the Associated Revenues (all monetary values in thousand $)

Probability of oil price falling		Probability that well is dry								
		.90	.80	.70	.60	.50	.40	.30	.20	.10
.95	sell later	163	163	163	163	163	163	163	163	163
.95	drill	0	40	80	120	160	200	240	280	320
.90	sell later	181	181	181	181	181	181	181	181	181
.90	drill	0	40	80	120	160	200	240	280	320
.85	sell later	198	198	198	198	198	198	198	198	198
.85	drill	0	40	80	120	160	200	240	280	320
.80	sell later	216	216	216	216	216	216	216	216	216
.80	drill	0	40	80	120	160	200	240	280	320
.75	sell later	234	234	234	234	234	234	234	234	234
.75	drill	0	40	80	120	160	200	240	280	320
.70	sell later	252	252	252	252	252	252	252	252	252
.70	drill	0	40	80	120	160	200	240	280	320
.65	sell later	269	269	269	269	269	269	269	269	269
.65	drill	0	40	80	120	160	200	240	280	320
.60	sell later	287	287	287	287	287	287	287	287	287
.60	drill	0	40	80	120	160	200	240	280	320
.55	sell later	305	305	305	305	305	305	305	305	305
.55	drill	0	40	80	120	160	200	240	280	320
.50	sell later	323	323	323	323	323	323	323	323	323
.50	drill	0	40	80	120	160	200	240	280	320
.45	sell later	340	340	340	340	340	340	340	340	340
.45	drill	0	40	80	120	160	200	240	280	320
.40	sell later	358	358	358	358	358	358	358	358	358
.40	drill	0	40	80	120	160	200	240	280	320

seen that the position with the two probabilities at 0.5 and 0.85 is a highly sensitive one: any small change in either probability could make another option preferable.

A more interesting way of illustrating the sensitivity of decisions to uncertainties in the values of the probabilities used in the decision tree is given in Table 7.2.

This table shows in a much starker fashion that the situation with the combination of a probability that the well will be dry of 0.5 and a probability that the oil price will fall of 0.85 is sensitive to small changes in these probabilities. This might call for an additional effort to determine these probabilities more precisely.

On the other hand, it can instantly be seen that if the probabilities had both been 0.5 for example, then the option to chose on grounds of maximum expected monetary value would not be sensitive to quite large changes in the probabilities. The robustness of the solution to changes in the data is something that management would find attractive.

Computer Software for Decision Tree Systems

For small decision tree problems it is not necessary to employ packages that have been specifically designed to provide decision tree support, since most spreadsheet packages can be used to develop decision tree models. Using a spreadsheet has the advantage that a well known package is used, and thus an additional learning overhead is avoided.

For larger scale decision tree problems specialist packages are available. Supertree and DATA are two such easy-to-use packages. They provide the ability to enter data without the need to replicate entries, to easily manipulate, change and reorder entries and to perform probabilistic and risk attitude sensitivity tests. Additionally they provide intrinsically many forms of tabular and graphical output with the capability of linking to spreadsheet and other packages for the provision of other, more specialist outputs. Supertree allows up to 8,000 decision paths to be evaluated.

MULTIPLE ATTRIBUTE DECISION MAKING

The Multiple Attribute Decision Making Technique

Multiple-criteria decision analysis is a technique that can be used in situations which require different courses of action to be considered which cannot be evaluated through measurement of a single, simple criterion. Two types of

Table 7.2 Probabilities and the Best Option based on EMV

		Probability that well is dry								
		0.9	0.8	0.7	0.6	0.5	0.4	0.3	0.2	0.1
	.95	sell now	sell now	sell now	sell now	sell now	sell now	drill	drill	drill
	.90	sell now	sell now	sell now	sell now	sell now	sell now	drill	drill	drill
	.85	sell now	sell now	sell now	sell now	sell now	sell now	drill	drill	drill
Probability	.80	sell later	sell later	sell later	sell later	sell later	sell later	drill	drill	drill
of	.75	sell later	sell later	sell later	sell later	sell later	sell later	sell later	drill	drill
oil price	.70	sell later	sell later	sell later	sell later	sell later	sell later	sell later	drill	drill
falling	.65	sell later	sell later	sell later	sell later	sell later	sell later	sell later	drill	drill
	.60	sell later	sell later	sell later	sell later	sell later	sell later	sell later	sell later	drill
	.55	sell later	sell later	sell later	sell later	sell later	sell later	sell later	sell later	drill
	.50	sell later	sell later	sell later	sell later	sell later	sell later	sell later	sell later	sell later
	.45	sell later	sell later	sell later	sell later	sell later	sell later	sell later	sell later	sell later
	.40	sell later	sell later	sell later	sell later	sell later	sell later	sell later	sell later	sell later

such problems can be identified (*see*, for example, Belton (1990)). The first is what is termed the evaluation problem which is concerned with choosing between well-defined alternatives: the second is the design problem which is concerned with the selection of a preferred course of action from amongst a potentially infinite set of options that satisfy a set of constraints. A common approach to the design problem is to use mathematical programming techniques, particularly linear programming as described in Chapter 6. What will be considered in this chapter is the evaluation problem which is known in multi criteria decision making circles as multiple attribute decision making.

All multiple attribute decision making approaches follow broadly the same general steps: the identification of the feasible options, the determination of the criteria by which to judge these options and the process of evaluation and choice.

Consider the case of deciding on the purchase of a new car. First, the problem owner(s) would have to specify the options he has open to him: Volvo, Ford, Renault, Nissan, etc. Next, the several criteria upon which the choice would be made would need to be identified: continuing the car example, some of the criteria on which the choice of car might hinge would be the fuel consumption, the style and the facilities offered. Some or all of these criteria might best be broken down into sub-criteria – as has been done for facilities and extras in Figure 7.3.

		Options			
Criteria	Weight	Volvo	Ford	Renault	Nissan
Fuel consumption	0.1	90	0	100	80
Style	0.3	70	0	100	50
Facilities	0.6				
No. of seats	0.46	80	100	0	90
Extras					
Sunroof	0.045	70	0	40	100
Central locking	0.045	20	0	100	80
Safety	0.05	40	50	0	100

Figure 7.3   The Decision Matrix Associated with the Car Buying Issue

Creating a hierarchy of evaluation criteria is advantageous, because it enables the user to disaggregate highly complex and generic criteria into their measurable components. Expert judgement and existing data are likely to be more effectively incorporated when using the more concrete, lower-level criteria. In addition, the clustering of criteria within hierarchies simplifies across-criteria comparisons.

The most common approach to the evaluation of options is to proceed as follows. First weights are assigned to the criteria to reflect their relative importance. These weights are scaling factors: if criterion A has a weight which is twice that of criterion B this would indicate that the decision maker values one point on criterion A the same as two points on criterion B and would be willing to trade one point on criterion A for two points on criterion B. For a multi-level hierarchy the criteria should be considered in families: the weight assigned to a parent criterion (facilities in the car example of Figure 7.3) represent the total weight assigned to the members of members of the family (to the number of seats, extras and safety). It is generally accepted that these weights are measured on a ratio scale. It is usual to normalise them to 1.

Continuing with the car example, weights would be assigned at each level in the hierarchy of Figure 7.3 with the weights at each level initially summing to the value 1. Thus, for example, the extras of sunroof and central locking might be considered of equal importance and thus each given the weight of 0.5. Within facilities as a whole, number of seats might be considered five times as important as extras which might themselves be considered twice as important as safety. Thus the proportional importances are 10 : 2 : 1 and the corresponding weightings would be 0.77, 0.15 and 0.08 (10/13, 2/13 and 1/13) respectively. It can be seen, for example, that the importance of the sunroof within facilities is 0.08 (0.5 x 2/13). If weightings of 0.1, 0.3 and 0.6 are assigned to fuel consumption, style and facilities, it can be seen that sunroof has a weighting of around 0.05 (0.5 x 2/13 x 0.6) of the total weight for all elements of the decision. One way of looking at this is that only 5% of the decision depends upon the sunroof whilst 46% depends on the number of seats and 30% on style. The weights are shown in the second column of Figure 7.3.

The next stage in the process is for one or more of the problem owners to consider each criterion in turn and to assign a score for each option being considered. The most common procedure is for the score of 100 to be assigned to the option which does best on a particular criterion and to assign zero to the option that does least well. All other options are given a score between 0 and 100. Proceeding in this way a matrix of scores is determined as shown in Figure 7.3.

The weightings assigned to the criteria give guidance as to the accuracy required of the scores. Since style has a weight of 0.30 and the sunroof has a weight of around 0.5, it would be expected that much more effort would be made to arrive at scores for the options on style than on sunroof.

The calculations are then performed, combining criteria weights with the criterion-option scores to rank the options in order of preference. This produces the evaluations given in Table 7.4.

Evaluation 7.4a puts Nissan as the highest ranking option, with Renault just the lowest. Scanning the makeup of these totals indicates quite clearly that the dominant feature is the number of seats, with almost 50% of the weight given to this one dimension.

It could be that although the consensus had been to the weightings reproduced in Table 7.4, one member of the decision making team had given style much more importance than 0.3 – perhaps his weightings had been 0.1, 0.5 and 0.4 for fuel consumption, style and facilities respectively. Putting these values into the matrix produces Table 7.4b. The rankings have now changed, with Volvo now the preferred choice although there is very little difference between Volvo and Nissan and with Renault a close third.

It may be that in the decision what was important was that the number of seats wasn't less than 4 and that the decision makers were indifferent to the number of seats as long as there were 4 or more. Under this regime, the number of seats would no longer feature as a criterion in a multi attribute decision making: an option either passes or does not satisfy the requirement for a minimum number of seats – if it satisfies this requirement it is included in the set of options for multi attribute decision making; if it fails to satisfy the requirement it is not considered further.

Identification of Criteria and the Determination of Values

In the discussion above no mention was made of the difficulties that may occur in identifying the criteria to use and in obtaining measures of the weights and scores used in the evaluations.

Often the criteria to use in evaluation would be obvious to the decision makers, and the inclusion of 'too many' criteria would be taken care of

Table 7.4   The Weighted Scores for the Car Buying Issue (values rounded)

(Table 7.4a)

Criteria	Weight	Options			
		Volvo	Ford	Renault	Nissan
Fuel consumption	0.1	9	0	10	8
Style	0.3	21	0	30	15
Facilities	0.6				
No. of seats	0.45	36	45	0	41
Extras					
Sunroof	0.05	4	0	2	5
Central locking	0.05	1	0	5	4
Safety	0.05	2	3	0	5
Total scores		73	48	47	78

(Table 7.4b)

Criteria	Weight	Options			
		Volvo	Ford	Renault	Nissan
Fuel consumption	0.1	9	0	10	8
Style	0.5	35	0	50	25
Facilities	0.4				
No. of seats	0.31	25	31	0	28
Extras					
Sunroof	0.03	2	0	1	3
Central locking	0.03	1	0	3	2
Safety	0.03	1	2	0	3
Total scores		73	33	64	69

through the assignment of very low weightings to some of them. However, in some cases the criteria to use will not be obvious and the decision makers will need guidance on their identification.

One method of structuring the unearthing of criteria is through the use of triads of options in which decision makers are asked to specify the differences and similarities between randomly selected sets of three options, following Kelly's (1955) minimum context or Fransella and Bannister's (1977) difference method. Continuing the car example, Volvo and Renault might be grouped together and compared with Ford; the differences might be itemised as style and facilities; the similarities as fuel consumption. Style, facilities and fuel consumption would then be prime candidates as evaluation criteria. The words used to describe the differences and similarities, such as 'nice' and 'poor', 'high' and 'low', 'expensive' and 'inexpensive' would be used to specify the end points of a scale for the respective criterion.

Having identified the criteria it would seem obvious that scores could be assigned to each option for each criterion, either numerically or on a defined scale (generally 0–9). However, there is considerable evidence that simply to ask people to score a list of options against a criterion is not a reliable way of obtaining the scores. A more valid approach is that of pair-wise comparison in which the scorer is asked to consider two options and to rate one against the other. For example, for the criterion of style the scorer might first be asked which of Volvo and Ford he preferred and to indicate whether this preference was strong or weak. Then he might be asked to do the same with the Volvo-Renault pair, then the Volvo-Nissan pair and so on. With the 4 options of Volvo, Ford, Renault, and Nissan six different pairings are possible. More generally, with N options the number of possible pairings is $N(N-1)/2$: thus, for example, with 10 options there would be $10 \times 9/2 = 45$ pairings. To ask the user to make a choice for each of a large number of pairings *for each criterion* would generally prove unacceptable. Fortunately however, a complete set of relative scores can be obtained by considering only N-1 pairs of options for each criterion. To see this consider the case where relative scores are available for the pairings Volvo-Ford, Volvo-Renault and Volvo-Nissan: if the relative scores for Volvo-Ford is 5:2, for Volvo-Renault is 1:2 and Volvo-Nissan is 3:1, then the overall relative scores can be inferred as shown in the final column of Table 7.5.

The number N-1 is the minimum set of pairs required to establish the relative priorities for all options. However, if data for more than this minimum number of pairings is obtained the impact of a poor or erroneous response can be reduced and an assessment of the consistency of judgement can be obtained. There would be a gross inconsistency in scoring if, for

Table 7.5   Relative Scores from 3 Pairwise Comparisons

Volvo	5	1	3	3
Ford	2			1.2 (2/5 * 3)
Renault		2		6
Nissan			1	1

example, for the same criterion Volvo were scored more highly than Ford, Ford more highly than Renault and Renault more highly than Volvo. There would be a lesser inconsistency if Volvo were scored much more highly than Ford, Ford were scored only slightly better than Renault yet Volvo were scored only slightly better than Renault. Data from more than the minimum set of pairings would allow such inconsistencies to be determined and brought to the attention of the decision maker.

The Analytic Hierarchy Process

One approach to multi attribute decision making that differs significantly in its theoretical basis from that described above, is the analytical hierarchy process developed by Saaty (1980) and (1982). There is considerable debate in the academic literature concerning the validity of some aspects of the process (for example, interpretation of criteria weights and the assumptions made about the scales of preference used). However, given that the main aims of DSS are to facilitate the thinking of decision makers about the issues they have to confront rather than for the DSS to provide precise answers, such validity issues are unlikely to have much practical effect. These points are well discussed by Belton (1990).

Computer Software for Multi Attribute Decision Making Systems

One significant feature of the latest software is the support for what is termed the visual interactive approach. In this there is a very easy link between graphical output and alterations in the values of key variables. VISA is a package expressly designed to facilitate this approach, very well suited to sensitivity and 'What if?' analyses. Lightyear has a very good user interface, making excellent use of graphics. As well as very simple numeric input, Lightyear allows graphical input and for the user to specify a vocabulary and then use that vocabulary to evaluate alternatives. HIVIEW is another well known package.

Priorities has the apparently unique feature that in the situation where a group of decision makers is involved, a further weighting can be applied to the results coming from each decision maker acting individually in order to calculate overall team scores for the options. (This may sound fine, but who will bell the cat? – who will introduce the weightings for each decision maker?). Measures of team consistency and consensus are available as output.

Criterium and Expert Choice are packages based on Saaty's analytic hierarchy process. Basic to the process is the pairwise comparisons of alternatives to establish the relative values. Such comparisons allow inconsistencies of judgement to be monitored and controlled.

Buede (1993) provides a survey of 25 decision tree and multi attribute decision making software packages.

SUMMARY

The main attraction of Preference Determination Systems to many managers is the few constraints that these systems impose on thinking. The general absence of mathematical complexity means that they have the potential to be used directly by managers much more widely than is likely with Extrapolatory Systems.

As the number of decision points increases, Decision Tree Systems become difficult to handle. This difficulty does not lie in the logic model but with the calculation of the relevant probabilities: the difficult area of conditional probabilities has to be confronted. This will require specialist skills, and in this respect, Decision Tree Systems are similar to Extrapolatory Systems and illustrate that Decision Tree Systems span the Extrapolatory and Preference Determination System classes of DSS.

The software now available to support Preference Determination Systems is extensive. Most of the software is very easy to use.

REFERENCES

Belton V., (1990) *MCDA – Practically the only way to choose, Operational Research Tutorial Papers,* edited by Hendry L.C. and Eglese R.W., associated with the 32nd Annual Conference of the Operational Research Society, Bangor, July.

Buede D., (1993) *Aiding Insight, OR/MS Today*, April, pp 52–60.

Fransella F. and Bannister D., (1977) A Manual for Repertory Grid Technique, Academic Press, London.

Kelly G.A., (1955) *A theory of personality: The Psychology of Personal Constructs*, Norton, New York.

Saaty T.L., (1980) *The Analytical Hierarchy Process*, McGraw Hill, New York.

Saaty T.L., (1982) *Decision Making for Leaders*, Lifetime Learning Publications.

8 Scenario Development Systems

All the DSS discussed in detail in Chapters 5 through 7 have been systems that concentrate on helping decision makers with the problem understanding phase of tackling a problem (see Figure 1.1). This phase assumes that a problem has already been detected and defined, and the DSS used in this phase are overwhelmingly used to achieve convergence. These DSS help the decision maker choose between a rather narrow set of options around one broad direction: they do not help widen the thinking of the decision maker to allow him ultimately to explore a much wider range of options around several broad directions. DSS that help in this regard are termed Scenario Development Systems.

This name is used for these systems because Scenario Development Systems are concerned with the broad development of the whole or a large portion of manager's scenario rather than with detailed and deep analyses of his local scenario for which the other types of DSS are suited. In Figure 2.4 the local scenario for Scenario Development Systems expands to include all, or a very considerable portion of the scenario.

Over the last decade, Scenario Development Systems have been developed that impose a minimum of constraints on decision makers. Two types of Scenario Development System are considered in this chapter. The first comprise Cognitive Mapping Systems which allow the articulated thought processes of managers to be exposed and codified and subsequently analysed. The results are 'cognitive maps' that show the underlying concepts. The second type involves 'ideas generation' with systems to support the unearthing of novel ways for tackling problems.

COGNITIVE MAPPING SYSTEMS

Two types of Cognitive Mapping System are of interest. Unfortunately, Eden and his collaborators (1983) have taken the generic term 'cognitive mapping' and applied it to their own specific approach. This specific use of the term thus clashes with the more generic use employed in this book. This should not cause trouble to the reader, however, as long as he is aware of the possibility of confusion existing. The second type of Cognitive Mapping Systems is the Strategic Choice approach developed by Friend and Hickling (1985).

The Cognitive Mapping Approach

Eden and his collaborators at the Universities of Bath and Strathclyde have spent many years developing ideas on cognitive mapping. The work of Kelly (1955) and his theory of personal constructs provides one of the bases for their work. Very briefly, Kelly sees man as constantly striving to make sense of his world in order to predict and control it. This leads on to the view that man is an intelligent problem finder, who continually develops his (subjective) scenario, by fitting the events that are occurring around him into it. He does this by developing constructs, which are articulated and represented by a phrase that 'makes sense' to the individual using it. An individual's set of personal constructs constitutes his scenario.

Kelly's theory was developed at the level of the individual. Eden and his collaborators take the view that what is required is for the (individual) scenario of each member of a management team to be combined with those of the other members of the team: in this way all the individual scenarios will be modified, hopefully to form a consensus.

Working with a variety of organisations the methodology of 'cognitive mapping' has been developed. Put most simply, cognitive mapping is a graphical way of modelling the interconnection of ideas and argument that people use when they are thinking and describing their problem. A cognitive map is a network of ideas linked by arrows, and can be developed from both written and spoken statements.

The methods used to code the ideas and linkages in a person's scenario have been developed by Eden and his collaborators from the coding methods used by political scientists to describe decision making processes. It is important to capture 'meaning' rather than just language. An effective way of representing meaning is to contrast a phrase with its psychological opposite: in cognitive mapping a pair of contrasting phrases is called a construct or a concept. The resulting cognitive map is similar to the influence diagrams used by Systems Dynamics modellers (see for example the work of Forrester (1961)).

An Example of Cognitive Mapping

An example of cognitive mapping will illustrate the basic concepts. This example is a modified version of the example given in reference 1.

Members of the Marketing Department of a large organisation are dissatisfied with the information system that has been developed for them. The Marketing Director is seeking to replace this system with a proprietary marketing information system. Purchasing a computer system such as this has wide ranging consequences, and senior management, the Computer Department and the Accounting Department have all expressed concern about the proposals.

As a starting point the basic issue will be taken as *Acquire a new system*. To form a construct this would be contrasted with its 'opposite', which is clearly Retain existing system.

Reasons for acquiring a new system need to be identified. One might be Existing system is inadequate, and this would be contrasted with the idea that the existing system is adequate, i.e. with the phrase Existing system is adequate. Another reason might be that there is *Insufficient storage* capacity rather than the 'opposite' – Plenty of storage capacity.

Pictorially these ideas could be represented as in Figure 8.1.

In Figure 8.1, the links between constructs have been shown by arrows, with the direction of the arrows implying cause and effect. Additionally the link

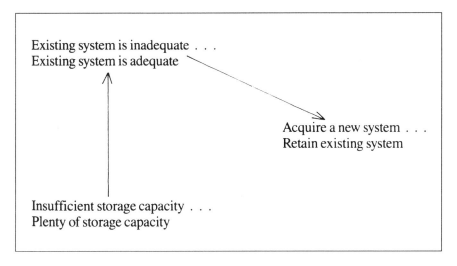

Figure 8.1   Linking of Constructs

implies that the first phrase of the 'tail' concept leads to the first phrase of the 'head' concept. For example, Figure 8.1 should be read as:

Existing system *is inadequate* leads to *Acquire a new system*, and *Existing system is adequate* leads to *Retain existing system*.

To show that the first phrase of one concept is linked to the second phrase of the second concept, a minus sign is used. To show this, consider the concept *Control is difficult* rather than *Planning and control is much easier*. If it were to be shown that *Acquire a new system* leads to *Planning and control is much easier*, this would be drawn as in Figure 8.2.

In Figure 8.2 the concepts are all expressed in bipolar form, i.e. they are all expressed as a phrase and its contrast. It is sometimes not helpful to do this, and in these circumstances one phrase would suffice. An example of this would be the concept *New computer applications* that affect the sufficiency of the storage capacity. This form of 'monopolar' concept is shown in Figure 8.3. Sometimes it is not possible to link concepts in a causal manner, although the two concepts are linked conceptually. These links are known as connotative links, and are illustrated by a short line (not an arrow) joining

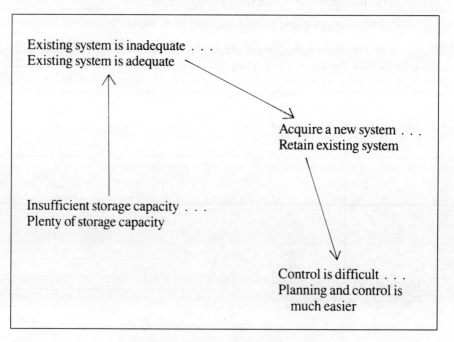

Figure 8.2   Linking of Concepts

the concepts. An example of a connotative link is the view that any changes in computer systems must not immediately precede or coincide with the end of a financial year. This could be expressed as the link between the concept *Make any changes after financial year end and the concept Acquire a new system*.

The map shown in Figure 8.3 is very simple: typically a cognitive map would contain several hundred concepts. Such a cognitive map representing the thinking of one person. In Eden's strategic management work where several managers would typically be involved, the map produced will be an aggregate of the cognitive maps of all the people in the team. This is called a 'strategic map'. The map is typically developed through cycles of workshops involving four to six managers attending a workshop focussed on a particular strategic issue. A complete strategic map would contain

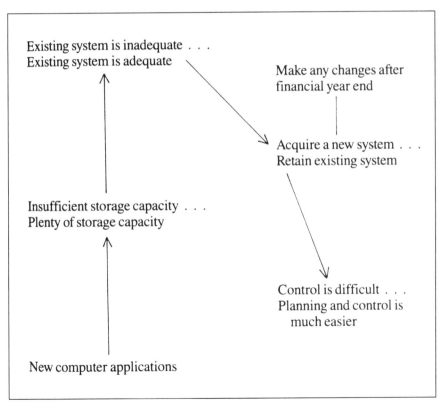

Figure 8.3   Linking of Concepts

several thousand concepts. The operation of a workshop within the Strategic Development and Analysis (SODA) overall decision framework is discussed in Chapter 14.

The Strategic Choice Approach

The strategic choice approach developed by Friend and Hickling (1985) consists of four modes of cognitive activity. Friend and Hickling call these the shaping, designing, comparing and choosing modes. These modes correspond very closely to the stages of problem definition, detailed system design, exploring courses of action and decision taking as discussed in Chapter 1 and set out in Figure 1.1. The one significant difference is that the choosing mode explicitly includes an action plan for change implementation.

Although the overall approach is very similar to that described in Chapter 1, the detailed way in which each stage or mode is carried out is different from other methodologies. To show this, the stages in the problem involving the marketing information system will be described.

There are several steps involved in each mode. These are:

- *Shaping Mode (Problem Definition)*
  - Defining the decision areas, which are opportunities for choice in which two or more different courses of action can be considered. Decision areas associated with the marketing information system are shown in Figure 8.4.
  - Identifying the links between decision areas, leading to a decision graph. A decision graph is shown in Figure 8.5.
  - Determining the problem focus, by selecting a set of linked decision areas for closer examination. One focus is shown in Figure 8.5 to include the decision areas of System, Accounting links, Overseas links and Computer department. Support and Top management would be seen to have only a weak link to the chosen problem focus.
- *Designing Mode (Detailed System Design)*
  - Within the problem focus, determine the decision options, which are the mutually exclusive courses of action. These are shown in Figure 8.6.
  - Identify the options from different decision areas that are incompatible.

DECISION AREA	LABEL
Which type of system should be obtained?	System?
What links should there be to the accounting systems?	Accountancy links?
What system should be used to satisfy top management?	Top management?
What are the consequences for the computer department?	Computer department?
What will be the linkages to the overseas branches?	Overseas links?
What technical support will be available?	Support?

Figure 8.4   Identification of Decision Areas

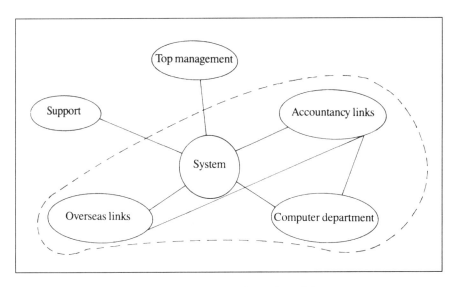

Figure 8.5   Decision Graph and Problem Focus

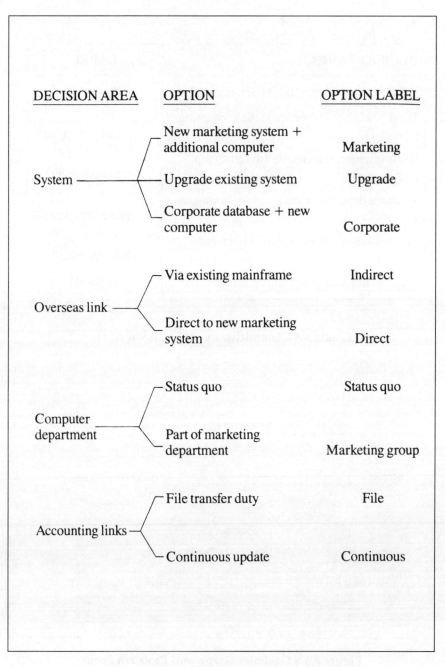

Figure 8.6   The Decision Options

- Build an option graph. This illustrates the links between options for all decision areas. This is shown in Figure 8.7. Note, for example, that it is considered incompatible for the Computer Department staff to join the Marketing Department unless the Marketing Department gets its own new computer system.

- Generate decision schemes. A decision scheme is any feasible combination of options containing one option from each of the decision areas within the problem focus. Decision schemes have been identified in Figure 8.8.

- Comparing Mode (Exploring Courses of Action)

  - Decide on the variables that will be used in the comparison of the decision schemes. Friend and Hickling term this set of variables a comparison area. For example, the variables chosen for the comparison area might be capital cost, the effect on computer department staff and the quality of the information provided to the Marketing Department.

  - By comparing one decision scheme with another, produce a relative assessment of these schemes.

  - State the balance of advantage between each pair of decision schemes.

  - Create a working shortlist. This is a subset of decision schemes in which it is intended to compare alternatives more closely.

- Choosing Mode (Decision Taking and Implementation of Change)

  - Define any uncertainty areas. An uncertainty area is a description of any source of uncertainty that is causing difficulty in the consideration of a decision problem. Examples would be uncertainty about the costs involved in upgrading the existing computer system and uncertainty in the feelings of Computer Department personnel about a possible move into the Marketing Department.

  - Produce exploratory options. An exploratory option is any course of action conceived as a means of reducing current feelings of uncertainty within some uncertainty area. For example, contact hardware and software suppliers, and question Computer Department personnel about their feelings. Produce an action scheme. This involves commitments within only some of the more urgent decision areas within a problem focus. This is akin to using a qualitative decision tree approach.

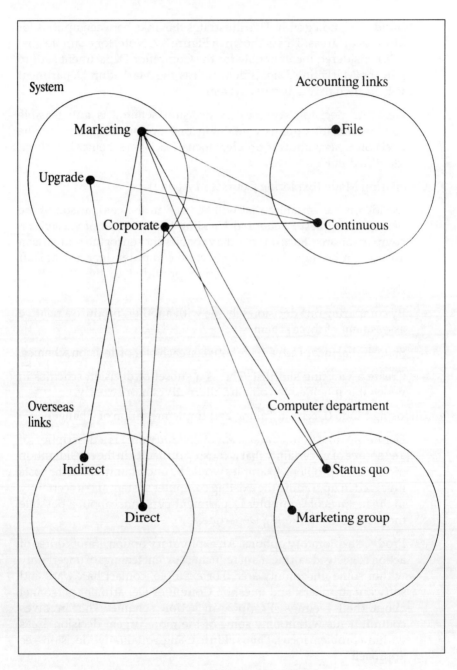

Figure 8.7   An Option Graph

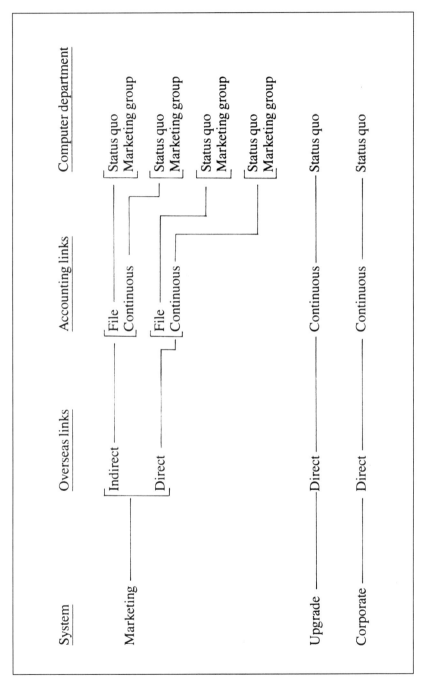

Figure 8.8   Decision Schemes

– Devise a commitment package. This is a combination of actions, explorations and arrangements for future choice designed as a means of making progress in a planning process. An example is given in Figure 8.9.

The emphasis on uncertainty and its reduction is interesting, and fits well with the view expressed in Chapter 4.

Computer Software for Cognitive Mapping Systems.

The cognitive mapping approach of Eden is supported by the specially written software package COPE (Cognitive Policy Evaluation). COPE stores concepts and their relationships to one another so that a hierarchical system of connected thoughts is recorded. It enables this system of ideas to be projected as a graphical representation. It can be used to reveal key decision areas and critical options, as well as revealing the implicit goal system embedded in the way a management team discusses an issue.

Eden and Huxham (1988) list some of the more important facilities offered by COPE. These are the ability to:

– search for concepts containing key words, so that only concepts containing these key words are extracted;

– find clusters of concepts that exists without connection to the rest of the map. Note that the concept of clustering will be discussed in Chapter 14;

– find all final outcomes (statements without consequences);

– search for statements that are central to many lines of argument;

– find those statements with the most supporting argumentation;

– conduct logical tests on different parts of the data: for example, 'Which statements relate to a particular option and have implications for one part of the company but not for another, and yet have no financial implications?'

The use of colour within COPE helps to make the linkages between concepts more easily intelligible. In one coding, concepts are coded red for goals, purple for strategic issues, blue for potential options, white for assumptions and yellow for argument linking other concepts.

The Strategic Choice Approach is also supported by specially written

DECISION AREAS	Immediate Decisions		Future Decisions	
	ACTIONS	EXPLORATIONS	DEFERRED CHOICES	CONTINGENCY PLANNING
System	Recruit database administrator	Database software availability	Whether marketing department and other databases have separate development or not	
Accounting links				
Computer department		Discuss moves with computer department staff		Buy in software programming expertise
Overseas links		Investigate consequences of indirect and direct links		Maintain existing interface

Figure 8.9   A Commitment Package

software that is faithful to the well tested 'manual' approach as described by Friend and Hickling (1985). The software is called STRAD (short for Strategic Adviser) (reference 2). This software is extremely user-friendly with a wide selection of graphical interfaces.

IDEAS GENERATION SYSTEMS

One very well known method of unearthing ideas is Brainstorming, in which ideas, concept and solution alternatives are generated as freely and rapidly as possible. This free-flowing session would typically be followed by a more analytical session at which the options generated through brainstorming would be exposed to 'the cold light of morning'.

It is important that inhibitions are removed for the initial ideas generation session. In the group sessions in which brainstorming commonly takes place, it is often a basic rule that no criticism is permitted of any idea that is put forward.

Computer Software for Ideas Generation Systems

Any current computer software is bound to impose some sort of structure on the user. However, BrainStorm is a computer package, developed by an experimental psychologist, that imposes very little. It works by building a description of a problem in terms of themes and then allowing the user to examine 'novel aspects' of these themes through the generation of 'ideas probes'. Ideas probes are generated by the computer randomly selecting one item from each theme. One example of an ideas probe is shown in Figure 8.10.

Here is a problem confronting a sales team. The team has already decided to hold a series of seminars to extol the virtues of its products. The problem is to decide the clientele it wishes to address, the sales strategy to adopt, and the date and location of the first, pilot seminar. In addition to deciding on these themes, the possible variations on each theme need to be decided upon.

It can be seen from this example that BrainStorm operates like a 'buzz word generator', constantly selecting one item from each set to form a possible option. Once the options have been generated, it is for the user to sift out the feasible from the infeasible.

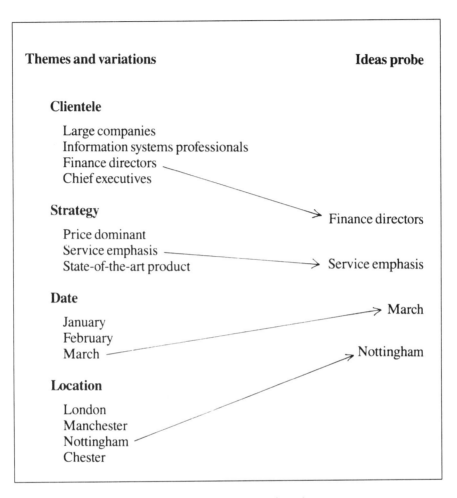

Figure 8.10   The Operation of Brainstormer

SUMMARY

Scenario Development Systems are systems offering an approach that can be used wherever there is a need for assistance in widening the scope of an original problem area and to structure these wide-ranging thoughts. The Cognitive Mapping Systems (cognitive mapping of Eden and colleagues and Strategic Choice) look for cause and effect constructs and structure accordingly. The Ideas Generation Systems offer the capability of encouraging the surfacing of ideas and their structuring.

The COPE software has been used to structure project reports, and to aid agenda setting for meetings. However, its main use has been as a tool to use within the SODA metasystem, which is described in Chapter 14.

REFERENCES

1.   Cope User Guide Version 7.0, Bath Software Research, 1985.

2.   STRAD User's Manual version 1.0, Stradspan Ltd, 1991.

Eden C., Jones S., and Sims D., (1983) *Messing about in Problems: an informal Structured Approach to their Identification and Management,* Frontiers of Operational Research and Applied Systems Analysis, Vol.1, Pergamon.

Eden C. and Huxham C., (1988) *Action-Oriented Strategic Management,* Journal of the Operational Research Society, Vol.39, No.10, pp 892–893.

Forrester J.W., (1961) *Industrial Dynamics,* The M.I.T. Press, Cambridge, Massachusetts.

Friend J. and Hickling A., (1985) *Planning under Pressure: The Strategic Choice Approach,* Pergamon Press, Oxford.

Kelly G.A., (1955) *A theory of personality: The Psychology of Personal Constructs,* Norton, New York.

9 Group Decision Support System

In his remarks at the closing plenary session of the First International Conference on DSS, Keen (1981) pointed out that the model of managerial decision making on which the design of DSS is generally based – that of the lone decision maker making decisions in isolation – is true only in rare cases. Overwhelmingly, decisions are taken only after extensive consultation, and involve several people. This view is in line with the activities of managers described in Chapter 1. Decision makers spend a considerable amount of time in decision making situations dealing with conflicting views and different areas of expertise. Tools and processes that have been devised for individual managers acting alone are unlikely to provide the full range of support.

Most studies on the value of single-user DSS have found that they enhance interaction amongst managers, leading to deeper analysis and to more focused discussion. However, this enhancement of managerial interaction generally takes place outside of the DSS: it is the outputs from the single-user DSS that are used by managers to discuss problem situations. It is only relatively recently that it was realised that the group processes involved in most managerial decision making could be improved by direct support *inside* the DSS.

Huber (1984) describes Group DSS as a set of software, hardware and language components and procedures that support a group of people engaged in a decision related meeting. DeSanctis and Gallupe (1985) give a similar definition – an interactive, computer-based system which facilitates solution of unstructured problems by a set of decision makers working together as a group. These definitions of Group DSS are wide enough to include the provision of communications to support the group in its deliberations. This inclusion was not explicitly stated in the definition of DSS discussed and arrived at in Chapter 3, but it was included by implication. Put simply, a Group DSS is a DSS that supports a group of people engaged together in a decision related process.

REQUIREMENTS FROM GROUP DECISION SUPPORT SYSTEMS

Group DSS subsume single-user DSS within them. The components of a single-user DSS (viz. logic model, data model and human-computer interface) are all present. As the group size shrinks to one, a Group DSS reduces to a single-user DSS. Conversely, in moving from a single-user DSS to a Group DSS, there are some additional requirements.

The aim of a Group DSS is to reduce the 'process losses' associated with conventional group decision making, namely disorganised and unfocused activity, dominance by one or two members of the group and the consequent inhibition of others, and the social pressures to conform. It is to be hoped that Group DSS would help a more democratic decision process to emerge, and reduce the 'muddling through' apparent in many group meetings. A necessary condition for success with a Group DSS is that it should satisfy the social needs of the group. The group wants to be rewarded as the decision making session proceeds, and this requires interim milestones of progress to be made available. An example of a poor DSS in this regard, a DSS that would require that all the data has to be entered before any analysis could be made. A Group DSS needs to be highly interactive to show the group that it is providing decision support, even if this support is simply that of 'minute-taker'. Another form of 'reward' that the support should offer the participants is to give members of the team a belief that they are making more intelligent/thoughtful decisions than would otherwise be the case.

As well as rewarding the individuals and the team, a Group DSS also needs to be able to facilitate negotiation amongst members of the team whilst the group session is underway, rather than simply as a result of informal discussions after the session. Although a Group DSS could be used to seek compromise, the ideal is to develop consensus about what should be done. If consensus or an amicable compromise is achieved, then this should provide the context to facilitate the conversion of agreement into a commitment to action. The emphasis is on sufficing rather than achieving a 'best' decision.

These requirements call for a Group DSS to offer:

- communication facilities between participants;

- enhanced modelling and interface facilities to permit voting and ranking for developing consensus;

- both qualitative and quantitative decision aids as appropriate;

- decision aids with which the participants are comfortable;

- decision aids that are transparent in operation, so that the participants will understand and so use the results;

- decision aids that are flexible, so that they do not constrain problem formulation.

Effective group decision support hinges on the ability of the support to respond in something like real time. What this means is that support must be forthcoming at a rate close to the speed of working of the group, with output available while the group is concerned with the same issue. This puts a considerable burden on the facilitators and on the information technology, since it is considered unreasonable if the support system cannot respond in less than 30 seconds.

The effects of Group DSS would not be expected to be universally favourable. Kiesler (1986) has pointed out that the inclusion of electronic aids in meetings can have negative effects. He cites the use of keyboard input increasing the level of information to such an extent that the increased cognitive effort required of the participants lowered group efficiency. He also surmised that heightened awareness of participants' views may increase the level of conflict within the group.

SETTINGS FOR GROUP DECISION MAKING

Although almost all group decision meetings are face to face, information technology is starting to make it possible for participants to be at different locations. DeSanctis and Gallupe (1985) have identified four types of Group DSS. These are the decision room, the local decision network, teleconferencing and remote decision making.

These arrangements are shown in Figure 9.1. Note the two axes: DeSanctis and Gallupe's view is that it is the physical proximity and the duration of the decision making process that determine the form of technological help that group decision making requires.

The Decision Room

The decision room is the traditional conference or board room augmented by electronic aids: the formalism associated with the use of information technology is married to face-to-face verbal interaction to produce a more efficient decision making process. Information can be communicated to and from participants via a network or by use of one or more public screens fed from the computer. Graphic pads may be available for the participants to

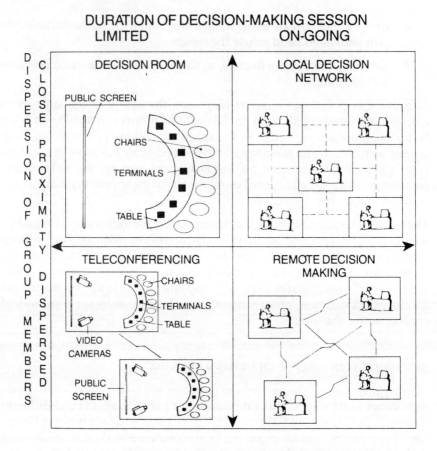

Figure 9.1   DeSanctis and Gallupe's Typology of Group DSS

project their graphs and sketches onto the public screen. The facility to take hardcopy of 'blackboard' activity is also often available. In general, facilitators would be available to ease the group decision process: they would allow the participants to concentrate on the issues at hand rather than have their concentration blunted by struggling with the technology.

There are three ways in which groups of decision makers can obtain the use of a decision room. First, there can be a permanent installation at the user's site. It is usually a conference room that is fitted out with terminals, public displays, etc. This is the manner used by the company ICL plc. in its own POD installations (see later). Second, there are portable installations brought to the user's site on an ad-hoc basis. Eden and his collaborators in the UK often use this method, as do Hammond Associates and the Wilson Learning Corporation in the USA. The skills of the vendor's staff in setting up the meeting can be a crucial element in the success of the decision making session. Third, use can be made of a permanent installation at the vendor's site: this is what is offered by the decision room housed in the London School of Economics and Political Science and that made available for outside use by ICL plc.

The discussion has concentrated on the 'high-tec' aspects of decision rooms. Harvey-Jones (1989) points out the importance of the 'low-tec' environment, and discusses the need to carefully consider the seating arrangements, to provide comfortable chairs and to have a flexible arrangement of tables, so that different configurations can be set up for different types of meeting. Room configuration can be most important: at one extreme it could reinforce the dominance of a leading individual - as in the typical 'older style' boardroom: at the other extreme it could facilitate a climate of openness and readiness to fully discuss issues.

Other Settings for Group Decision Making

Teleconferencing   This type of group decision support is conceptually similar to the decision room approach, and is appropriate where the participants are geographically separated from each other. Two or more decision rooms are linked together by visual or simply voice communication: where the link is a visual one the conferencing is termed videoconferencing.

Local Decision Network   Instead of the decision room where the participants must all be in the same room at one time and the decision meeting is of short duration, the local decision network allows participants to remain in their offices and to communicate over a much longer period of time – and not necessarily at the same time. Through their own workstations, each participant would be provided with access to each other (most often by electronic mail) and to a central base of data, perhaps to work which they are jointly authoring, and to decision support software. 'Public screens' would be available on their own terminals. Decision rooms and face-to-face meetings would be used to augment the interactions available on the local decision network.

Remote Decision Making   This approach is fundamentally the same as the local decision network, but with the offices of managers not now in close proximity. The 'electronic' augmentation of the meetings is not easy, and more is required of the technology to make it work.

SUPPORT OFFERED BY GROUP DSS

Group DSS may support only one or a few types of decision making forms. A full-service Group DSS would be able to support a diversity of tasks, for example, financial planning, personnel planning and crisis management: they would be what are sometimes termed 'wide-band' systems. However, most Group DSS offer only a very limited range of support. For example, Executive Information Systems generally offer simply the facility to display (past) data; only exceptionally are Extrapolatory System facilities other than forecasting made available. As further examples, a system may simply provide the capability for a group to use a decision tree approach and that is all; a system may simply provide a multi-attribute decision system.

Group DSS may be classified by the directness of the way in which members of the group interact with the system. First, there are the systems in which only a facilitator or his assistants interface directly with the computer: participants offer ideas and information and these are subsequently input to the computer as the facilitator deems appropriate. This form of Group DSS will be termed 'single facilitator workstation' systems. A well-proven example of this approach is Decision Conferencing (to be described in the next section). Second, there are keypad systems in which each group member has a keypad that allows him to vote: the facilitator controls from a central workstation the questions posed and the treatment of responses. Examples here are the approach taken by Decision Dynamics and Option Technologies (to be described in a later section). Finally, there are approaches in which each group member has his own workstation and can work without a facilitator being present, although working without any facilitation at all is rare. These types of system will be termed 'workstation-centred' Group DSS.

SINGLE FACILITATOR WORKSTATION SYSTEM – DECISION CONFERENCING

As well as being a generic term, Decision Conferencing is the name given to one form of single facilitator workstation Group DSS. The approach was introduced to Europe in 1981 by Phillips and his collaborators of the Decision Analysis Unit of the London School of Economics and Political Science (1986). Since 1984, further developments have evolved in collaboration with ICL plc., initially for the company's own use and now as a product for its customers. Many conferences have now been conducted in the UK.

Decision Conferencing is a problem solving session, typically lasting two days, attended by the owners of the problem. Important aspects of the differing scenarios of the participants are combined into a computer model by the group during the session. By examining the implications of the model, then trying 'What if?' and sensitivity analyses, participants deepen their understanding and are helped to reach an agreement about what to do.

The process is generally guided by three support staff, who are process consultants, not specialists in the content of the problem. First, there is the facilitator, who helps the group focus on the task, model the problem and interpret the results. Second, there is the analyst who attends to the computer modelling. Third, there is the recorder, who uses a projected word processor to help the group agree and own the words that describe critical issues and to record the thinking of the group as it occurs. This recording also provides the group with documentation to take away after the conference.

Several stages are common to most decision conferences. After an initial introduction by the facilitator, the group is asked to discuss the issues and concerns that are to be explored. Thus the problem has already been detected and the problem is being defined.

An initial attempt to construct a model is then made. The facilitator has available several DSS of the sort described in Chapters 6 and 7. In the light of the discussions to define the problem, it is he who decides which of these types of DSS is most appropriate and should be used. The analyst will then assist the participants to add both data and judgement to the model.

It should be noted that the availability of a battery of (individual) DSS to aid group deliberations is both a boon and a drawback. It is a boon in that tried and tested techniques are available in a fairly user-friendly manner, without time being spent 'reinventing the wheel'. On the other hand, it is a drawback because it will constrain the problem tackling approach: the technique will structure the discussion. The outputs from the model are typically projected onto a large screen for the participants' comments. The initial results are rarely fully accepted by the group, and iterations of the cycle of – model changes – results – model changes – then take place. An acceptable level of consensus is generally reached after several iterations, and this agreement forms the basis on which the group can work in formulating an action plan.

Phillips (1986) provides guidance on the features of organisations that increase the chances of a Decision Conference being a success. The organisations that are likely to benefit from Decision Conferencing are those where:

(a)   consultation proceeds decision-making;

(b)   communication links across the organisation chart, so that information flows laterally as well as vertically;

(c)   a climate of problem solving exists, in which options can be freely explored rather than manipulated to serve predetermined solutions;

(d)   authority and accountability are well distributed throughout the organisation.

Keypad Systems

In keypad systems each member of the group is provided with a personal handset that generally provides a 2-line display and a numeric keypad. Typically, the numeric keypad is configured like a telephone layout and in appearance can best be likened to a simple hand calculator. The keypads are linked to a central microcomputer either by cable or by radio.

Very often in operation the facilitator will have agreed with the person calling the meeting on the questions that will be asked of the group. This is particularly likely to occur in situations where the activities are well-structured – such as the example of beer and lager tasting panels described by Gear and Read (1993). In other cases the questions to be considered will emerge during the initial portion of the meeting and be input to the computer during the meeting, either by the facilitator or by an assistant.

Following the posing of a question, the participants will be asked to respond using the keypad, typically entering a 1 to 4 digit number into the display. Participants can view their entry personally, edit it if necessary and then, when happy with the entry, transmit it as a digital message to the computer.

The computer is connected to a large public display and programmed to allow various aggregations of the individual responses to be displayed. The overall arrangement is shown in Figure 9.2.

At its simplest, histograms can be shown indicating the spread of the responses. More sophisticated and informative displays may result from the splitting of the whole set of responses: for example, it is common for keypad systems to allow the responses from individual handsets to be grouped according to the number of the handset – for example, with handsets numbered 1–9 given to salespeople and handsets numbered 10–15 given to production personnel. A distinction can be made between the aggregate responses of these two groups. Such distinctions can also be made dynamically: for example, to show the link between two responses –

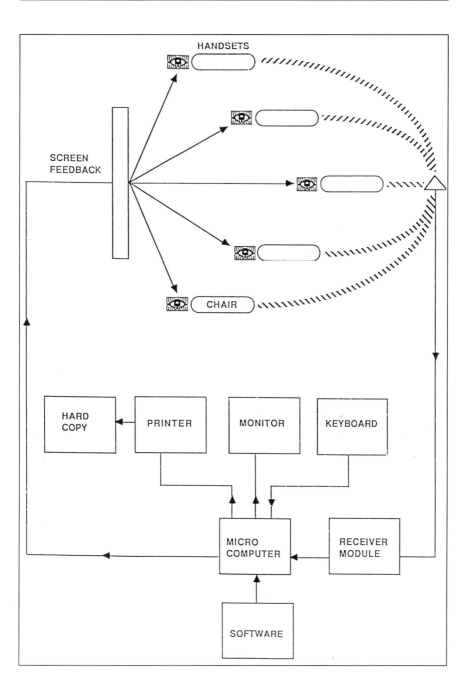

Figure 9.2   Typical Layout of a Keypad System

between age and pricing strategy, between years of service in the organisation and the relative importance of the issues the organisation is facing. Very many types of graphic display can be shown.

Workstation-centred Systems

Following Huber's work of the early 1980s, a number of research groups in the USA, from both academic and commercial organisations, have developed Group DSS featuring high levels of technological support. GroupSystems is typical of these approaches. Originating from research at the University of Arizona, it has been developed by IBM in the USA for internal use and as a client service, via a country wide network of more than 20 decision support centres. Other typical offerings are Meetingware VisionQuest and the Software Aided Meeting Management System (SAMM).

GroupSystems, Meetingware VisionQuest and SAMM operate with a set of PCs linked by a local area network, providing for direct individual input and for individual and aggregated information to be displayed to the group through projection facilities. A set of software modules are sequenced to support the different phases of decision making. This process is called 'script writing'. Given a particular problem context a suitable set of modules can be selected prior to the meeting to form a customised Group DSS.

Participants can draft ideas privately at their workstations, passing promising suggestions to the public screen for discussion by the group, whilst quietly discarding, without embarrassment, results which they judge to be weak. The display of many ideas on the public screen leads to productive discussion aimed at resolving issues. When voting takes place, preferences of individuals can be expressed confidentially; a valuable feature if it is difficult to express views contrary to the dominant person or group. An action plan is formulated at the close of a meeting, documenting concise recommendations for future activity and assigning actions to be carried out by each of the participants. Because much of the communication is electronic, a permanent record of the session is automatically created.

This software allows members of the client organisation to run the meeting on their own after some training of a person who operates the hardware and software and acts as a chauffeur.

To better understand the support offered by workstation-centred Group DSS, that offered by Meetingware (and discussed in detail by Atkinson and Marshall (1990)) will be considered in more detail. Meetingware consists of the set of software modules which are listed in Figure 9.3. Their sequencing

LIST:	This software combines ideas from each participant into one, publicly displayed list. Each participant would enter ideas at their PC independently of each other, and thus in parallel.
BRAINSTORM:	Similar to LIST, but with the ideas displayed publicly as they are typed in by the participant. Individuals can use this public list to further ideas.
DISCUSS:	A publicly displayed list of all the ideas that the participants wish to discuss. The facilities include a timer to ensure that discussion time is allocated appropriately.
EDIT:	A means of editing inputs.
ORGANISE:	An outliner similar to Think Tank allowing ideas to be organised.
RATE:	Enables each participant to rate an item, and for these individual ratings to be combined and for histograms and an average rating to be displayed.
RANK:	The same as RATE, but with participants ranking items in order.
VOTE:	Used to register a yes or no vote for a particular item.
CROSS-IMPACT ANALYSIS:	This provides a two-dimensional table where the axes of the table are lists whose cross impact is considered.
WEIGHTED FACTORS ANALYSIS:	This module is the Meetingware implementation of multi-attribute utility theory.

Figure 9.3   The Set of Software used in Meetingware

to support the different phases of decision making for a particular meeting is called 'script writing'. Given a particular problem context a suitable set of modules can be selected prior to the meeting to form a customised Group DSS. The process of 'script writing' is illustrated in Figure 9.4.

An example of a report produced using Meetingware is shown in Figure 9.5.

School of Information Systems
IS / BS Curriculum Planning Session

1. Introduction & MeetingWare Orientation (20 Minutes)
   * MeetingWare Description
   * Session Overview
   * Problem Boundaries / Levels

2. Identify and Organize Major Student Goals / Objectives (50 Minutes)
   * LIST
   * DISCUSS / ORGANIZE (Dual Screen)

3. Prioritize Retreat Goals / Objectives (20 Minutes)
   * RATE

4. Compare GOALS vs UNITS IS CURRICULUM (45 Minutes)
   * CROSS-IMPACT ANALYSIS

5. Compare GOALS vs UNITS BS CURRICULUM (45 Minutes)
   * CROSS-IMPACT ANALYSIS

**Figure 9.4   A meetingware script for a curriculum planning session
(from Atkinson and Marshall)**

Watson et al. (1988) carried out an extensive study of the use of workstation types of Group DSS, being able to compare their results with those from groups offered 'paper and pencil' help and groups offered no help at all. Their findings can be summed up as:

– The use of Group DSS tended to reduce face-to-face interpersonal communication in the group. This increased the social distance between members.

– The use of Group DSS presented a challenge to the groups, making their meetings more difficult than groups without Group DSS. This feature might reduce or disappear as experience with the technology was gained.

– The groups using Group DSS appeared to become very procedure oriented, rather than issue oriented. The researchers viewed this

---

Post-graduate Student Goals / Objectives for Course Study

– 1 To Update Previous Tertiary Goals
– 2 Build my Professional self Confidence
– 3 Extending Understanding of Current and Future IS Issue
– 4 Develop Broad Understanding of IS
– 5 Learn About Info. Mgt. for Orgs
– 6 Learn About Latest IT Trends
+ 7 Learn Appropriate IS and IT Techniques
    – 7.1 Learn ISP
    – 7.2 Learn IA
    – 7.3 Learn IRD
    – 7.4 To Learn a Structured Approach to Handle IT Problems
    – 7.5 Learn Theory and APP. of SSM
    – 7.6 Learn About Latest System Development Tools
    – 7.7 Learn DSS and EIS and GDSS and ES
+ 8 Career Development
    – 8.1 Prepare for Career Growth
    – 8.2 Help Determine Career Choices
– 9 To Review Knowledge Against Current Practice
+ 10 Stimulate Thinking About IS and Related Topics
    – 10.1 Sharing Ideas and Experience via Group Discussions

---

Figure 9.5   Report after having used the LIST, DISCUSS and ORGANIZER models of Meetingware (from Atkinson and Marshall)

orientation to be overly strong and as having adverse effects on decision making.

–   The levels of conflict in groups using Group DSS were not greater than those of other groups. Group DSS appeared to assist conflict management within the groups.

–   The imposition of structure, in both the Group DSS and the 'paper and pencil' groups seemed to have beneficial effects. This finding supports the value of structuring decision making sessions, rather than the value of Group DSS per se.

–   No differences were found in the equality of member influence between the three types of group. This was surprising, considering the potential Group DSS apparently have for reducing the dominance of forceful personalities.

The overall conclusion is that in general the workstation type of Group DSS appear to offer some advantage over no support but little advantage over the pencil and paper method of supporting group discussion. Needless to say, these views have not been universally accepted: the purveyors and many users of these systems have reported very substantial gains in meeting efficiency.

STRATEGIC DECISION SUPPORT

Group DSS could be developed for decision making at any level in an organisation. However, as discussed in Chapter 2, it is at the strategic level where decision making involves more factors, many of which are judgemental, and thus the more mechanistic features of DSS become less relevant. Also, the importance of strategic decisions means that support is most needed at this level, and it is deemed organisationally reasonable to fund such activity.

Strategic decision making is not normally an area addressed by information technology, except for financial planning models. This is because strategic problems are messy and complex and tend to be couched in qualitative terms. They also invariably involve groups. At the strategic level, DSS and indeed many planning processes themselves, fail to be effective because they tend to artificially constrain managers to concentrate on problems that are too small, or which are artificially constrained by the techniques used (this is especially true of Extrapolatory Systems). Strategic decision making is not so much about tackling problems as about handling issues: that is to say, it is much more about keeping the relationships in and around the organisation in balance.

Strategic considerations have always to fight for attention with the concerns all managers have for the short-term: the urgent tends to drive out the important. To be effective, any strategic decision making process has to be highly time-effective to stand a chance of success. This means that there is little chance of success unless managers can use their own terms and language. A feature of strategic decision making is the reliance on soft information. Soft information is present at lower levels in an organisation, but is less prevalent in the formal decision making processes. Soft information was defined in Chapter 2 as information that lacked objectivity, and was generally qualitative. Brookes (1985) has pointed out a number of problems that arise in efforts to build strategic DSS that can handle soft information. These he listed as:

(a)   its access and indexation is likely to be difficult;

(b) its existence is often not known to those who need it;

(c) its owners often place tight constraints on its distribution;

(d) its interpretation is intimately linked to the context in which it is received;

(e) it tends to have a very short lifespan.

Points (d) and (e) are covered by the context dependency seen to be a feature of MINTS.

Computer Software for Group DSS

In many of the situations in which Group DSS are employed the software available is the same as that used by managers individually. In the proceeding chapters many different forms of DSS have been described and all of these could be used under the direction of a facilitator to support groups. For instance, the most popular DSS package aids in use with Decision Conferencing are those based on multi-criteria decision making and the packages described in Chapter 7 are those that are employed. Spreadsheets are also to focus group discussions (see for example, the case described by Marples and Riddle (1992)) and both the COPE and STRAD software described in Chapter 8 are often used in group situations. Thus it is probably not far from the truth to say that when facilitators act as mediators between the participants and the computer support, they employ the same DSS that can also be used by individual managers. This has significant consequences for the use of DSS before and after group meetings.

Systems built to operate without a facilitator acting between participants and computer need to offer different support to that available from individual DSS. OptionFinder and TeamWorker appear to be the leaders in keypad systems. GroupSystems and Vision Quest appear to be the leading products for workstation-centred systems.

Electronic mail is now a widespread means of electronic communication between people who are geographically separated. Lotus Notes is now the de facto standard package for team working over distance.

SUMMARY

A Group DSS is a DSS that supports a group of people engaged in a decision related process. The extra organisational dimension present in a Group DSS is that the interaction that would take place outside of the DSS where single-user DSS are employed, is now encompassed within the formal group decision making process – within the Group DSS. In addition to the requirements of a single-user DSS, a Group DSS should:

(a)   facilitate negotiation amongst members of the team;

(b)   develop consensus or an amicable compromise about what should be done;

(c)   develop a commitment to action (rather than the 'right' decision);

(d)   give members of the team a belief that they are making more intelligent, thoughtful decisions than would otherwise be the case.

The additional technological feature of a Group DSS is the ability to communicate electronically between participants and four different configurations have been described. Three types of Group DSS have been identified, classified according to the directness and completeness of the computer-human interface. Single facilitator workstation systems can employ all of the software and techniques described in previous chapters as only one person directly interfaces with the computer. Keypad and workstation-centred systems require facilities over and above those suitable for the single-user. Keypad systems require communications software, keypads and projection equipment: workstation-centred systems also require communication facilities and additionally many specialist software modules.

Strategic decision making is singled out for a brief discussion since it is the type of decision making, with its many judgemental inputs, that perhaps most calls for the use of Group DSS.

REFERENCES

Atkinson D.J. and Marshall P.H., (1990) *A Comparison of Group Decision Support System Approaches* Illustrated via LSE Decision Conferencing and Meetingware, Proceedings of the 10th Annual Conference of the Australian Operational Research Society, Curtin University, Perth, Australia, pp 295–327.

Brookes C.H.P., (1985) *A Framework for DSS Development*, Proceedings of DSS-85, San Francisco, California, pp 80–97.

DeSanctis G. and Gallupe B., (1985) *Group Decision Support Systems: A New Frontier*, Database, pp 3–10, Winter.

Gear A.E. and Read M.J., (1993) *Using TeamWorker for Management Meetings*, OR Insight, Vol.6, Issue 2, April–June, pp 24–28.

Harvey-Jones J., (1989) *Making It Happen: Reflections on Leadership*, pp 279–282, Fontana.

Huber G.P., (1984) *Issues in the Design of Group Decision Support Systems,* MIS Quarterly, Vol.8, pp 195–204.

Keen P.G.W., (1981) *Value Analysis: Justifying Decision Support Systems*, MIS Quarterly, Vol.5, No.1, pp 1–16.

Kiesler S., (1986) *The hidden messages in computer networks,* Harvard Business Review, Vol.64, No.1, pp 46–60, January–February.

Marples C.G. and Riddle D., (1992) *Formulating Strategy in the POD* – an Application of Decision Conferencing in Welwyn Hatfield District Council, OR Insight, Vol.5, Issue 2, pp 12–15.

Phillips L.D., (1986) *Computing for Consensus*, Datamation, pp 68–2 – 68–6, October

Watson R.T., DeSanctis G. and Poole M.S., (1988) *Using a GDSS to Facilitate Group Consensus: Some Intended and Some Unintended Consequences*, MIS Quarterly, pp 463–478, September.

10 The Human-Computer Interface

In Chapter 2 the three major elements of DSS were introduced: the logic model, the data model and the human-computer interface. Although many forms of DSS have been introduced and discussed in subsequent chapters, considerations of the human-computer interface have only been peripherally addressed. This chapter redresses this deficiency and is devoted to considering the major requirements of the interface in the design of DSS. It begins with a short consideration of the role and importance of ergonomics in the design of a computer-human interface. This naturally leads on to a discussion of the concept of usability. Types of input and output interfaces of significance in the design and use of DSS are introduced and discussed. Finally, the requirements of the interface are discussed in terms of response times, help messages and other interactions.

THE ROLE AND IMPORTANCE OF ERGONOMICS

Consideration of the design of the interface in DSS is the domain of ergonomics (the equivalent term 'human factors' is used in the USA). There are two main reasons why the findings from studies of ergonomics are an essential input into DSS design. First, the complexity of the design process often physically separates designer from user and this separation often prevents effective user feedback as the DSS is developed. This is particularly a problem with packaged software, although the sheer number of offerings in each category of DSS means that those packages with features that happen to satisfy users remain, whilst the less user-friendly disappear. Second, as described in Chapter 12, the designer is likely to have had a different educational background from the user and be motivated by different concerns: this emotional/behavioural separation again acts to prevent effective user input to the design process.

Human-computer interaction may be defined simply as the direct, close-coupled computer usage by users. It covers both the human-computer processes and functions themselves and the hardware and software components which facilitate these interactions. In the design of DSS it must be borne in mind that the concern is with human-computer interaction rather than with each component separately: the concern is with a socio-technical system with each part complementing the other. It is for this reason that Shackel (1991) bemoans the recent use of the term 'end-user': he points out that the very use of the term may well betray an attitude that the user is the last person to be considered in the design of a system – thus leading to bad design and user-unfriendly systems. He pleads for designers to see the user as in the centre of a human-computer system instead of as a mere peripheral. This book circumvents the problem of using the term end-user because the focus is on a particular type of user – on managers. However, this largely ignores the fact that DSS are very often used by secretaries and other office staff!!

THE CONCEPT OF USABILITY

An important consideration in the design of a DSS is its usability. Shackel (1991) provides a convenient definition of the term as 'the capability to be used by humans easily and effectively'. This illustrates the necessary balance between ease of use and the increasing costs that are incurred as a design is improved to incorporate more and more user-friendly features.

There are several dimensions to the concept of usability. There is the issue of the ability of the user to learn how to use the DSS and the time taken to absorb the training required. What is appropriate will depend on the type of user, whether use is for the first-time or not and whether use is frequent or whether it is intermittent with considerable time between system use. There is also the question of the 'cognitive coupling' between the computer outputs and the user: for example, can the user understand the output from the extrapolatory systems described in Chapter 6? Achieving satisfactory levels of system flexibility can pose problems: for example, can a range of ad hoc queries be satisfactorily answered or is the system inherently limited as, for example, are most Data Retrieval Systems. The most appropriate form of computer prompts and help messages needs to be considered as must the users' ability to navigate around the associated manuals. There is the question of errors in data inputs and other responses. Consideration needs to be given to the question of whether the system satisfies Health and Safety legislation.

Shackel (1991) provides a context for understanding usability and this is reproduced in Figure 10.1.

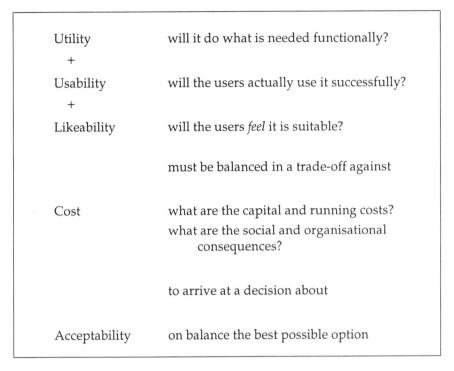

Figure 10.1 The Context of Usability (from Shackel (1991))

This view suggests that a DSS will not be used unless the combination of utility, usability and likeability outweighs the associated costs.

Shackel (1984) lists eight responses to the lack of usability and these are reproduced in Figure 10.2.

Although there are many factors contributing to a lack of usability, one major feature is the inappropriateness of the human-computer interface. The requirements of this interface will now be considered.

PHYSICAL FORMS OF HUMAN-COMPUTER INTERACTION

There are now a great many input and output devices for facilitating human-computer interaction. Input devices range from the standard keyboard to the hand-held consoles, joysticks, trackballs and foot pedals employed in many of the modern computer games to the devices that have been developed to utilise the remaining facilities of the disabled. Perhaps

Response	Meaning	Comments
Disuse	100% reliance on and use of other information sources	Needs other sources and (senior) discretionary users
Misuse	"Bending the rules" to short-cut difficulties	Needs "know-how". May damage system integrity.
Partial use	Use of only a limited subset of system capabilities	Users may not learn to use the most relevant facilities.
Distant use	Use delegated to an operator	Typical response of managers to bad usability
Task modification	Changing the task to match capabilities of the system	Typical for rigid tools and unstructured problems.
Compensatory user activity	Compensation for system inadequacies by additional activity	Typical with users of low discretion, such as clerks.
Direct user/ programming	Programming by user to make system fit needs	Computer-sophisticated e.g. scientist or engineer.
Frustration, and apathy	Response of user when above actions are inadequate or unsatisfactory	Involves lack of user acceptance, high error rates, poor performance.

Figure 10.2   Typical User Responses to Inadequate Systems (Shackel (1984)

the best known of these is the device used by Professor Steven Hawkins (5), the author of the best-seller 'A Short History of Time' and a sufferer from Motor Neurone Disease. He uses a speech synthesizer to allow his voice to be heard. Computers can recognise speech, albeit in rather constrained form, and thus can accept speech input for certain simple tasks.

There are also a range of output devices available, many of which provide 'hard copy' – a term usually applied to permanent paper output. These include printers, graph plotters and devices for producing presentation slides and overhead transparencies. Microfiche and microfilm records can also be directly produced by computer. Computers can also 'talk' in much more sophisticated ways than the bleeps of the microcomputers of a decade ago.

Whilst there are a great many ways for humans to communicate with computers and vice-versa, the range of devices for use with DSS is much more limited. With DSS the emphasis is on direct or quasi-direct interaction by managers either with a microcomputer or with a terminal of a mainframe or mini computer. In such circumstances, input is usually via a keyboard and output through a visual display unit (VDU). Additionally, there is likely to be a link to a printer for hard copy outputs and communications links to other people and systems.

That keyboard entry is by far the most used form of computer input means that the user needs to have some familiarity with typing. This requirement has traditionally inhibited the use of DSS by some of the very people they are devised to assist – senior managers. However, this impediment to use is now no longer as significant as in the past, partly because using computers is now a much more acceptable activity amongst senior management and partly because other means of interacting with a computer have been devised. These alternative methods either obviate the need to use a keyboard altogether or mean that simple keyed inputs are all that are required. Part of the success of the Executive Information Systems that are described in Chapter 5 arises from the development of these more 'senior-manager friendly' interfaces.

There have been three crucial developments in human-computer interfaces over the last decade. First there has been the development of menus. This term is taken from their use in restaurants where normally you are offered two menus – one for food and one for drink – although the latter is termed the wine list. In a menu the dishes that are on offer are listed, usually in some sort of logical order – hors d'oeuvres first , then the main course dishes, etc. In computer usage, menus allow the user to navigate around a system by selecting from a 'menu' of items presented on a screen. Selection can be by simply moving a cursor (very often using the 'arrow' keys of the keyboard) to the item to be selected and then pressing the 'Enter' key. The selection of an item in one menu often leads to the presentation of a second menu and so on. An example is given in Figure 10.3. With such a hierarchy of menus the user can easily and safely select the support that is required.

In menu design there is the question of 'breadth versus depth' In Figure 10.3 the menu system shown has a maximum depth of 8 levels (from top to bottom) with a breadth of 11 at the first level and 15 at the second. As a rule of thumb, research suggests that menus should not generally contain more than 7 or 8 items, although having more does not seem to have great disadvantages. However, having an extended hierarchy of menus can be most infuriating. Taken to its extreme one could envisage a set of menus in

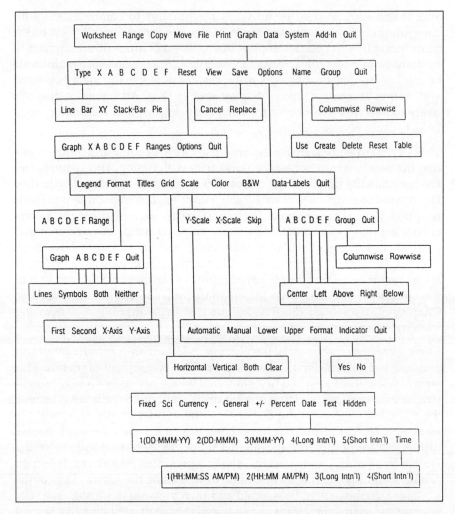

**Figure 10.3   A Sample Menu from the Lotus 1-2-3 Speadsheet
(reproduced by kind permission of Lotus Corporation)**

which the user is simply offered a yes-no choice at each level, requiring
many levels to be employed for the user to make a single selection.

The second crucial development is that of mouse and icon systems
that allow the user to navigate through the elements of a computer system
by simply pointing to the icon or picture that illustrates the service required.
The mouse is a small, hand-held device looking somewhat like a small

rodent that allows an arrow or other pointer shown on the screen to be moved until it is over the icon that offers the service sought. The mouse also carries switches that can be 'clicked' to effect selection when the pointer is over the required icon. An example of a set of icons is given in Figure 10.4.

The third development has been in the field of light pens and touch screens. For interested readers, the technologies are well described in the book by Rubin (1988). A light pen is a device that looks very like an ordinary pen which is used to point to an area of the screen display. The light pen can sense where on the screen it is positioned, can transmit this knowledge to the computer and the appropriate action taken. With a touch screen, the user points with his/her finger at the screen to select the service required. These technologies have been developed to mirror what one would do naturally if you were viewing a piece of paper – you would point out interesting items with your finger or with a pen. Light pens and touch

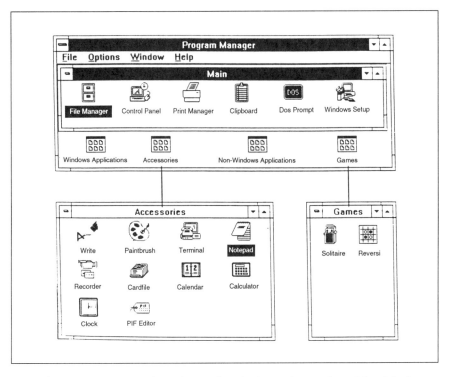

Figure 10.4   Icons in Microsoft Windows (reproduced by kind permission of Microsoft Corp.)

screens allow intermediary devices such as mice and keyboards to be eliminated and thus the computer-human interaction to be more intimate.

Many of the features described above are brought together in what are termed WIMP environments. This acronym stands for Windows, Icons, Menus and Pointers. A common approach to the design of WIMP interfaces had been to consider that the most appropriate layout for a computer screen is that which mirrors the user's desktop. Thus documents, folders and files can lie open on/in it, with any one of them selected to be worked on as and when required. An example is shown in Figure 10.4.

INTERFACE REQUIREMENTS

A crucial feature in the design of any DSS are the response times of the computer to user input. Readers of this book who have restricted their use of DSS to simple spreadsheets may not have experienced the frustration of the delays that can accompany what seem like the simplest of requests. It might be thought that the increase in the speed of working of computer hardware would have minimised these frustrations: however, the increased capabilities have allowed much more complex systems to be implemented. One has only to think of the initiation of macros using function keys to realise that one keystroke can set in train many operations of tedious duration.

Rubin (1988) has produced a set of recommended response times associated with various user tasks. These are reproduced in Table 10.1.

Interestingly, frustration at long system response times may not lead to a lowering of user productivity. Martin and Corl (1986) have indeed shown that user productivity for simple data-entry tasks increases as the system response time is reduced. However, they also showed that in problem solving tasks – of the sort for which DSS are developed – there is no link between system response times and productivity over the range of response times they investigated.

Even if the user is very experienced in the use of computers in general and a specific DSS in particular, help will be needed to ensure that the system is used efficiently. More and different forms of help would be needed for a new user or for a user who is using the system intermittently – which is often the case with DSS.

Manuals do have a place for a certain type of user but are not now the usual major source of help. More and more often this is provided by on-screen messages. However, it is not feasible to provide a fully appropriate form of

**Table 10.1   Recommended System Response Times (Rubin 1988).
Reproduced by kind permission of Ellis Horwood Ltd.**

Activity	Recommended Response Time (in seconds)
System activation	3.0
Tracking the movement of an input device such as a mouse	0.1
Request for a 'simple' service such as selecting a menu item	2.0
Request for a 'complex' service such as the step selection task	5.0
Response to a 'simple' inquiry query from a database	2.0
Response to a 'complex' inquiry	4.0
Error feedback	2.0

help for each user since this would require the computer to be able to respond to a user's specific knowledge and requirements. An approximation to this ideal is obtained by providing a set of help messages with each set geared to a perceived general requirement. For example, the most rudimentary level of help would simply be in the form of an aide-memoire, with very short explanations of input commands. This form is often found in the abbreviated menus at the top or bottom of the normal screen (and offering such help as X = eXtract, Q = Quit for example). The next level might typically give a short explanation of what a term means (eXtract means make an ASCII copy of the item being considered). Finally, the explanation could become fulsome, covering a screen or more. Obviously the best arrangement is for the user to be able to choose the levels of help that he/she deems appropriate at that time: as experience is gained, less fulsome help would normally be required.

Error messages are messages initiated by the computer to tell the user that some action is either inappropriate or simply not understood by the computer. An example of inappropriate behaviour is the message 'Non-Systems disk or disk error. Replace and strike key when ready' that the operating system MS-DOS gives when an attempt is made to start a PC with a data disk in drive A.

The term 'error message' is rather an infelicitous one since it suggests that the computer, and thus the systems designer, is chastising or at the very least chiding the user for not doing as the designer expected. The assumption is that the user made the mistake, not that the designer provided an inappropriately fragile design.

Often considered as error messages are those messages that warn a user that some proposed action is likely to have undesirable results. For example, when quitting a spreadsheet, a good DSS interface would ask whether the user wanted to save the latest version if the spreadsheet had been altered since the last save. If the answer were yes, then a further warning might be issued to say that unless otherwise instructed the previous version of the spreadsheet would be overwritten.

There are similarities in the good design of error messages with those for the help messages discussed above. They should be polite, concise and clearly stated in the language with which the user is most comfortable. They should be constructive: a message that simply says that an error has occurred is of little use. A user often needs to know what sort of mishap has occurred and always needs to know what has to be done to put it right.

SUMMARY

In this chapter the common means of communicating with DSS have been introduced and some of the main considerations associated with the design of computer-human interfaces have been discussed. The importance of not considering the user as the 'end-user' has been stressed: user characteristics and needs are not peripheral considerations in the design of a DSS but central ones.

REFERENCES

Shackel B., (1991) *Usability – Context, Framework, Definition, Design and Evaluation*, in Shackel B. and Richardson S. (eds) Human Factors for Informatics Usability, Cambridge University Press.

Shackel B. (1984) *The Concept of Usability*, in Bennett J., Case D., Sandelin J. and Smith M. (eds) Visual Display Terminals, Prentice-Hall Inc., Englewood Cliffs, New Jersey, USA.

Rubin T. (1988) *User Interface Design for Computer Systems*, Ellis Horwood Ltd, Chichester, UK.

Martin G.L. and Corl K.G. (1986) *System response time effects on user productivity, Behaviour and Information Technology*, Vol.5, No.1, pp3–13.

11 Measures of Success for Decision Support Systems

Designing and building a DSS takes time and money. Justification for the use of organisational resources for such activity will only be forthcoming if previously implemented DSS are seen to be successful and if any proposed system is likely to contribute to organisational goals. This means that it is important to have suitable measures by which systems success can be gauged.

Broadly, MIS are primarily designed to improve the efficiency of organisations, MINTS with improving their effectiveness. Correspondingly, appropriate measure of success would be expected to involve the impact of MIS on organisational efficiency and the impact of MINTS on organisational effectiveness. It can be argued that in the case of commercial organisations, both efficiency and effectiveness should ultimately show in the profitability, and that enhanced profitability is the most appropriate measure of the success of a DSS.

DIFFICULTIES WITH MEASUREMENT

The problem is that in practice it is extremely difficult to determine the influence of a DSS on organisational efficiency, effectiveness or profitability. The problem is one of comparing costs with benefits, and whereas the costs associated with a DSS are very often easy to establish, the benefits are much more difficult to determine. For transaction processing systems such as one for order processing, it is probably possible to determine the benefits that accrue from the introduction of the system in terms of the reduction of personnel employed and other cost savings. For simple MIS the same is likely to be true. For example, the introduction of a Data Retrieval System may directly reduce the costs associated with providing the required information: however, even in this simple case, the benefits of having more up-to-date or more precise information are less tangible and much less easy to determine.

169

This difficulty in determining benefits – and particularly their financial value – and managerial indifference to their detailed assessment may be illuminated by an anecdote. Some years ago in a consultancy study, the author was under pressure to justify a new computer system that would help a manager better plan and control wrapping material procurement. In reply to the question of what were the benefits likely to be, he retorted "Just tell me the costs and I'll tell you the benefits". He wanted the system and believed the overall benefits (including the intangible benefits) would outweigh the costs however high they might be. On reflection this was right: he was a manager responsible for spending millions of pounds of the organisation's money, and it was for him to make the decision whether resources were well spent on a new system.

This brings the discussion to a central point – that it is the view of success taken by a manager or a group of managers that is paramount. The view taken by some systems designers that technical elegance can be a measure of overall systems success is inappropriate, although such factors may contribute to the success of the system.

Three strands can be discerned in the development of measures of success for DSS. The simple types of DSS being developed in the 60s and early 70s enabled single measures of success to be postulated. As DSS were developed to support more complex situations, more complex measures of success were seen to be needed and were derived. Later, process considerations were seen to be important.

MEASURES OF SUCCESS

Single Measures of Success

Given the difficulties in determining the nexus between DSS and profitability, organisational efficiency and organisational effectiveness, several indirect criteria of success have been proposed. One set of proposals revolve around the use of DSS: widespread use and the application of a DSS to a major problem in an organisation have both been proposed. Another set of measures considers improvement in the quality of decisions and in the level of performance. The conventional commercially used measures of success such as Return on Investment, Return on Equity and Return on Assets may also be used for investments in information technology.

Recently, Strassmann (1990) has publicised the idea of Return on Management as the key to measuring organisational performance and, by extension, the most appropriate measure for MIS success. He defines return on management as the ratio of management value-added to management costs, with management added-value being the residual after every contributor to an organisation's inputs has been paid.

Attempts have been made to quantify the benefits of DSS by conducting a survey within a firm and obtained a perceptual measure of the monetary value of existing reports by asking the users how much they would be willing to pay for each report.

The measures of success given above are all concerned primarily with organisational impacts, seek to be quantitative and are product oriented. Others have looked more widely. User satisfaction has been proposed as a criterion of success by many authors (see Kim (1989) for a listing). In his article, Kim has summarised the results of much of the work that has been published dealing with user satisfaction for individual MIS.

Multiple Success Criteria

Single measures of success are unlikely to be satisfactory for anything but the simplest forms of DSS. Thus one must look for more complex measures.

Several studies have defined systems success in terms of satisfying a list of success factors. The number of factors suggested range from 25 to almost 60. In all cases weightings and scores are given to the factors and these values are combined mathematically to produce an overall systems success score. Some researchers have simply given a list of factors, whilst others have used a 'two-level' approach. In this, the first level consisting of dimensions of success and the second of the success factors contributing to each dimension. The work of Miller and Doyle (1984) with Information Systems is a good example of the general approach. They categorise 38 success factors into 7 dimensions as shown in Table 11.1.

Keen (1981) has produced a list of benefits frequently cited by users of DSS (other than Data Retrieval Systems). This list is reproduced in Table 11.2.

Sanders (1984) used 13 success factors for measuring the individual user's perception of DSS success. These can be grouped into those factors that relate to the user's perceived overall satisfaction with the system, and those that indicate improved decision making. These are listed in Table 11.3.

The sets of measures proposed by Keen and by Sanders have the merit of consisting of a much smaller number of items than most other composite measures. They are geared to measuring user satisfaction rather than the wider organisational requirement.

Table 11.1   Benefits from the Use of DSS (Miller and Doyle (1984)

(a) *Characteristics of conventional systems:* completeness of output information, accuracy of output information, more monitor systems, relevance of report contents, currency of output information, volume of output information, report availability and timeliness, more exception systems.

(b) *Strategic management issues:* top management involvement, strategic IS planning, business-related systems priorities, using database technology, overall cost-effectiveness of IS, use of steering committee.

(c) *User involvement:* users' feeling of participation, users's control over IS services, IS-user management communications, users' understanding of systems, user confidence in systems.

(d) *Responsiveness to new system needs:* prompt processing of change requests, short lead time for new systems development, responsiveness to changing user needs, IS support for users, preparation of new system proposals, flexibility of data and reports.

(e) *End-user computing:* more analysis systems, more inquiry systems, effective training of programmers or users, ease of user access to terminals.

(f) *Information System staff quality:* user-oriented systems analysts, competence of systems analysts, technical competence of IS staff, larger IS effort to create new systems, positive attitude of IS to users.

(g) Reliability of service: low % hardware and systems downtime, efficient running of current systems, data security and privacy.

Process Considerations

Some studies have extended the definition of information system success to include factors other than those relating directly to the finished (or 'signed-off') product. As cited above, Miller and Doyle's measures of system success includes some that address the quality of the organisational support for developing and maintaining the system. User satisfaction with the procedures required to obtain reports has also been suggested.

In general however, there has been little research on the success of DSS where the process of supporting decision making is as important or more important than any products developed. (This is especially so where the

Table 11.2   Benefits frequently cited by users of MINTS (Keen (1981)).

1. Increase in the number of alternatives examined
2. Better understanding of the business
3. Fast response to unexpected situations
4. Ability to carry out ad hoc analysis
5. New insights and learning
6. Improved communication
7. Control
8. Cost savings
9. Better decisions
10. More effective teamwork
11. Time savings
12. Making better use of data resources

development of the decision aid is an evolutionary one). In some ways this would be looking at the success of the providers of decision support over a long period in the organisation's life: that is, at the success of a Management Science Group, Information Centre and the like.

Forghani (1989) emphasises the interactions between the people involved with a DSS, particularly those between the designer and the manager for whom the system is being built. He views DSS as products but not as finished products; i.e., they are developed and extended as the need arises. His view is that as one moves away from MIS towards DSS the emphasis in DSS development shifts from a product orientation to one of establishing and maintaining good relations with people in the organisation.

Measures of Success for Group Decision Support Systems

Single-user DSS can be considered a special case of Group DSS where the group has reduced to one. Thus it would be expected that all the measures of success proposed for single-user DSS would be just as applicable for Group DSS. However, given the preoccupation with process within Group DSS – with negotiation and with communication – additional measures of success need to be used to cover these additional dimensions.

Table 11.3   List of Success Factors (Saunders (1984))

A) Overall Satisfaction:

I have become dependent on DSS in performing my job.

DSS is extremely useful.

All in all I think that DSS is an important system for this organisation.

I have personally benefited from the existence of DSS in this organisation.

I have become dependent on DSS.

As a result of DSS, I am seen as more valuable in this organisation.

B) Decision Making Satisfaction:

DSS has improved the quality of decisions I make in this organisation.

Utilization of DSS has enabled me to make better decisions.

As a result of DSS, the speed at which I analyse decisions has increased. Use of data generated by DSS has enabled me to present my arguments more convincingly.

As a result of DSS, more relevant information has been available to me for decision-making.

DSS has led me to greater use of analytical aids in my decision-making.

As a result of DSS, I am better able to set my priorities in decision-making.

According to Eden (1991), a necessary condition for success with a Group DSS is that it should satisfy the social needs of the group. The group wants to be rewarded as the decision making session proceeds. One form of 'reward' is to give participants a belief that they are making more intelligent and thoughtful decisions than would otherwise be the case. As measures of success, Pinsonneault and Kraemer (1989) use the participants' satisfaction with the process and the willingness of the group members to work in groups in the future, whether in this particular group or in other groups. Kraemer and King (1988) identify focusing on key issues and whether meetings are interesting as measures of success.

Nunamaker et al. (1989) suggest both the quality of session process and quality of outcome as the measures of group support effectiveness. Quality of session process involved the help given to generate ideas, to identify key ideas, to ensure that the problem solving process was fair and the degree to which the participants took part in the process (and thus owned the outcome). The quality of outcome is measured by the degree to which the system provided the product that the session initiator desired.

The concept of communications thoroughness has been proposed as one measure of process success. It is measured as the number of recorded thoughts, the number of verbal remarks and the number of task-related remarks as a proportion of the total verbal remarks.

Eden (1991) considers political commitment and emotional commitment as measures of success for group meetings. Two supports for political commitment are substantive (or means-ends) rationality (as Eden says "it makes sense") and procedural rationality ("we followed an appropriate process").

HIERARCHY OF MEASURES OF SUCCESS

All of the measures of success that have been identified by the author have been detailed in Finlay (1993). The number of measures that have been proposed is large and a choice must be made from them for any particular situation. This is helped through considering the hierarchy of these measures.

It is now generally recognised that DSS should support the goals of the organisation in which they are to be used. By extension, the measures of success of DSS must be sought in terms of their help in achieving these goals. Organisational goals form a hierarchy: indeed, such a hierarchy is implicit in the foregoing discussion: for example, enhanced profitability, quality of decisions and user satisfaction are measures at different levels in the organisational hierarchy.

Enhanced profitability is likely to be only one dimension of corporate success. Other measures might be productivity, growth, innovation, adaption to change, contribution and survival, market share, cash generation and technical excellence. The particular measures used by an organisation will be contextually determined. For commercial organisations the ultimate measure of success is likely to be increased competitive advantage.

Within the overall thrust of competitive advantage the measures of organisational success may be grouped into those associated with organisational effectiveness and those associated with organisational efficiency. The organisation would be more effective and more efficient through making better decisions; i.e., with more effective and more efficient decision making. It would be hoped that these improvements in decision making would result from the implementation of effective DSS.

This hierarchy of organisational measures is shown in the upper portion of Figure 11.1. Where possible, success of an DSS would be sought in terms of how well it helped the organisation meet goals on these dimensions. These measures are supra-DSS measures.

As previously discussed, in practice it is likely that the effects of an DSS on these organisational goals will be difficult to identify. Thus the search for indirect measures of DSS success – measures that can more likely be operationalized. A broad indication of the form of these indirect measures is provided in the lower portion of Figure 11.1, where intra-DSS measures are listed.

This lower portion is a modified and augmented version of the interaction of effectiveness, use and information quality proposed by Kim (1989) for MIS. The augmentations are the inclusion of Intelligence Quality to take account of the intelligence generation aspects of MINTS, Process Quality to incorporate the unique contribution of Group DSS and Validity.

The implication of the discussion so far is that it is possible to identify the changes wrought by the introduction of a DSS into an organisation: at the highest level through enhanced organisational success, at the lower levels by such things as information quality. For some types of DSS, particularly with Group DSS used at strategic levels where the decision making is complex, ill-structured and non-recurring, it is appropriate additionally to address the question of success in a different manner, and in doing so develop another dimension to success. Here, the output measures need to be augmented by 'internal' measures through a validation of the DSS itself. Whilst the measures of success already discussed represent a form of validity, since they measure the appropriateness of the DSS, the validation considered here is of the form of the DSS itself. For example, as described in Chapter 7 the use of pair-wise comparisons within multi attribute decision making provides a more reliable and thus more valid way of obtaining ratings than does simply scoring a list of items. A DSS that uses pair-wise comparisons is thus more valid than a similar one that does not. A further discussion of validation is given in Chapter 13.

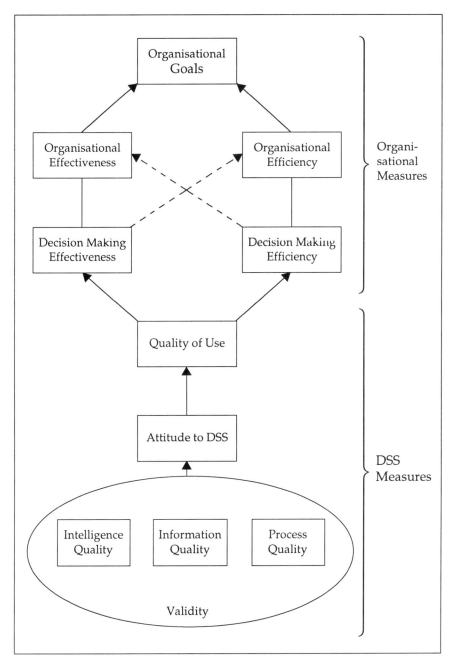

Figure 11.1 A Hierarchy of Organisational and DSS Measures of Success

APPROPRIATE MEASURES OF SUCCESS

In general, all classes of DSS should contribute to all organisational goals. However, the size of the contribution will differ across the range of goals. Given the difficulty of determining the link between DSS and organisational success, only the first order contributions will be considered. It would be expected that the link between a DSS and the measurement of its impact would be stronger and more direct the lower down the hierarchy one is operating.

Organisational Measures

Organisational Effectiveness

Effectiveness may be defined as doing the right thing (Drucker (1974)); organisational effectiveness with doing the right things for the organisation as a whole. MIS provide information about the past and present. On the other hand MINTS are future oriented, providing intelligence and option-generating features and are used for planning. This suggests that MIS will have a second order impact on organisational effectiveness (through providing information for decision making) whilst MINTS should make a considerable impact. Thus it would not be appropriate to seek success for MIS in terms of enhancements to organisational effectiveness. However, it would be appropriate to do so for MINTS.

Previously identified measures of success that may be considered appropriate dimensions of organisational effectiveness are: faster and better adaption/response to 'the new', improved cash generation, greater growth, more and better innovation, increased market share, enhanced profitability, satisfactory return on investment and technical excellence. These terms are listed in Table 11.4

Organisational Efficiency

Efficiency may be defined as doing the thing right (Drucker (1974)). MIS are concerned with providing information about the past, particularly about the operations of the organisation itself. They are geared to control; hence it would be appropriate to seek success for an MIS in terms of increased organisational efficiency. Given that the definition of MINTS used in this paper excludes those DSS that are extrapolatory in nature, there would be a less significant contribution expected of MINTS.

Table 11.4   Appropriate Measures of Success for DSS

ORGANISATIONAL MEASURES

Organisational Effectiveness
Faster and better adaption/response to 'the new'
Improved cash generation
Greater growth
More and better innovation
Increased market share
Enhanced profitability
Satisfactory return on investment
Technical excellence

Organisational Efficiency
Enhanced communication between stakeholders
Greater and more appropriate control
Cost savings
Enhanced productivity
Greater team work
Time savings

Decision Making Effectiveness
The ability to carry out ad hoc analysis
Increased depth of the analysis undertaken
More alternatives examined
The procedural and substantive rationality of the process

Decision Making Efficiency
The better use of available data
A reduction in the time taken for decision making
Improvements in the predictive accuracy of the decision making process
Greater focusing of the process on key issues

INTRA-DSS MEASURES

Attitudes to DSS
Enhanced employee welfare
Improved tangible and intangible relationships
Satisfaction with the procedures for getting reports
Satisfaction with the procedures for getting systems enhancements and maintenance

---

Table 11.4   Appropriate Measures of Success for DSS (continued)

Quality of Use of DSS
The application of the DSS to a major problem area
Repeat use
Utilization ratio
Widespread use.

Information Quality
Accuracy/reliability of the information
Communications thoroughness
Format and contents of reports
Information scope
Timeliness of this information
Value of information

Intelligence Quality
Better understanding of the organisation and its environment
Generation of ideas
New insights and learning

Process Quality
An enhanced commitment to action
Improved negotiation quality
Fuller consensus formation
A belief that more intelligent decisions are being taken
Increased confidence in the decision
More participants
More and more equal participation
Enhanced openness of the process
Less emotive meetings
Decreased domination by one or a few individuals
A fuller and deeper ownership of the outcomes
Enhanced meeting interest
Willingness to work with the group again

Validity
Construct validity
Content validity
Theoretical validity

Previously identified measures of success that may be considered appropriate dimensions of organisational efficiency are: enhanced communication between stakeholders, greater and more appropriate control, cost savings, enhanced productivity, greater team work and time savings.

Decision Making Effectiveness

MIS help change decision making effectiveness through the provision of better information. MINTS attempt an improvement in decision making effectiveness by providing decision aids that provide managers with insights and intelligence and allow options to be generated. This suggests that both should make a considerable impact on decision making effectiveness, but with MINTS making a stronger impact.

Previously identified measures of success that may be considered appropriate dimensions of decision making effectiveness are: the ability to carry out ad hoc analysis, increased depth of the analysis undertaken, more alternatives examined and the procedural and substantive rationality of the process.

Decision Making Efficiency

Decision making efficiency is concerned with the resources used during the decision making process. The efficiency of decision making would be enhanced through the provision of better and more timely information and improved process. Thus it would be expected that MIS and Group DSS in general would contribute significantly to this organisational goal: individual MINTS only peripherally.

Previously identified measures of success that may be considered appropriate dimensions of decision making efficiency are: the better use of available data, a reduction in the time taken for decision making, improvements in the predictive accuracy of the decision making process and greater focusing of the process on key issues.

Intra-DSS Measures

Attitude to DSS

Attitude to DSS is an overall, subjective measure of user satisfaction. Previously identified measures of success that may be considered appropriate dimensions of attitude to DSS (in addition to those contributed by the other intra-DSS measures) are: enhanced employee welfare, improved tangible and intangible relationships, satisfaction with the procedures for getting reports, satisfaction with the procedures for getting systems enhancements and maintenance.

Quality of Use of DSS

Since use of a MINTS tends to be voluntary, system use is a valid measure of success. This is not so for MIS where use tends to be mandatory and thus success cannot be sought in terms of system use. It is for this reason that 'Quality of Use' rather than simply 'Use' of DSS is considered a measure of DSS success: it allows the mandatory use associated with MIS to be incorporated in the same framework of success factors.

Previously identified measures of success relating to the quality of use of DSS are: the application of the DSS to a major problem area, repeat use, utilization ratio and widespread use.

Information Quality

Information quality is a primary user measure of success for MIS. With MINTS it becomes less applicable as the outputs are managerial insights and learning. Previously identified measures of success that may be considered appropriate dimensions of information quality are: the accuracy/reliability of the information provided by the DSS, communications thoroughness, the format and contents of reports, the value of information generated by the DSS and the timeliness of this information. A measure for the information scope of the system is also needed: for example, whether the system is restricted to providing information on intra-organisational matters alone, or whether it also provides information from the environment in which the organisation is operating.

Intelligence Quality

Intelligence quality is a primary user measure of success for MINTS. Previously identified measures of success that may be considered appropriate dimensions of intelligence quality are: the generation of ideas, new insights and learning and better understanding of the organisation and its environment.

Process Quality

It is only for Group DSS that process quality is significant. Previously identified measures of success that may be considered appropriate dimensions of group processes are: an enhanced commitment to action, improved negotiation quality, fuller consensus formation, a belief that more intelligent decisions are being taken, increased confidence in the decision, more participants, more and more equal participation, enhanced openness of the process, less emotive meetings, decreased domination by one or a few individuals, a fuller and deeper ownership of the outcomes, enhanced meeting interest, and willingness to work with the group again.

Validity

The validation of DSS is the process of checking of the appropriateness of the system for the purpose for which it is being used: validity is the sought after result of this process. The requirement is first to critically examining the theory that lies behind the design of the DSS (to establish theoretical validity). Second, to compare the implementation of the DSS with what theory suggests (to establish construct validity). Third, to ensure that the DSS is of appropriate scope and detail (to establish content validity).

SUMMARY

No single measure of success is really appropriate and none has found widespread acceptance. For MIS, for which use tends to be mandatory, user satisfaction would probably be the best single measure of success to use if one were needed. For MINTS, where use tends to be discretionary, the amount of use of the system is probably a more appropriate single measure of success.

Several researchers have considered the factors that contribute to system success, and the importance to be attached to each. Success is measured by weighting the score that a system achieves for each factor by the importance of the factor, and then combining these weighted scores. Unfortunately, typically 30–40 factors have been identified in these studies.

Most of the published work on measures of success has put the emphasis on the success of a product. This emphasis is inappropriate where the DSS is primarily concerned with the process of decision making, and where the longer-term considerations associated with an evolving DSS are significant. Here, establishing and maintaining relationships is important.

It would be preferable to have a suitable measure of success associated with goals at the highest level in the organisation, but practicalities mean that reliance must often be placed on indirect measures. A hierarchy of organisational and DSS goals has been developed. Measures of success for each level in the hierarchy have been listed, and the most appropriate for each types of DSS have been suggested. These suggestions have been encapsulated in Table 11.4.

It is recognised that the nature of the measurement process must be related to the purpose for which the measurement is to be used. If the purpose is to compare the investment in an DSS with other investments then organisational measures would be sought. If the purpose is to discover whether an DSS meets user needs then intra-DSS measures would be more appropriate.

REFERENCES

Drucker P.F *Management, tasks, responsibilities and practice* Heinemann, London, 1974.

Eden C., A Framework for Thinking About Group Decision Support Systems (GDSS), *ESRC Seminar Series on Problem Structuring and the Management of Complexity*, No.4 May, 1991.

Finlay P.N., Measures of success for lone-user management support systems, Journal of Information Systems, Vol.3, pp 47–67, 1993.

Forghani S.M., The likelihood of Success in Management Intelligence Systems: Building a Consultant Advisory System, PhD thesis, Loughborough University of Technology, 1989.

Keen P.G.W., Value Analysis: Justifying Decision Support Systems,MIS Quarterly, pp 1–15, March 1981.

Kim K.K., User Satisfaction: A Synthesis of Three Different Perspectives, *Journal of Information Systems*, Fall, 1989, pp 1–12.

Miller J. and Doyle B.A., Measuring the Effectiveness of Computer- based Information Systems, MIS Quarterly, March 1984, pp 17–25,

Nunamaker J., Vogel D., Heminger A., Martz B., Grohowski R. and McCoff C., Experiences at IBM with Group Support Systems: A Field Study, *Decision Support Systems 5*, 1989, pp 183–196.

Pinsonneault A. and Kraemer L., The Impact of Technological Support on Groups: An Assessment of the Empirical Research, *Decision Support Systems 5*, 1989, pp 197–216.

Sanders G.L., MIS. DSS Success Measure, Systems, Objectives, Solutions, Vol.4, 1984, pp 29–34.

Strassmann P.A., *The Business Value of Computers: an Executive's Guide*, The Information Economics Press, New Canaan, Conn., USA, 1990.

12 Developing Decision Support Systems

It is now becoming increasingly recognised that organisations need an information management strategy to use information technology efficiently and effectively. The development of all but the simplest DSS need to be placed in this context. Whilst a discussion of information technology strategy development is beyond the scope of this book, two approaches that readers might like to follow up are Business Systems Planning and the Business Information Control Study. Zachman (1982) has usefully reviewed these two approaches.

It is useful to recall the discussion at the beginning of Chapter 2 concerning recipes (Johnson and Scholes (1993)). Where a similar situation is encountered to one in the past, a recipe can be used to bring about the desired result. In this case the link between problem detection and action is a direct one as shown in Figure 12.1a.

Where a new situation is encountered for which no recipe exists, then the detection-action nexus is not so direct, and the stages of problem tackling listed in Figure 1.1 cannot be short-circuited. A system is needed to explore possible courses of action: in particular, a detailed model may be required at the heart of the system. This requires that the problem situation is translated from the manager's world into the system designer's world, and some manifestation of it returned for the manager to use. (Of course the manager and designer could be the same person, but operating in two ways). This link of managerial and designer's worlds is shown in Figure 12.1b.

As explained in Chapter 4, the rationale for categorising DSS that has been used in this book is that each type of DSS calls for a different emphasis in development and implementation. As would be expected, the major differences in methodology are between those used in MIS and MINTS developments, and these were listed in Table 4.1. For convenience, this table is reproduced as Table 12.1. Further differences between systems were set out in Figure 4.7, and these are reproduced as Figure 12.2. These differences have a large impact on the way in which DSS are developed.

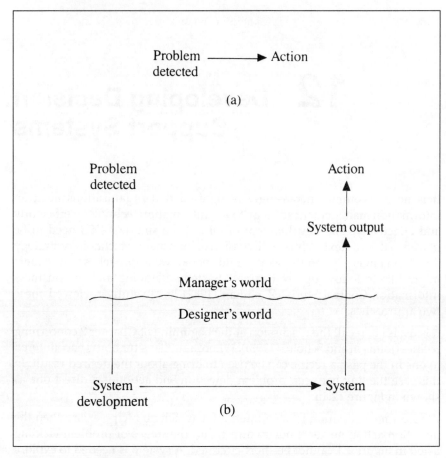

Figure 12.1   Modes of Problem Tackling

GENERAL CONSIDERATIONS

The Systems Development Cycle

The 'classical' systems development cycle was initially developed in the computer context for data processing systems associated with operational control. The cycle consists of nine stages and is briefly described below. For a full discussion of this approach the reader is referred to Clifton (1987). In brief the stages are:

  – *Feasibility Survey* Looking broadly at the operational, financial and organisational feasibility of the proposal. The output will be a feasibility report.

Table 12.1   The Emphases Associated with Types of IT System

	Management Information System	Management Intelligence System
Type of system	Internal control/budgeting	Planning
Focus	On efficient, structured information flows and data structures Efficiency	On effective decisions, flexibility, adaptability and quick response Effectiveness
Objectives	Prespecified	Ad hoc/contingent
Type of situation	Within fixed policies	Within a given scenario
Created by	IT specialists/business analysts	Users/business analysts
Design perspective	Organisational	Individual/small group
Design methodology used	'Classical' systems approach and prototyping of inputs and outputs	'Breadboarding'
Hardware/software orientation	Hardware and software	Software
Models i) **ii)** **iii)** **iv)** **v)**	Fixed logic Mainly deterministic relations Mainly arithmetic and mathematical Mainly deterministic data Ratio and interval scales	Evolutionary logic Judgemental relations Mainly logical Probabilistic data Nominal and ordinal scales
Output i) **ii)** **iii)** **iv)**	General format Standardised/interrogative reports An answer Management information	User created Iterative/interactive ill-structured reports Insight, learning, dialogue Intelligence
Time scale	Past, present and future	Present and future
Context	Context independent Structured	Context dependent Ill-structured
Exactitude	Precision and accuracy	Accuracy
Validation	'Classical' systems methodology	Appropriateness
Usage	Largely mandatory	Discretionary

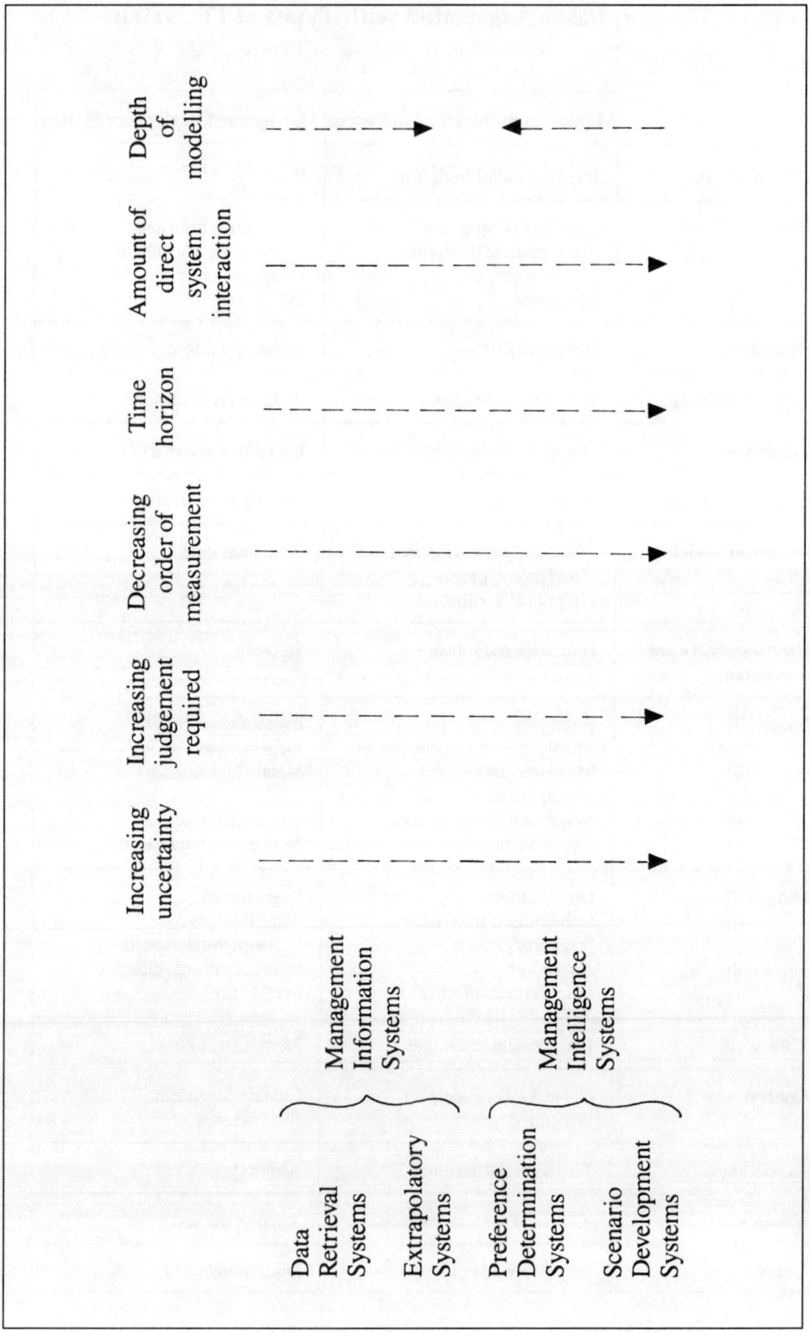

Figure 12.2 Features of Types of Decision Support Systems

- *Systems Analysis* Investigating the situation to determine what needs to be done. Specifying to management what the new system will do for them, what they and their staff will be required to do, and what the system will look like. The output will be a systems specification.

- *Systems Design* Creating a design for the system specifying how the requirements identified in the systems specification will be achieved. This will identify and define all data items, all file structures and the programs and program structure. If necessary, the systems software that will be needed will also be specified. The logic model (in terms of a suite of programs) will be defined. Validation procedures will be defined.

- *Systems Programming* Creating the logic models (programs).

- *Systems Testing* Creating a test pack for validation, and running it against the system.

- *Systems Documentation* Writing down how the system works, the names and definition of variables, collating program listings, job descriptions for personnel involved in the maintenance of the system.

- *Systems Implementation* Getting the system up and running.

- *Review* Evaluation of the stages of the system development cycle and of the system itself.

- *Systems Maintenance* Making sure that the system runs as intended throughout its life.

The systems development cycle is a tried and tested approach for the development of operational systems. However, it must not be inferred that the cycle should be used in its entirety for all forms of DSS. The cycle has been introduced here as a well-defined, successful model against which the design and implementation of each type of DSS can be discussed.

The People Involved in the System Development Cycle

In the world of information technology there are several terms used for what will be termed 'system designer' or more simply 'designer'. Management scientists would use the term 'modeller', showing their emphasis on the (logic) model rather than on the whole system: data processing people would use the term 'systems analyst' or 'analyst', which gives scant acknowledgement to the synthesis that must accompany any analysis for a system to be designed. Expert system developers use the term 'knowledge engineer', again a term that covers one aspect of these people's work but not all that is required to produce a system. Because of these deficiencies, the term 'designer' or 'system designer' will be used in this book, unless the specific and different skills associated with modellers, analysts and engineers are to be emphasised.

Thus far the discussion about system design and usage has implied that there are but two people involved, a manager and a designer. These are indeed the principal characters but there are other people in the process who it is important to recognise and who may play a significant role.

A manager may be the problem owner in the sense that a problem exists in the part of the organisation for which he has responsibility. However, it may be that he has been forced to recognise and do something about the problem by someone else – very likely by his own boss. If this situation occurs, then the designer has to deal with this boss as well, since it is he who has initiated the search for a decision aid. It is also likely in these circumstances that the boss is the person with the power to change the organisation if he feels this is needed.

Again, the designer himself is likely to be a member of a hierarchy of specialists, and he has to be aware of his own boss's predilections and the place of this specialist grouping in the total organisation. I once worked for the Ministry of Defence where 100 designers worked in a country house 20 miles from London, attempting to influence managers working in Central London. As a junior designer, my work was vetted by my boss and by his boss before being transmitted to the centre. To compound matters, many of the decision-makers in London were military personnel who moved post every two or three years. Thus it was hardly ever possible for direct contact between designer and decision maker to exist.

Forghani (1989) has additionally identified what he terms 'political actors' as potentially significant people in the success of a DSS. He and Checkland (1981) also cite the importance of problem sponsors as important individuals. Introducing a DSS is an innovatory act, and as Pinchot (1985) forcefully points out, one very important prerequisite for a successful innovator is to have a powerful sponsor. Forghani also considers the custodians of data to be significant people in the implementation of DSS. (See later in the discussion of MIS development for further consideration of the importance of databases).

Systems Infrastructure

Any DSS is built on a systems 'infrastructure', having at its lowest level the 'computer' and other associated hardware, and the systems software that is needed to make the hardware function (such as an operating system). One level up from this there are the DSS generators (such as those described in Chapters 5 through 8) that allow DSS to be developed. At the highest level there are the DSS themselves, which deliver decision support to managers. This hierarchy of hardware and software is sketched in Figure 12.3.

General Factors for Success

The conventional wisdom has it that managers must be intimately involved in the building of any system that they use. By being so involved they then know that their views have been put into the system, they understand the system, feel that it is theirs and have some responsibility for it.

It is argued that user participation will lead to increased user commitment, and decreased resistance to change. User participation should lead to improve user understanding of the system, as well as resulting in a more accurate and complete assessment of user information requirements.

Alter (1978) supports the argument for user involvement and the user's perception of need as crucial elements of a successful system. His study of 56 DSS showed that those systems that suffered significant implementation problems were characterised by a lack of user involvement and user initiation. He found relatively few problems in systems in which the users had an active role in the initiation or implementation stages.

Alter further argues that it is too simplistic to say that users must be involved in system development. The question to be asked, he argues, is not that users must be involved, but what measures should be taken to ensure user involvement and a real need for the system. To achieve this, he suggested the following:

- spend more time to find out what the users really want;
- pay serious attention to user capabilities and management style;
- maintain close contact with the user throughout development;
- provide users with service rather than a product;
- design a simple system which does not overload the user;
- use an evolutionary approach that exploits the user's learning curve.

Ives & Olson (1984) believe that the appropriate level of user involvement differs according to the type of information system and/or the stage in the development process.

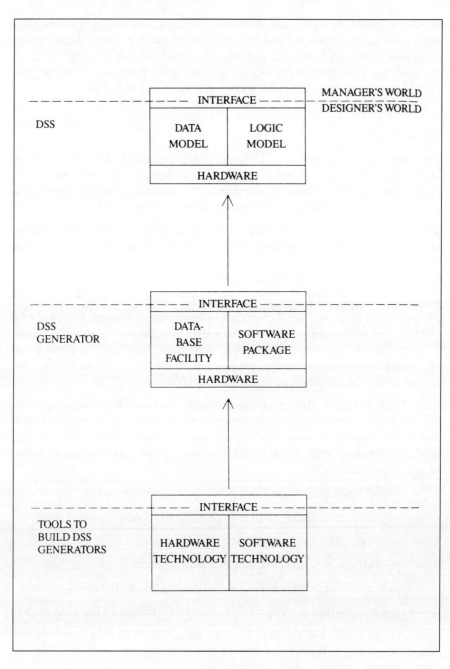

Figure 12.3   The DSS Information

For example, they argue that user involvement/participation may even be inappropriate for a system which requires considerable technical expertise or systems where the product is invisible or unimportant to users.

Ginzberg (1981) carried out a study of user expectations as predictors of project success or failure. The results of his study suggests that users who have a more realistic expectations of their system prior to implementation, are more satisfied with the system and use it more often than those users whose pre-implementation expectations are unrealistic. He argues that the definition stage of a project is most crucial. It is during this stage that early warnings about the success or failure of a project can be noticed.

Traditionally, management support has also been regarded as a crucial factor for a successful system. Sanders and Courtney (1985) give further support to this view, and confirm the importance of top management support in the implementation stage of a DSS. They further found evidence relating to the role of training in DSS development, and showed the length of use as a critical factor contributing to DSS satisfaction. It is been argued that effective management of DSS development requires:

- an explicit plan for the full development life cycle;
- careful assignment of responsibility for DSS developments;
- appropriate user involvement and direction;
- on-going user needs assessment and problem diagnosis.

Overall, it is management, rather than hardware, software, or technical expertise, that is becoming viewed as the missing ingredient in the recipe for successful DSS development efforts.

In the firms with successful DSS development efforts, top management made more effective use of six planning and control mechanisms: executive steering committees, written overall development plans, agreed development priorities for system implementation, long-term funding commitments by top management, system planning objectives, and project development policies.

THE MANAGER-DESIGNER INTERACTION

Cognitive Types

McKenny and Keen (1971) put forward the view that there are significant differences in the way people deal with information for decision-making: in the way a person 'captures' information and on how he deals with it. They call these two dimensions 'information gathering' and 'information evaluation'. Where a person lies on these dimensions defines the way he thinks; i.e. it defines his cognitive type.

The world provides an infinity of stimuli, and everyone must develop a way of accepting some of these stimuli and rejecting others, otherwise he would be swamped. How he does this characterises his information gathering style. In McKenny and Keen's terminology, receptive individuals use detailed and highly structured models to filter out unwanted stimuli: a stimulus that conforms to the model is accepted, others are not. (This fits the model shown in Figure 2.4). For example, a clerk dealing with customer orders would reject orders for which the order quantity was specified as negative or given as alphabetic characters: he is trained to reject such orders by a model that demands acceptance only of positive numbers for a quantity ordered. Again, a receptive manager considering the problem of falling sales may have a model that involves monthly aggregate sales figures. In such a case, the more detailed weekly, daily or even individual order details would be ignored as inconsequential. For the receptive person, modelling precedes information gathering.

On the other hand a preceptive individual would have a much less well-defined model with which to filter the incoming stimuli. He would use the stimuli to paint a picture, to form his scenario. So, to revert to the case of the manager investigating falling sales, a preceptive individual would look at a great deal of the data available and try to find the cause of falling sales from them. Some focusing and filtering would be applied, but he would not prescribe and narrow-down the types of data that he would consider to anything like the same extent as would a receptive individual. For the preceptive person, information gathering precedes modelling.

Some individuals approach the information evaluation associated with a problem by structuring the problem in terms of some method that, if followed through, is likely to produce a useful answer. McKenny and Keen refer to such thinkers as systematic thinkers. Such individuals do well in structured problem situations, where a method often exists by which the problem can be tackled. In ill-structured situations, which are novel and require judgement, it is intuitive thinkers who are likely to be most successful. Intuitive thinkers generally do not decide on a method and follow it through, but move quickly from one method to another, working very much on a trial-and-error basis.

Using the two dimensions of information gathering and information evaluation, McKenny and Keen formed the matrix reproduced in Figure 12.4.

		Information evaluation	
		Systematic	Intuitive
Information gathering	Preceptive	Management scientist Production & distribution managers	Marketing manager
	Receptive	Accountant Auditor Systems analyst	Salesman

Figure 12.4   McKenny and Keen's Cognitive Classification

In Figure 12.4 examples of business jobs are associated with the four cognitive types. If management scientists were to be placed in this matrix, it is likely they would be placed in the first quadrant – that of systematic, preceptive thinkers. This might suggest that their way of thinking, and consequently methods of work, approximate closely with those of production and distribution managers. It might further be concluded that it would be for the production and distribution functions that Extrapolatory Systems (the products of management scientists) would have been most frequently developed and successfully applied. This has indeed been the case. Many systems analysts would be placed in the lower left quadrant – as receptive and systematic thinkers, very concerned with formal methods and showing detailed concern with data. In this respect they are operating somewhat closer to clerks than to managers.

All designers are likely to be systematic thinkers in their professional life (though not necessarily elsewhere!) and thus think differently from intuitive managers. Summarising differences in thinking styles, Table 12.2. has been constructed (after Hobbs (1974)).

Obviously table 12.2 represents a very black and white picture; for example the fact that production and distribution managers tend to be systematic thinkers, though probably not so much as designers, waters down the dichotomies. However, the table does indicate areas where thinking styles may differ and where difficulties may be encountered for a manager and designer working together.

Table 12.2   Managers' and Designers' Thinking Styles

Designers think	Managers think
Systematically	Intuitively
Mathematically, abstractly	By analogy and example
Using evidence and logic	Usingprecedent and logic commonsense
In logical sequence	Emotionally
Rationally – before the event	Rationally – after the event
Of model form	Of model content
Objectively	Politically

Other Factors in the Manager-Designer Interaction

The relationship between a manager and designer may also be affected by their having different objectives. Whilst the manager's declared objectives are likely to be those acceptable to his organisation – such as cutting costs, getting impartial outside advice – other more personal objectives are likely to be significant, and may be dominant. For example, a manager might like to be the first manager to try something out, or wish to block any changes until he retires. Any system that looks as if it might adversely affect these personal objectives is going to have a difficult time being built and accepted. On the other hand, the designer may be keen to follow some particular line in order to meet his own personal objectives, which may at best be irrelevant to the manager and at worst may clash with the manager's objectives. Examples of objectives irrelevant to the manager would be the desire to publish a paper in a learned journal, or to try a technique that the designer has not used before: an example of an objective that would clash with a manager's objectives would be the designer's wish to develop a system that might incorporate some of the manager's expertise, and thus appear to reduce the manager's own contribution to problem solving.

In terms of information gathering, McKenny and Keen classified people as preceptive and receptive. Managers' apparent keenness for meetings has been mentioned in Chapter 1. Mintzberg (1975) points out that managers much preferred verbal channels – meetings and telephone conversations – to the written. No doubt part of this preference reflects the content of the media: that verbal channels tend to give up-to-the-minute information and almost any line of enquiry can be pursued, whereas written channels are often associated with out-of-date information and do not easily allow for a range of supplementary enquiries to be handled. However, the ability to handle written material is partly a matter of training. System designers have selected themselves for a job that requires 'book learning', and at university and elsewhere they have been trained to garner information from books and other written material. By and large managers do not have this predilection or training or the time to read. Thus for managers the preferred source of information is often verbal.

The preference that managers have for discussions rather than documents, and the extreme bittiness of their working day means that a designer must develop skill in verbal presentation. He must be able to interpret what the manager is saying in the small time he has for discussion, and be willing to discuss the system and results from it in the restricted time available. Written reports should not be more than one or two pages or they will hardly ever be read and never digested: model representations should be attractively laid out and appropriate to the message.

In developing systems there should never be a long gap between designer – client interactions. If there is, it becomes increasingly difficult to maintain energy, and cognitive developments by both parties begin to leave the other party behind.

MANAGEMENT INFORMATION SYSTEMS DEVELOPMENT

From Table 12.1 it can be seen that in general, MIS tend to be organisationally based; are dealing with context independent, well-structured situations; and are used to improve the efficiency of an organisation.

Any DSS can be considered to be composed of three parts, the logic model, the data model and the computer-human interface. Primarily, it is the differences in the models that gives rise to the different approaches to the development of DSS.

In MIS, systems design follows the path shown in Figure 12.5. Recalling from Chapter 2 that the scenario is the manager's world view, the local scenario represents his view of that portion of his total scenario which encompasses the problem situation. The MIS will help with a portion of his local scenario and that of any other manager who is also to use the system.

A detailed explanation of the logic modelling process is given in Finlay (1985). A detailed explanation of the data modelling stages can be found in

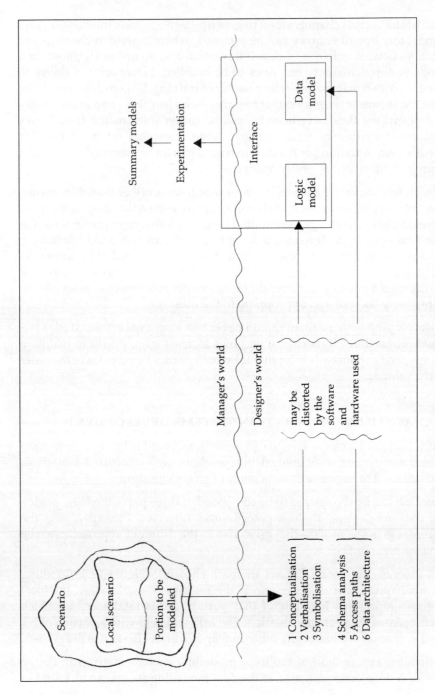

Figure 12.5   Modelling in Management Information Systems

many texts – for example, the CIMA Summary text (1986) and Law and Longworth (1987). In summary, the stages are as shown in Figure 12.6.

Note that the conceptualisation stage of systems design is the consolidation of the findings of the feasibility study and systems analysis stages of the systems development cycle.

The emphases placed on the various stages will depend on the type of DSS being designed. These emphases will now be explored.

Data Retrieval Systems

Data Retrieval Systems would be used to help with problem detection (see Figure 1.1), and to supply data values to the data models of other forms of DSS (see Figure 2.4). They are systems for very well-structured situations.

1	Conceptualisation	Detailed definition of the problem and the intended range of application of the system. Identifcation of any techniques and tools that might be appropriate. Identifcation of the information requirements.
2	Verbalisation	Precisely stating in English the relations between informational variables, noting any assumptions made.
3	Symbolisation	Assigning symbols to the variables and to activites and stating the units and conventions used.
4	Schema analysis	Data analysis, probably using entity and functional analyses to determine the data that is needed, where it originates, how it is used and when it is needed. Definition of the precision required of the data values.
5	Data structure	Definition of the file contents and structures to be used.
6	Access paths	Definition of the access paths required to satisfy managerial information requirements.

Figure 12.6   Stages in Systems Design

The systems development cycle is almost completely applicable to the development of Data Retrieval Systems, although if the system is a small one, such as a file drawer system holding the personnel records for a few employees, then it may be acceptable to short-circuit some of the stages. With systems of any size however, for example, those to serve the whole organisation or where the data covers many areas of business activity, then there is a need to follow all or most of the stages of the systems development cycle. As given in Table 12.1, the general design perspective is an organisational one.

Features listed in Table 12.1 that are of particular significance to the development of Data Retrieval Systems are those relating to the models and outputs. The logic models are conceptually very simple, using definitional relations. Linked to this is the restriction of data values within the data models to 'facts' – data about the past or present about which there is no disagreement. Apart from simple retrieval, any manipulation that is required is at the arithmetic level (such as averaging or aggregating). The levels of measurement (see Appendix B) are on ratio and interval scales.

What this tells us about developing and implementing such systems is that the organisational context requires a long look at requirements, no particular manager can define the system, and this gives power and responsibility to the information centre. Because the logic model is based purely on definitional relations, then there is little need for the analyst who is building the system to work closely with any individual manager to determine his requirements. The exception is with Executive Information Systems.

The social, organisational and social problems associated with Executive Information Systems tend to be more difficult to resolve during development than do the technical ones. A survey carried out in 1988 by Business Intelligence found that defining the actual information needs of senior executives was rated as one of the most challenging tasks facing Executive Information System developers. This was brought about by the executives frequently changing their priorities, and lacking clarity as to what they needed. Also, getting executives to change to computer-presented information has proved difficult.

Although the logic modelling tends to be very straightforward with Data Retrieval Systems, this is not generally the case with the data modelling, especially with large systems for use by many different people within an organisation. In large organisations, data modelling is the province of the database administrator and systems programmers. These people have to be concerned with the quality of the data held on the database and with providing file structures within which the data is held to allow efficient access paths to satisfy information requirements.

Figure 12.7 sketches out the process whereby at the database underpinning a Data Retrieval System would be created. The terms used here are in keeping with their use throughout the book and does not accord with the use made by database specialists. [Very unfortunately, they tend to use the term 'logic model' for 'data model'].

The form of data modelling associated with databases is not normally the province of non-information specialist managers. The one area in data modelling of concern to him might be with data definition; for example, what constitutes a fixed cost in an accounting system.

The third part of the system is the interface between the model and the user. There will be many interfaces, each needing to satisfy an individual manager and his staff.

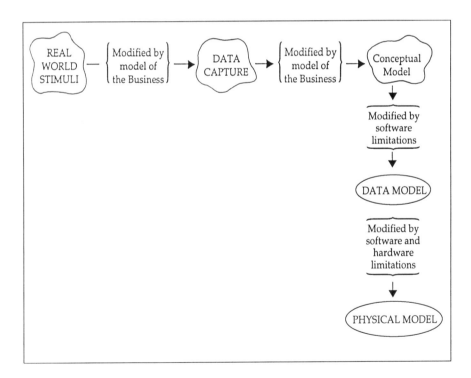

Figure 12.7 Three Steps in Developing a Database

Prototyping is the approach whereby these individual needs can be met. The term is borrowed from Engineering: a prototype is an early version of a system that exhibits the main features of the later, operational system. Prototyping is done because theory and experience are not powerful or detailed enough to define every element of the final system.

The term 'prototyping' can be applied to any system that is developed rapidly and which is exposed to the user for interactive, hands-on development and modification. The approach is for the user to provide a general specification and for the systems designers to quickly develop an initial version. The user would then try this version and, in the light of the experience gained, modifications would be suggested. The cycle of modification – trial – modification would be continued until an acceptable system were developed.

With MIS of any substantial size, it is just not possible to prototype significant portions of it. Prototyping of the input and output screens is possible however, and is a valid approach to involve the manager and his staff in development, and to show them that progress is being achieved. One of the major problems with the development of large Data Retrieval Systems is the extended time-scale of development, with manager's expectations raised at the first (feasibility survey) stage, and with them not significantly involved until late in the systems cycle – perhaps many months later.

Linking back to the stages of the systems development cycle, manager and designer will typically be involved in the feasibility survey, with a designer and the manager's staff heavily involved in the systems analysis stage. The manager and probably his immediate superior will then only have a significant involvement towards the 'end' of the cycle where decisions concerning implementation have to be taken. The systems design, programming and the initial parts of the testing stages are likely to be ones carried out by the information system specialists. These will include the programmers, designers, database manager and possibly systems programmers (see Clifton (1987) for a discussion of the roles of these people). Final testing will involve the manager's staff. Documentation will only peripherally involve the manager's staff. The review will heavily involve the manager.

Extrapolatory Systems

Extrapolatory systems differ from Data Retrieval Systems in that they extrapolate less well-structured situations into an uncertain future. Thus they are not concerned solely with 'facts' and 'definitions' but with logic and data that are open to dispute. Whilst the emphasis within Data Retrieval Systems is with data modelling, the emphasis within Extrapolatory Systems is with logic modelling. With Extrapolatory Systems the schema analysis, data structuring and access path determination are almost always treated in a very rudimentary fashion, since the data models are of such limited scope.

The most obvious difficulty lies in the use of non-definitional relations in the logic model: justification of these types of relation can be difficult. For example, the relations might have been developed using a sophisticated statistical technique and it may be very time-consuming, if not impossible, to explain the technique to a statistically naive manager. Again, the relations may have been devised by a designer from managerial statements that make the relations inevitable. However, the consequences of these relations may be such that the manager later wishes to disown his own relations!!

Whilst user involvement is to be sought and welcomed, model building is often a difficult and time consuming business and, with the time pressures on them, managers can very seldom afford the time that an intimate involvement demands.

Figure 12.2 indicates some of the differences between types of DSS. In Extrapolatory Systems the depth of modelling is substantial: the logic models are mathematical – and thus in a form very different from the typical manager's scenario. It is this separation of the designer's and manager's views that causes a great deal of the heartache in the development and implementation of Extrapolatory Systems. Not only is the modelling mathematical, but it can be probabilistic, another area causing great difficulty for most managers.

The Use of Intermediaries

In these conditions of conceptual difficulty, the use of intermediaries acting between the manager and the DSS has been suggested as an important factor in building and implementing DSS successfully. DSS involving specialised languages and techniques should be made available to managers through intermediaries, rather than trying to get managers to interact directly with the systems. There is too much opportunity for misuse when DSS is left in the hands of users who do not understand their capabilities or limitations.

Overdependence on intermediaries may result in a reduced level of involvement by users in the exploration stage of problem-solving. The exploration stage is a crucial one, for it is during this stage that users obtain a better understanding and deeper insight into their decision problems and decision environment.

Whilst the use of intermediaries is likely to be unavoidable, the time pressures on managers may well lead to a split of responsibility between designer and manager. This split may widen into a yawning gap: managers and specialist system designers may be operating in two separate cultures, each with its own goals, languages and methods. Under such circumstances effective co-operation, and even communication, between the two is just about minimal.

In summary, the deeper into the designer's world the modelling technique goes, the more likely it is that the manager will not be able to use the system or to understand its output. This gap may mean that any system built is inappropriate to the manager's needs and has little impact on decision-making.

Product or Service?

A significant feature of systems design is whether the designer is seen as providing a product or a service. If he is providing a product, this suggests that the requirement is well defined before development takes place, and that once the system has been accepted by the manager, the link between designer and manager ceases except for maintenance. Extrapolatory Systems call for a more service orientated approach; the designer becomes part of the support system. Although the designer will be providing a product – in the shape of a set of computer programs – he will be available to augment these programs, derive new summary models for example, and be in a position to help the manager both in his explorations with the system and in his interpretation of the results.

Applicability of the Systems Development Cycle

The last paragraphs should have given some indication that the systems development cycle would not be generally applicable to Extrapolatory Systems. The use of the cycle presumes that the problem situation is well structured, and thus the system can be defined at the outset. There is also the assumption underlying the systems cycle that the setting for the completed system, in terms of environment, managerial preferences and decision making styles is largely unchanging (i.e. context independent). None of these assumptions holds well for many Extrapolatory Systems (and indeed hardly holds at all for MINTS – see the next sections).

As the situation becomes less structured, there appears to be a case for extending prototyping from the design of inputs and outputs, to other elements of the system. However, the techniques associated with Extrapolatory Systems mean that a certain amount of structure is imposed on the situation. Where this imposition leads to cognitive mismatch between system and manager, the success of the DSS is in doubt, unless intermediaries are skilful in fully mitigating the effects of this mismatch.

MANAGEMENT INTELLIGENCE SYSTEMS DEVELOPMENT

Referring to Table 12.1, it can be seen that MINTS are concerned with ill-structured, context-dependent situations. As was discussed in the summary to Chapter 4, MINTS seek to improve systems effectiveness through an improvement in the efficiency of problem tackling.

Systems Design in Management Intelligence Systems

The systems development cycle has been discussed earlier, and a model for systems design in MIS was set out in Figure 12.5. It is illustrative to consider how appropriate these models are to the development of MINTS.

MINTS are developed in situations where users don't really know where they are going, and thus with objectives not clearly definable at the outset. The approach is an evolutionary one, in which the user(s) can experiment with a small portion of their problem situation and expand their area as they think appropriate (rather than as the designer thinks appropriate). An appropriate approach is unlikely to be that of the systems development cycle where objectives must be clearly agreed from the outset. A more appropriate approach is the 'breadboarding' approach.

The term breadboarding is borrowed from electronics. A breadboard is a board with a matrix of holes in it, which allows transistors and other electrical components to be attached to it in such a way that their interconnections can be changed very easily. The reason why this arrangement is so valuable in electronic system design is because it is not easy to define beforehand what the final system is to look like. This difficulty arises out of the subtle linkages between transistor outputs and inputs. Due to these linkages, the build up of the system needs to be gradual, relying to some extent on trial and error to achieve the desired outcome. This is a common situation, where the means influences the ends and vice-versa, and the lack of structure means that the ends are not known with any precision.

The Use of Intermediaries

MINTS are used in much less structured situations than are MIS. Consequently, the role of intermediaries is different. The emphasis is not on structuring relatively well defined problems – often to be able to use a well established technique – but on a much wider structuring. Where MINTS are used in a group context, the role moves from that of a 'techniques consultant' to that of a process consultant. The intermediary becomes more a facilitator, facilitating the discussions and negotiations that generally accompany problem tackling.

The roles of facilitators in Decision Conferencing were described in Chapter 9. In Chapter 14 the parts played by facilitators in the use of Metasystems are described in detail. Facilitators in Metasystem usage are acting in a similar way to facilitators involved with MINTS.

Preference Determination Systems

As described in Chapter 7, these systems do little to constrain the thinking of managers, except in forcing them to think of options and, in the case of Decision Tree Systems, with placing probabilities on outcomes. The systems would be developed with very little input from intermediaries or facilitators: all that they would be required to do is to explain the use of the computer and how the session would proceed. The available software would carry out all the calculations. In the case of Decision Tree Systems there might be an additional requirement on the facilitator to help with sensitivity analyses.

Scenario Development Systems

Scenario Development Systems are concerned with the development of the scenarios of one, or more generally, several managers and are often used in a group context. The ability of the facilitators as a process consultant is a very important influence on the success of the group sessions. Often a large amount of work takes place before the first session, with the facilitator discussing with the eventual participants how they see the problem, what their knowledge is, and what ways they see for tackling the problem.

SUMMARY

Research findings seem almost unanimous that three factors are vital for successful systems development and implementation. These are user involvement, senior managerial backing, and the management of user expectations. The findings of Ives and Olsen suggest that the importance of user involvement may be overrated, and indeed even counter productive in the development of some kinds of DSS.

The system development cycle was originally used in the context of information technology with Data Processing Systems. It was found that it could be used almost unchanged to develop the type of DSS most closely related to these systems, i.e. to Data Retrieval Systems. A recent development has been the move to the prototyping of inputs and outputs. The systems development cycle has less to offer other forms of DSS. With Extrapolatory Systems, the rigid sequencing of stages begins to break down. Because of the difficulties managers have with features of Extrapolatory Systems such as probability and judgemental relations, intermediaries play a significant role in such systems.

Through training, selection and predilection, managers and designers are likely to be different types of thinkers with different personal objectives. The solution to the difficulties often encountered between managers and designers working together is for each to try to understand how the other thinks. However, except marginally, it is not possible to retrain a systematic designer to be intuitive or to change an intuitive manager into a systematic one. Even if this retraining were possible it would not be sensible to carry it out, since neither designer nor manager should dilute the expertise he has and which is important to the DSS building process.

The system development cycle has little to offer the MINTS developer. In theory there are still the same stages to be gone through, but they are tackled in a very loose and iterative way. With Scenario Development Systems, a very great deal appears to depend on the abilities of the facilitator. The emphasis is on the process of decision making rather than merely on a tangible finished product, as is the case with MIS.

For successful implementation, the designer must realise that he is not just a provider of systems, but a seller of a means by which the manager can improve the performance of the unit for which he has responsibility. A little thinking as a salesman on his part would be an advantage.

REFERENCES

Alter S., (1978) *Development Patterns for Decision Support Systems*, MIS Quarterly, Vol.2, No.3, pp 33–42

Business Intelligence, (1988) The EIS Report

Checkland P., (1981) *Systems Thinking, Systems Practice,* John Wiley and Sons.

CIMA Study Text, Stage 2, (1986) *Information Technology Management,* BPP Publishing, London

Clifton H.D., (1987) *Business Data Systems, A practical guide to systems analysis and data processing,* Prentice-Hall International

Finlay P.N., (1985) *Mathematical Modelling for Business Decision-Making,* Croom Helm

Forghani M.S., (1989) *The Likelihood of Success in Management Intelligence Systems*: Building a Consultant Advisory System, PhD thesis, Loughborough University of Technology

Ginzberg M.J., (1981) *Early Diagnosis of MIS Implementation Failure: Promising Results and Unanswered Questions,* Mangement Science, Vol.27, No.4, pp 459–478

Hobbs J.A., (1974) *Some Do's and Don'ts in Selling O.R.,* Annual Operational Research Conference, 22-25 October, Brighton

Ives B. and Olson M.H., (1984) *User Involvement and MIS Success: A Review of Research,* Management Science, Vol.30, No.5, pp 586–603.

Johnson G. and Scholes K., (1993) *Exploring Corporate Strategy,* Prentice Hall International, 3rd edition

Law D. and Longworth G., (1987) *Systems Development: Strategies and Techniques,* NCC Publications, Manchester UK

McKenny J.L., and Keen P.G.W., (1974) *How managers' minds work,* Harvard Business Review, May–June, pp.79–90

Mintzberg H., (1975) *The manager's job: folklore and fact,* Harvard Business Review, July–August, pp 49–61

Pinchot G.III, (1985) *Intrapreneuring: Why you don't have to leave the corporation to become an entrepreneur,* Harper and Row.

Sanders G.L. and Courtney J.F., (1985) *A Field Study of Organizational Factors Influencing DSS Success,* MIS Quarterly, pp 77–89

Zachman J.A., (1982) *Business Systems Planning and Business Systems Control Study: A comparison,* IBM Systems Journal, Vol.21, No.1, pp 31–53

13 Validation of Decision Support System

The validation of DSS is the checking of the appropriateness of the system for the purpose for which it is being used. This often means the testing the agreement between the behaviour of the DSS and that of the real world system being modelled. However, this is not always the case since a real world system against which to test the DSS may not always be available. A valid DSS would be one that has stood up to the testing during the process of validation.

A major conceptual problem with the validation process is that validation can never be fully carried out. This problem arises because it is not possible to prove that a law or a relationship about the real world is valid, only that it is invalid (Popper, 1959). [This statement naturally does not apply to definitional relations – these are correct by definition]. The fact that the sun has been observed to rise in the East for many thousands of years has led to the law 'the sun always rises in the East'. The observations and the resulting law only make it very probable that the sun will rise in the East tomorrow – it does not and cannot guarantee that it will. On the other hand, if on only one day the sun failed to exhibit this behaviour, then the rule that the sun always rises in the East would have been disproved. Thus, although a law cannot be proved, one genuine, contradictory finding can make a law invalid.

The validation of DSS is not concerned with proving the absolute truth of the underlying relationships that make up the DSS – since this is impossible – but with demonstrating that, with a reasonable probability, the relationships are appropriate. The term 'appropriate' has been used rather than 'right' or 'the truth' since with DSS for managerial decision-making the search is for usability, and usability depends on the user's viewpoint and the context in which he finds himself.

When considering MIS it is possible to test the outputs of the system against a real world system (or, for systems not yet built, against surrogates for them). This is a more difficult concept for MINTS where it is often the process of decision making that these systems support.

With this difficulty in mind and incorporating the concept of usefulness in the definition, the process of validation will be defined as the checking of the appropriateness of a DSS to help tackle real world problems as seen from the viewpoint of those using the system.

VALIDATION OF MANAGEMENT INFORMATION SYSTEMS

The Need for Validation

Validation is a process that should take place throughout the DSS building process. Ideally all those people who will be using the DSS should be intimately involved in its creation. However, managers very often do not have the time to get deeply involved in building models, and so a great deal of the responsibility for validation rests with the designer. Even if an individual manager were deeply involved, often he does not stay long in the job for which the DSS was designed, and a new manager, who has had no involvement in the DSS building, has to validate a DSS that already exists, or simply accept the DSS as 'correct'. So much of the managerial validation (as opposed to the designer's validation) is concentrated on the completed DSS, or at the end of a phase in the development process.

Finlay and Wilson (1987) have demonstrated that little validation is carried out during and after the building of mathematical DSS. This may not have mattered much when the systems were small and limited to aiding a single manager. However, as the tools available to create quantitative and qualitative computer decision aids develop and become more widely available, as DSS are developed by non-specialist information systems staff and used at higher levels within organisations, the need to validate systems becomes more pressing: the penalties for using invalid DSS become potentially more severe.

Verification

One special and well developed area of validation is that of verification, which is the process of testing computer programs to see that they perform as expected – for example, that totals are calculated correctly, and that exceptions are reported appropriately. Verification, therefore, is the testing and debugging of programs. It is not concerned with the appropriateness of the relations that make up the logic model, only with whether the translation of the relationships into a computer representation has been done correctly. Here, in contradistinction to all other aspects of validation, it is theoretically possible to test that the representation is 'correct', since to the programmer all relations will be presented to him as though they were definitional. However, it may be impracticable to verify the DSS over all possible situations.

From the foregoing, it can be seen that for Data Retrieval Systems verification is all the validation that needs to be carried out.

A note of caution here. The terms validation and verification have been used as they are in the U.S.A. British designers tend to switch the definitions and use validation for verification and vice-versa. The author's view is that standardisation of terms is helpful: the American nomenclature has been chosen purely on the grounds that there are more American designers than British ones.

VALIDATION OF THE LOGIC MODEL

It is possible to validate a DSS in two broad ways:

1. by checking out each part of the DSS;

2. by checking that an acceptable output is achieved for each of a set of inputs.

For a manager a third method of validation exists: he can simply have so much faith in the designer that he leaves all the validation to him. The association of the designer with a DSS is sufficient to give the DSS a good name. The first validation method is an analytical one, in that each part is checked individually and in conjunction with other, interacting parts. The second method is a synoptic method, where an overview of the DSS is taken, and the total DSS performance is checked. Since the synoptic method checks out the interactions between relations, but not explicitly each relation, use of both methods in combination is preferred.

Analytical Validation

In checking out an individual relation, there are four broad steps to be taken. First there are checks on the definitions of the variables used in the relation: second, checks as to the consistency of these variables, and third, checks on the broad 'shape' of the relation, i.e. on the feasibility of the relation. The fourth step is to check that the range of application of the relation fits the intended range of application, and to specify areas where the two do not match.

Checks on Definitions

It is important when designing a DSS for all the people concerned in its creation and use to be sure of the meaning of the variables used. For instance, a rather poor DSS would be created if there was confusion over what costs are to be included in the various cost variables – such as fixed, semi-variable and direct.

Checks on Consistency of Variables

An important second step in validation is to check that the variables used within a relation are consistent. Consistency involves both the dimensions of the variables and the units of measurement used.

The variable 'number of peas in a pod' is a simple number, unlike the variable 'distance between Paris and London' which is not, since this has associated with it a dimension – in this case the dimension of length. The actual value of the distance would be specified as the number of units along the dimension of length – as 350 kms or 200 miles: for a distance, to state a number without specifying the units, is meaningless. Checking the consistency of the units used is the second step after checking on the consistency of the dimensions. In practice, both checks are likely to be performed at the same time. However, conceptually they are different and linked to different stages of the mathematical modelling methodology (see Figure 12.5). The first step should be done at the verbalisation stage, the second during the symbolisation stage.

Checks on the Consistency of Dimensions

Consider the following attempt to relate the fuel used on a journey to other journey characteristics:

$$\text{FUEL USED} = \text{DISTANCE TRAVELLED} \times \text{SPEED}$$

By considering the dimensions of the three variables, it can easily be seen that this cannot be a valid relation. The dimension of FUEL USED is a volume (or more fundamentally, length x length x length), that of DISTANCE TRAVELLED is a length, and SPEED has the dimension of length/time.

In dimensional terms this relation becomes:

$$\text{volume} = \text{length} \times \text{length} / \text{time}$$

Since volume itself has the dimensions length x length x length (or length^3), this relation is saying

$$\text{length} = 1 / \text{time}$$

which cannot be correct, ie. it is dimensionally invalid.

Checks on the Consistency of Units

Even with the dimensions in balance, an inappropriate DSS would be derived if inconsistent units of measurement were used. Continuing the same example, if DISTANCE TRAVELLED were in miles and the DISTANCE / UNIT OF FUEL CONSUMPTION were specified in km/litre, then in unit terms the above relation would read:

$$\text{FUEL USED} = \frac{\text{miles}}{\text{km/litre}}$$

$$= \frac{\text{miles} \times \text{litres}}{\text{km}}$$

i.e. the variable FUEL USED would be in no recognised units, and therefore very difficult to work with: this relation is unlikely to be considered to have consistency of units

Checks on the Feasibility of a Relation

The checks on the consistency of the dimensions and units are a form of verification in that the tests applied are rigorous and standard: a relation failing the tests would be deemed 'incorrect'. Any relation that has passed these tests must then be scrutinised for appropriateness, and here the primary considerations are the 'shape' of the relations and the range over which the relation remains appropriate. The range of application of the DSS will be discussed in the next section.

Consider the case where a relation purports to show the link between the financial contribution from the sales of a product and its price in a competitive market. A relation with the shape shown in Figure 13.1 might be sketched. Whilst this relation might not be the most appropriate one to put forward, (and only the judgement of the sales and marketing staff can be used to assess this), there are simple tests that should be applied to check on its feasibility.

The first check is to look at the behaviour of the relation at the 'extremes', i.e. when the values of the variables are very high and very low within the range of application of the model. With Figure 13.1 the test would be at high values of price and for zero price. With a very high price it might be expected that the number of the product sold would fall off very rapidly – and make a more rapid decline in the contribution than the higher price would to an increase in the contribution. Thus at high values of price the curve of Figure 13.1 looks feasible.

Towards a zero price the curve looks more problematical. Would one expect the curve to flatten out, implying that the loss of revenue on each item as the price is reduced, is closely counterbalanced by the increase in the number of items sold? Perhaps, but the relation needs to be checked in this area.

Having checked at the extremes, another check is of the 'bumps' in the curve. Reverting to Figure 13.1 once more, there is a maximum contribution expected when the price is P. Is this reasonable, or would a consistent increase or decrease in the contribution as price is increased be more reasonable?

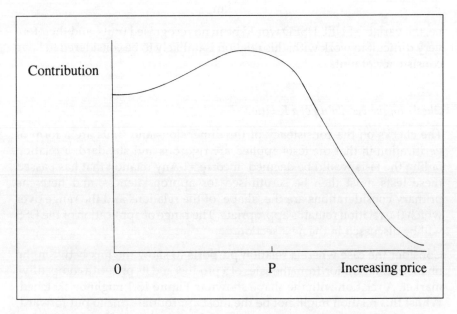

Figure 13.1   The Relationship Between Contribution and Price

Checks on the Range of Application of Individual Relations

Consider the case of a department in a manufacturing organisation where the manager has said that the number of people he would require to produce given levels of output are as follows: for an output of 20 million packs per year he estimates that he requires 75 people; for 25 million packs per year, 90 people; for 27 million packs per year, 100 people; for 30 million packs per year, 110 people, and to produce 35 million packs he requires 130 people.

Plotting these values produces Figure 13.2. The points suggest that a straight line relation between output and number of people required may adequately represent the real world situation.

As shown in Table 13.1, the fit of the straight line to the points is very close for all output volumes between 25 and 35 million packs per year. A difference of five people is shown for an output of 20 million packs per year and this may be too large a discrepancy for the relationship represented by the line to be acceptable. If it were too large, then the straight line relationship would not be valid for outputs below 25 million packs.

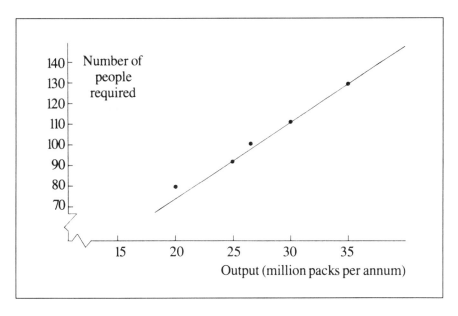

Figure 13.2   The Relationship between Output and Number of People Required

Table 13.1   Comparison of the Number of People Required for the Production of Normal Sized packs

Output million pa	Numbers of people specified	Required from graph	Difference
20	75	70	−5
25	90	90	0
27	100	98	−2
30	110	110	0
35	130	130	0

Around outputs of 35 million packs the fit of the line to the points is perfect and thus the relationship would be considered valid in this range. So good is the fit that there must be a temptation to extrapolate the line to cover cases where the output is greater than 35 million packs per year.

Sometimes the situation in which the DSS is being used forces such extrapolation, but it is always a risky procedure since the relationship is being used in unfamiliar territory, where the comfort of firm data does not exist. Perhaps there are physical constraints that prevent an output of more than 35 million packs per year being possible, or perhaps a double shift would be needed and this would require a great many more people to be employed.

Because the line drawn in Figure 13.2 is linear, the algebraic representation of the relationship between the number of people required and the output volume must be of the form:

NO OF PEOPLE REQUIRED = A + B x OUTPUT

A and B are constants, with values of −10 and 4 respectively, giving

NO OF PEOPLE REQUIRED = −10 + 4 x OUTPUT

where output is measured in million packs per year.

This equation is not sufficient to define the relationship; the range over which it is valid needs to be expressed as well. This appears to be for outputs between 25 and 35 million packs per year. Thus, the relationship must be expressed with the caveat:

$$25 < OUTPUT < 35$$

Listing the Assumptions Made

Validation should expose all the assumptions made in selecting the relationship. It is worth noting that in arriving at the above relation it has been assumed that it was possible to interpolate between the values specified by the manager, by joining up the points with a straight line. In fact this may not have been valid. It would not have been valid had the relationship been a 'stepped' one, i.e. if at one or more production volumes it had been necessary to make a sharp change in the number of people employed.

Synoptic Validation

Synoptic validation is concerned with checking 'around the model', by being satisfied that acceptable outputs are obtained from a set of inputs applied to the model. This form of DSS checking is often done by auditors checking on the operation of computerised business systems, and by the programmers and systems analysts who build them.

These DSS are DSS of existing real world systems and they are 'hard' systems in the terms used by Checkland (1981). Under such conditions it is fairly easy to check around the model, since data generated by the DSS can be checked against that from the system itself, or of some close approximation to it. Samples of proposals to alter the layout of checkouts in an existing supermarket can be tried out, and checked against what happens when this is done 'for real': stock control rules can be changed in a DSS and in the stockroom and the results compared. If the DSS outputs from the sample of changes match the outputs obtained from the real world, then those concerned in the development and use of a DSS will have greater confidence in its use in situations not tested against the real world. A DSS is considered to be replicatively valid if the data it produces matches data already produced by the real world system.

A DSS is predictively valid when the chronology is reversed and a data match is obtained, i.e. when data produced by the DSS is matched to those subsequently observed in the real world. Predictive validity is a more stringent test than is replicative validity. The reason for this is that a DSS is created using history – past data and experience. To use historical data again to test the DSS is a weak test since the test is over the same ground as already incorporated into the DSS and is not venturing into untried territory. With predictive validity the DSS is being tested as to its ability to predict, not simply its ability to describe. A well known example of this is the predictive validity of Maxwell's mathematical model of electromagnetism, which predicted properties whose physical reality were first shown to exist 20 years later by Hertz.

The Role of the Manager in Validation

Inevitably many DSS will be more complex than the graph shown in Figure 13.2. For that DSS the manager has a "feel" that simple increases in the output will lead to simple increases in the number of people employed within the limits defined by the designer. For more complex DSS there is a real danger that a manager may accept the DSS as a "black box". What he must do is to calibrate the DSS as best he can. His current operating situation gives him a point of origin and the designer should have defined the limitations of the model. The manager must tentatively explore the modelled world with the designer in two ways:–

(a) The designer will have included certain variables and excluded others. The manager must establish broadly the outcomes resulting from the use of different values of the variables, and so establish that all the sensitive variables have been included in the system.

(b) Starting from the point of origin, the manager should seek to establish the effect of changing variables: why, for example, do certain discontinuities appear in outputs? The manager should be able to relate such discontinuities to specific features of the model. The manager should also seek to establish that outputs are in line with his expectations. Even when the manager is in unfamiliar territory he should ensure that results match his expectations, or if they contradict them, then evidence should be available to back up these unexpected results.

The manager is now gradually calibrating the DSS and learning a great deal in the process.

VALIDATION OF THE DATA MODEL

Validation of the data model within a DSS is concerned with the precision and accuracy of measurement and with whether there has been any bias in the data. One area where bias could arise is from a (deliberate) lack of consistency; for example, where the 'twin deceits' of flattering sales forecasts and very low costs are used in a financial planning exercise. Another area of bias can arise because the sample of data collected is not representative of all the data. This might happen for example, where the results of a sales promotion in one test area subjected to unusual effects, (say the testing coincided with distribution difficulties faced by a major competitor), are used as a guide to the results to be expected nationally.

Rather surprisingly perhaps, high imprecision in one or more variables can greatly ease the difficulties of data specification. This point is covered fully by Finlay et al. (1988).

VALIDATION OF MANAGEMENT INTELLIGENCE SYSTEMS

Apart from the obvious need to verify a DSS, one major reason that validation is carried out is because the system is designed and built by people other than the user. Validation is one means of bridging the gulf that can arise between designer and manager, and which was discussed in Chapter 12. The second major reason relates to DSS that will be used several times, possibly by different managers, and here some form of objective quality assurance is needed.

Many fewer of these concerns are present in the use of MINTS. Partly this is because the gulf between manager and designer is generally much reduced, since the designer is now a facilitator, concerned primarily with helping the process of decision making, and not much with the content of the decision making. Partly it is due to the transitory nature of the use of the MINTS.

SUMMARY

Validation of DSS involving only a few relations is relatively simple, since each relation can be subjected to close scrutiny, and the interaction between the relations is unlikely to be complex.

With DSS involving many relations, validation becomes much more difficult, and there is a great tendency for the manager for whom the DSS has been built, to simply accept/reject the system, having neither the time nor inclination to understand it. This is a very dangerous position to take and one that should be strongly resisted.

Less objective validation is possible with MINTS, where the significant contribution is primarily a process one, and the process and any associated DSS are controlled directly by the user.

REFERENCES

Checkland P., (1981) *Systems Thinking, Systems Practice*, John Wiley and Sons, New York

Finlay P.N., Forghani M. and Wilson J.M., (1987) *A Logical Way of Controlling the Cost of Data Acquisition*, The British Accounting Review, Vol 19, No.2, pp1–10

Finlay P.N.and Wilson J.M., (1987) *The Paucity of Model Validation in Operational Research Projects*, Journal Operational Research Society, Vol 38, No 4, pp 303–308

Popper K.R., (1959) *The Logic of Scientific Discovery*, Basic Books, New York.

14 Metasystems

The approaches to be described in this chapter do not feature in the typology of DSS developed in Chapter 4. This is for two reasons. First, they do not rely on computer software, and thus they cannot be classified as DSS according to the definition developed in Chapter 3. Second, they offer a methodology for tackling problem situations rather than a technique. For this reason they are termed Metasystems: they overarch and encompass any specific DSS, and provide a framework within which specific DSS may be used more effectively.

Two metasystems will be described. These are the Strategic Options Development and Analysis (SODA) approach (Eden et al., 1986) and the Soft Systems Methodology (SSM) devised and developed by Checkland (1981). These approaches have many common themes; in particular, that every problem exists in an organisational context, and that this context will be perceived differently by different people. These themes have led to the development of group decision support structures rather than the enhancement of individual decision making or of improvements in meetings per se. In this chapter the focus is on describing the overarching methodologies within which individual and group DSS might be employed.

STRATEGIC OPTIONS DEVELOPMENT AND ANALYSIS

Strategic Options Development and Analysis (SODA) has been used for helping teams of between 4 and 20 people work on messy problems. It is the methodology within which Eden and his colleagues use their Cognitive Mapping System (*see* the discussion in Chapter 8).

Eden (1985) has given a detailed description of one application of the SODA methodology. The application involved the majority of a 40-strong publishing team and was concerned with strategic change to one of its publications. This example was not fully typical, and in order to describe a typical SODA programme and to build on the discussion of cognitive mapping given in Chapter 8, the example of the acquisition of a marketing information system is again used here. This example will also be used to show the approaches adopted by the other metasystem to be described later. This use of the same example will allow the similarities and contrasts to be more easily appreciated.

To reiterate, the problem concerning the marketing information system is that members of the Marketing Department of a large organisation are dissatisfied with the information system that has been developed for them. The Marketing Director is seeking to replace this system with a proprietary marketing information system. Purchasing a computer system such as this has wide ranging consequences, and senior management, the Computer Department and the Accounting Department have all expressed concern about the proposals. Figure 14.1 sets out the activities associated with a typical full-blown SODA programme.

The activities shown in Figure 14.1 would proceed as follows:

1   Discussions would be held between the facilitator, the senior (decision making) manager and the analyst from the organisation who would be helping the facilitator. The discussions would aim to determine the structure of the whole planning activity, who would participate in the sessions and the way the sessions would be conducted. A timetable of activities would be drawn up – as in Figure 14.1.

2   The facilitator would carry out individual interviews with each of the participants. Each interview would last around one hour. The interviews would be planned to introduce the facilitator and manager to each other, and for some of the issues of importance to the manager to be unearthed.

3   From his notes of each interview, the facilitator would construct on paper a cognitive map for each interviewee. (See Chapter 8 for a description of cognitive mapping and for an example of a typical map).

4   The second interviews would again involve each member of the group individually. The aim of these interviews would be to further develop the cognitive map that the facilitator had drawn as a result of the first interview. Amendments to the map would be drawn in as the discussion proceeds.

5   The set of cognitive maps would be analysed by the facilitator and common concepts, thoughts and cognitive threads identified. This would allow the facilitator to produce a set of composite cognitive maps, which

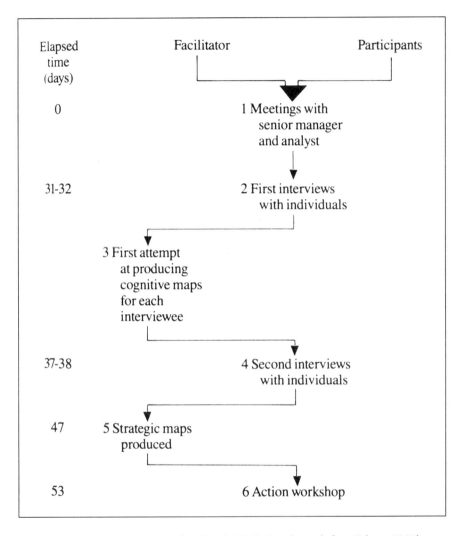

Figure 14.1   The Plan for the SODA Sessions (after Eden, 1985)

are termed 'strategic maps'. A small example of this process is given in Figure 14.2. This process would be aided by the use of the COPE computer software (see Chapter 8 for a description). Each strategic map would be associated with a cluster of concepts that would identify an issue of general concern to the group. Examples of these issues would be *The type of system to be acquired,* and *The consequences for the computer department.*

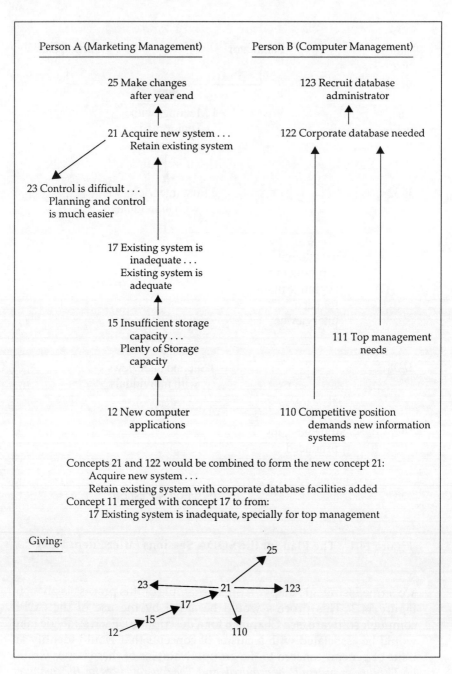

Person A (Marketing Management)   Person B (Computer Management)

25 Make changes   123 Recruit database
   after year end   administrator

21 Acquire new system . . .   122 Corporate database needed
   Retain existing system

23 Control is difficult . . .
   Planning and control
   is much easier

17 Existing system is
   inadequate . . .
   Existing system is
   adequate

15 Insufficient storage
   capacity . . .   111 Top management
   Plenty of Storage   needs
   capacity

12 New computer   110 Competitive position
   applications   demands new information
                                                   systems

Concepts 21 and 122 would be combined to form the new concept 21:
   Acquire new system . . .
   Retain existing system with corporate database facilities added
Concept 11 merged with concept 17 to from:
   17 Existing system is inadequate, specially for top management

Giving:

Figure 14.2   An Example of Merging Two Cognitive Maps

6   The action workshop is where the group would meet, typically for a day, to discuss the issues of concern identified by the facilitator in step 5. Definite proposals would be developed here, including agreements as to whether a new system were required, and if so, how the system should be acquired, the timetable for acquisition and who would be responsible for implementing the new system. The end result would be an agreed action plan.

From this account of the operation of a SODA programme, it can be seen that the effort involved may be large, with the requirement for preliminary interviews (especially with senior management) often leading to extended elapsed times between the first interviews and the action workshop. Much shorter SODA applications are undertaken, with short circuiting of some of the stages (omitting interviews for example).

THE SOFT SYSTEMS METHODOLOGY (SSM)

The SSM devised by Checkland (1981) consists of 7 stages of enquiry. These stages are sketched in Figure 14.3.

An enquiry begins, not with an identified problem, but rather with the local scenarios of the problem owners. At its least structured, this scenario will be the organisational setting within which one or more people have a feeling that something is not as it should be. Examples might be The existing system is inadequate and *How will we cope with the new computer applications?*. It is during this stage that the problem owner(s) would be identified.

Stage 2 is the stage where what Checkland calls a 'rich picture' of the situation is first developed. This picture includes both quantitative and qualitative factual and subjective information. The analyst helping the problem owners with the situation will look at the rich picture, seeking general patterns, themes or issues which encapsulate the symptoms of the situation (ie. those points that make people angry, depressed or have other strong emotions). Examples would be *The accountants have foisted their system on us* and *The computer's storage facilities are hopelessly small*.

Working from these issues, the next step is to develop notional systems that, if implemented, would help with the mess. To continue the same example, an effective steering group might be helpful in the issue of the dominance of accountants in determining information systems requirements: the use of a business systems planning system might help in determining the organisation's future needs for information systems and for helping prioritise information systems developments.

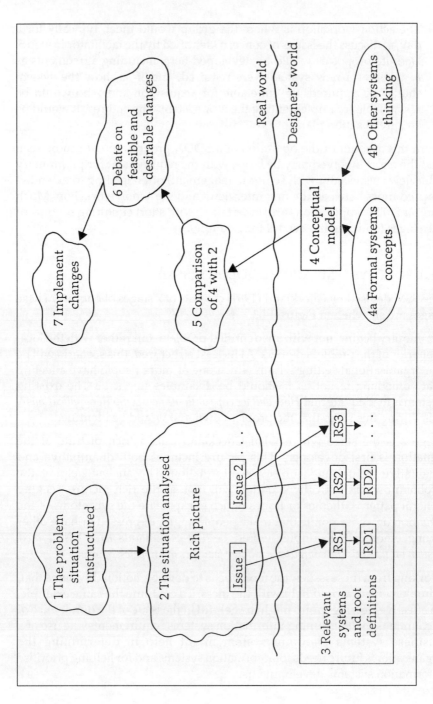

Figure 14.3   The Checkland Methodology (SSM)

All the remaining stages are designed to trace through the logical consequences of taking a particular view of the problem situation (as encapsulated in the notional system). The first move in this direction, within stage 3, is to produce what Checkland calls a 'root definition'. This is the equivalent of the system specification that is produced for well-structured systems such as Data Retrieval Systems. A root definition is a precisely-defined statement of what the relevant system should be. For example, the business systems planning system might have as its root definition "a company-accepted method for the determination of information systems to support the organisation's business needs and for the prioritising of information systems developments."

In stage 4, working solely from the root definition, a conceptual model is created. The process of creation might call on the use of individual DSS (in stage 4a) and on other systems thinking (for example, on accounting 'theory' and principles in stage 4b). The conceptual model will be the set of activities that the notional system must be able to carry out in order to operate. For example, the business systems planning system might call for; the commissioning of outside consultants; the setting up of a steering group to monitor the consultants activities, and a firm statement of the organisation's business strategy.

Stage 5 sees the comparison of the activities that the notional system must contain with the activities carried out by the present system. If there are differences, then either the notional system or the present system (or both) are deficient. If the fault lies in the notional system, then further iterations of stages 2, 3 and 4 will be called for: if the fault is deemed to lie in the present system, then the move is to stage 6 and then to the implementation of the desired and feasible changes in stage 7.

From Figure 14.4 and the associated discussion it would appear that the overall process is linear, starting at phase 1 and proceeding through the phases in strict sequence to end at phase 7. Whilst it is easier to describe it in this sequence, in practice it is possible to start with almost any of the phases. The process is usually highly iterative.

THE PLACE OF DECISION SUPPORT SYSTEMS WITHIN METASYSTEMS

Computer software (COPE) has been developed to support the SODA approach and can be used as an integral part of the process – by a facilitator rather than by the participants. In SSM, DSS may be used as an adjunct to stage 4 (in stage 4a).

Humphreys and Wisudha (1987) have taken the SSM and considered the types of management support that would be needed at each stage. They have identified 4 types of what they term 'intelligent resources'. These are as follows:

- Methods and systems that can facilitate the problem owners' use of their own problem expressing language in generating initial descriptions of issues of concern. These provide help in the SSM stages 2 and 3.

- Systems that assist in the generation and development of a conceptual model of the problem from the rich picture. These provide help in the transition from the SSM stage 3 to stage 4.

- Expert consultant systems that facilitate and guide the exploration of a conceptual model. These provide help in the SSM stage 4 and in moving from the SSM stage 4 to stage 5.

- Systems that support preference structuring. These systems will be of use when the options under consideration have already been well defined. These system would seem to support stages 5 and 6 of the SSM.

[Humphreys and Wisudha do not include systems for alerting managers to the occurrence of a problem: presumably this is because they do not consider problem detection as part of decision analysis].

From the characteristics of the types of DSS as listed in Chapter 4 and discussed in Chapter 5 through 8, it can be seen that Humphreys and Wisudha's 'intelligent resources' fit closely to these systems. The Scenario Development Systems correspond to the first category. Depending on where uncertainty lies, Preference Determination and Extrapolatory Systems might be able to help generate the conceptual model. Humphreys and Wisudha's third category corresponds to the 'chauffeured' use of DSS, either through a user-friendly computer system or through the intermediary of an analyst. Their final category corresponds to Preference Determination Systems.

From the foregoing discussion, it can be deduced that there is likely to be recurring chronological patterns to the use of different types of DSS. At the outset a manager needs clues to indicate that a problem or opportunity exists (through an internal Data Retrieval System if looking in at the organisation, or environmental scanning if looking outwards). Then possibly a Scenario Development System would be employed to help understanding of other participants' points of view and to generate ideas, followed by the use of a Preference Determination System to help decide what should be done. This might be followed by the use of an Extrapolatory System if the situation were close to one that had been tackled previously. Ultimately, the procedure might become so commonplace that the cycle of DSS use would form part of a standard control process within a metasystem. This sequence is shown in Figure 14.4, parallel to a conventional, normative view of the stages of decision-making which was illustrated in Figure 1.1.

SUMMARY

Metasystems have been developed in order to ensure that the organisational context and group feelings associated with a problem situation are fully taken into account in tackling the problem. All metasystems share the common emphasis on the importance in involving the group that 'owns' the problem in the problem tackling sessions. The approaches end with an action plan, agreed by the participants.

Metasystems use English as the means of communication and for recording ideas. This means that there is a minimum of time spent by the participants learning how to 'use' the system.

In the SODA approach there is considerable interaction between the facilitator and the participants on an individual basis before the participants tackle their problem in a group context.

The SSM does not require computer tools as an integral part of its approach. However, there are many areas where computer assistance could be used as adjuncts to all metasystems.

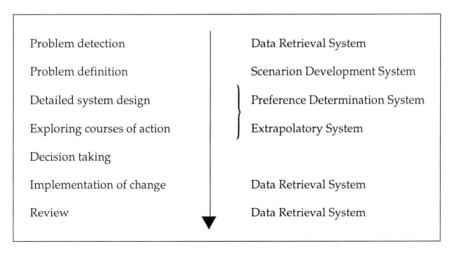

Figure 14.4   The Possible Chronological Use of Types of Decision Support System

REFERENCES

Eden C., Jones S. and Sims D., (1986) *Messing About in Problems: An Informal Structured Approach to their Identification and Management*, Frontiers of Operational Research and Applied Systems Analysis, Volume 1, Pergamon Press

Checkland P., (1981) *Systems Thinking, Systems Practice*, John Wiley and Sons

Eden C., (1985) *Perish the Thought!*, Journal of the Operational Research Society, Vol.36, No.9, pp 809–819

Humphreys P.C. and Wisudha A.D., (1987) *Methods and Tools for structuring and analysing decision problems*, Technical Report 87–1, Decision Analysis Unit, London School of Economics and Political Science.

15 Expert Systems

Expert Systems do not feature in Chapter 4 where the types of DSS are listed and described. Thus to devote a chapter to Expert Systems, albeit a small one, may appear something of an anomaly. The reasons for including a chapter on Expert Systems are the intense current interest in them, and to show how they may be incorporated within the typology of DSS described in this book. Interestingly, Expert Systems now appear to occupy a position similar to that held by DSS a decade ago. The term Expert System is used to sell many types of software, and in some cases all that is on offer is a facility for producing an interesting human-computer interface!

The chapter begins with a short introduction to Expert Systems. This allows a comparison between DSS and Expert Systems to be developed, first in terms of the components of these system, then in terms of the development methodologies used. Finally, Expert Systems are fitted into the typology of DSS.

THE BASICS OF EXPERT SYSTEMS

There are very many definitions of the term 'Expert System'. One that is simple and conveys the essence of such systems is that of Bramer (1982). He defines an Expert System as a computing system that embodies organised knowledge concerning some specific area of human expertise, sufficient to perform as a skilful and cost-effective consultant.

Looked at simply, the goal for an Expert System is to mimic an expert: for example, to mimic a doctor, a production manager, a marketing director. In order to do this, the expert's knowledge must be available within the Expert System. In Expert Systems parlance, the area of expertise covered by the Expert System is termed the 'knowledge domain', or simply the 'domain'.

To design an Expert System, the Expert System builder must first extract the knowledge associated with the chosen domain from the expert, and then codify it into a form which the computer can deal with. The jargon terms for these two processes are knowledge elicitation and knowledge representation. Together, the process is termed 'knowledge engineering'.

Not only must the Expert System contain within itself the 'facts' that the expert has, it must also be able to mimic the procedure by which the expert reasons with these facts. Thus both factual and procedural knowledge must be elicited and codified. The procedures by which the expert uses his factual knowledge is termed inference. The part of the system that performs these inferences is termed the inference engine. It is important to note that this arrangement separates the procedural knowledge from the factual knowledge.

The knowledge base and the inference engine are shown schematically in Figure 15.1. Also shown in this diagram are the natural language interface that allows the user to interact with the computer in a 'natural' manner – in his own natural language and using any jargon that he might use when normally consulting an expert.

Another feature required of a full Expert System is for it to be able to give an explanation to the user – for example, of how it arrived at a particular answer, or why a particular question is being asked. All these features are shown in Figure 15.1.

Also shown in Figure 15.1 is a knowledge refining program. This gives the person maintaining the Expert System the ability to alter the knowledge base as the knowledge improves or as the scope of the system is widened.

Readers wishing to know more about Expert Systems are referred to the books by Simons (1984) and by Waterman (1986).

DECISION SUPPORT SYSTEMS AND EXPERT SYSTEMS: CONTRASTS AND COMPARISONS

Over the past few years, several authors have discussed the links between DSS and Expert Systems, especially between the models developed by Management Scientists (primarily models to be used in Extrapolatory Systems) and the models central to Expert Systems. The similarities between the two approaches are masked by the different terminology used, which appears to be a consequence of the different backgrounds of the dominant groups within the Management Science and Expert System fraternities. Whilst both Expert Systems and Management Science groups like to pride

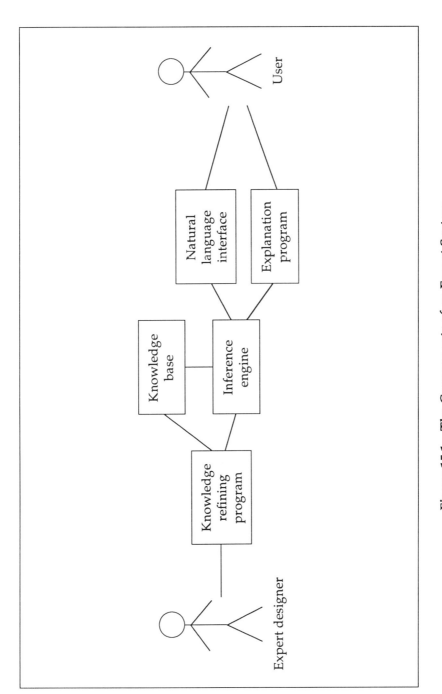

Figure 15.1 The Components of an Expert System

themselves on their multidisciplinary composition, the ethos within the groups is likely to be very different: with mathematicians, statisticians and physical scientists dominating the Management Science groups, whilst behavioural and computer scientists dominating the Expert Systems groups.

The differences between 'conventional' DSS and Expert Systems might appear at first sight to be great. Where are the DSS equivalents to the components of an Expert System as depicted in Figure 15.1: to the knowledge base, inference engine, natural language interface, explanation program and knowledge refining program?

The Knowledge Base

As described in Chapter 2, a DSS consists of a logic model and a data model linked to the user through a human-computer interface. The logic model consists of relations between variables: that is to say, it contains the knowledge of the situation being modelled. Sometimes these rules are definitional, sometimes they are judgemental.

Where the Expert System developers use the terms 'knowledge' and 'knowledge base', the DSS developers would use the terms 'logic' and 'logic model'. Expert Systems use the term 'rule' where the DSS fraternity tend to use the term 'relation' or 'relationship'. Interestingly, the financial modelling package FCS has for 20 years used the term 'rules' for the relations in a logic model. The concept of a set of rules or relations in the logic model of a DSS is identical to the concept of the knowledge base of Expert Systems. Whilst the concept is the same, the content of the rules appear very dissimilar.

It is illustrative to look at how a problem might be tackled in a 'typical' DSS and how it might be tackled in a 'typical' Expert System'. The example chosen is an amended version of that used in Chapter 12 where validation was discussed.

This example considered the case of a department in a manufacturing organisation where the manager has estimated that the number of people he would require to produce given levels of output are as follows: for an output of 15–20 million packs per year he estimates that he requires 65 people; for 20–25 million packs per year, 80 people; for 25–30 million packs per year, 100 people; for 30–35 million packs per year, 125 people, and to produce 35–40 million packs he requires 135 people.

These figures are for the production of normal sized packs; an additional 10% more people would be required if the packs were large size.

A Decision Support Systems' Approach

The DSS designer would look for the simplest relation that would generate appropriately accurate values for the number of people required. A straight line relation might be considered: plotting the values for normal sized packs produces Figure 15.2.

The points suggest that a straight line relation between output and number of people required may indeed adequately represent the real world situation, since as shown in table 15.1, the fit of the straight line to the points is very close for all output volumes between 20 and 40 million packs per year.

The relations to predict the number of people are as follows:

If PACK SIZE is NORMAL

Then NO. OF PEOPLE REQUIRED = –10 + 4 x OUTPUT

If PACK SIZE is LARGE

Then NO. OF PEOPLE REQUIRED = –10 + (4 x OUTPUT) x 11/10

There are just two rules to cover the whole range of outputs to be considered. The match of the predicted and specified data is set out in Table 15.1.

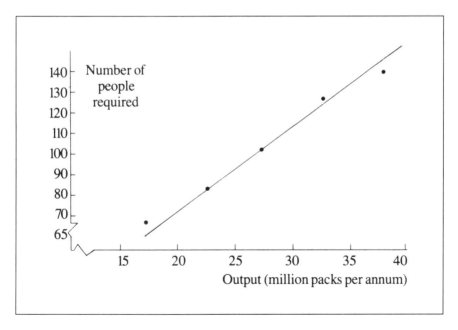

Figure 15.2   The Relationship between Output and Number of
People required

Table 15.1   Comparison of the Number of People Required for the Production of Normal Sized Packs

Output million pa	Numbers of people required		
	Specified	From graph	Difference
15–20	65	60	–5
20–25	80	80	0
25–30	100	100	0
30–35	125	120	–5
35-40	135	140	+5

An Expert Systems' Approach

A 'typical' Expert System would not convert the manager's knowledge into a mathematical model, but would attempt to construct a model that remained transparent to the manager. Thus the model might be as follows:

If OUTPUT is MORE THAN OR EQUAL TO 15 AND LESS THAN 20 MILLION
And the PACK SIZE is NORMAL
Then NO. OF PEOPLE REQUIRED = 65

If OUTPUT is MORE THAN OR EQUAL TO 15 AND LESS THAN 20 MILLION
And the PACK SIZE is LARGE
Then NO. OF PEOPLE REQUIRED = 72

If OUTPUT is MORE THAN OR EQUAL TO 20 AND LESS THAN 25 MILLION
And the PACK SIZE is NORMAL
Then NO. OF PEOPLE REQUIRED = 80

If OUTPUT is MORE THAN OR EQUAL TO 20 AND LESS THAN 25 MILLION
And the PACK SIZE is LARGE
Then NO. OF PEOPLE REQUIRED = 88

If OUTPUT is MORE THAN OR EQUAL TO 25 AND LESS THAN 30 MILLION
And the PACK SIZE is NORMAL
Then NO. OF PEOPLE REQUIRED = 100

If OUTPUT is MORE THAN OR EQUAL TO 25 AND LESS THAN 30 MILLION
And the PACK SIZE is LARGE
Then NO. OF PEOPLE REQUIRED = 110

If OUTPUT is MORE THAN OR EQUAL TO 30 AND LESS THAN 35 MILLION
And the PACK SIZE is NORMAL
Then NO. OF PEOPLE REQUIRED = 125

If OUTPUT is MORE THAN OR EQUAL TO 30 AND LESS THAN 35 MILLION
And the PACK SIZE is LARGE
Then NO. OF PEOPLE REQUIRED = 138

If OUTPUT is MORE THAN OR EQUAL TO 35 AND LESS THAN 40 MILLION
And the PACK SIZE is NORMAL
Then NO. OF PEOPLE REQUIRED = 135

If OUTPUT is MORE THAN OR EQUAL TO 35 AND LESS THAN 40 MILLION
And the PACK SIZE is LARGE
Then NO. OF PEOPLE REQUIRED = 149

This 'Expert System' model consists of 10 rules rather than the two of the mathematical model. However, it has the attraction that the rules will be readily understandable by the expert (their meaning being obvious or transparent). It also has the apparent attraction that it seems to reflect faithfully what the manager really meant. But is the production system such that the number of people required is a stepped; e.g. is the number of people required the same for all outputs of one size of pack between 15 and 20 millions? If so, then the rules typifying Expert System rules are a true reflection of the real situation, whilst the mathematical model relations are not. The reverse may be the case, and it is for the decision maker/expert and system designer to determine the appropriate form for the model.

The production modelling described above illustrates the combinatorial problems associated with many expert systems. With just 5 states of the variable OUTPUT and 2 states of the variable PACK SIZE there are $(5 \times 2) = 10$ rules. It can be seen that if one had 4 variables each with 3 states then the number of combinations of variables and thus the number of rules would be $3 \times 3 \times 3 \times 3 = 81$. In contrast, putting each variable as a mathematical relation would produce just 4 relations.

The states of the variables used in an Expert System are important in that their number determine the discriminatory power of the system. This is what Waterman (1986) calls granularity. This simply means the level of detail at which the knowledge should be represented.

A contrast is often made between the models in DSS and those in Expert Systems in that Expert Systems are dealing largely with heuristics and that DSS seldom do. Whilst on balance this difference undoubtably exists, it is a difference in emphasis. DSS do contain heuristics in the form of judgemental relations, and Expert Systems need to contain mathematical relations to overcome the combinatorial problems discussed above. The bank lending system quoted in O'Keefe et al. (1986) as an example of an Expert System contains many rules that are little short of definitional, or have been derived from prediction of failure models. Again, any management scientist worthy of his salt has devised judgemental rules and implemented these in a DSS.

One apparently fundamental difference between DSS and Expert Systems is that DSS has a data model, with the Expert System concerned solely with words – with text. However, whilst DSS in general are predominantly concerned with numbers, the Preference Determination and Scenario Development Systems (discussed in Chapters 7 and 8 respectively) are more concerned with text. Also, Expert Systems often include a database and a further quantitative data model may be constructed from the user's responses to the questions asked. In fact, one of the standard methods of representing data in Expert Systems is through the use of frames, an approach that is almost identical to that taken in database design.

Thus in terms of data and logic models and knowledge bases, Expert Systems and DSS have much in common.

The Inference Engine

The inference engine of an Expert System takes the rules that define how the expert processes his factual knowledge and interprets them as appropriate. Unlike a simple conventional computer program, the steps are not sequentially determined by the programmer, but follow from the data input and the results obtained at earlier stages in the use of the system. This difference is not as marked as this brief description might suggest, since DSS invariably have 'branching' instructions within them. Again, some of the DSS tools now available allow a DSS developer to put in the rules in any sequence he likes, allowing the most appropriate sequence of rule firings to be determined by the inference engine: this facility has been offered by the financial planning package System-W since the early 1980s.

The inference engine works in either forward chaining or backward chaining mode or both. Suppose in a very simple Expert System to determine the number of MANAGERS to employ for two production situations. The following set of rules might apply.

If OUTPUT is BETWEEN 15 AND 20 MILLION
And the PACK SIZE is NORMAL
Then NO. OF PEOPLE REQUIRED = 65

If OUTPUT is BETWEEN 15 AND 20 MILLION
And the PACK SIZE is LARGE
Then NO. OF PEOPLE REQUIRED = 72

If NO. OF PEOPLE REQUIRED is 65
Then MANAGERS = 1

If NO. OF PEOPLE REQUIRED is 72
Then MANAGERS = 2

In forward chaining, the required factual knowledge is asked of the user to provide values for the output and then the pack size. This allows the number of people required to be calculated. With this information the rules assuming knowledge of the number of managers required would be searched and the appropriate one 'fired'. In the above example, for an output of between 15 and 20 million large sized packs, the number of people required would be calculated as 72. This value would fire the fourth rule above specifying that two managers should be employed.

In backward chaining, the ultimate goal would first be examined. This is the number of managers to employ. To determine this requires that the number of people required be known, and this in turn requires that the output and pack size be known. This information would then be sought.

Interestingly, a parallel exists with the operation of financial planning software. Usually the forward chaining mode is used. However, it is becoming increasingly commonplace for backward chaining (sometimes known as Backward Iteration or Goal Seeking) to be available. In this mode, the user is able to ask 'What must?' questions such as 'What must Sales be in order that the company makes a Profit of 1Mn?'

The Natural Language Interface

Over many years the information technology industry has moved progressively towards making computer systems more accessible to the end user. One way this has been accomplished is through improvements in the interface between user and computer, so much so in fact that even Board members (albeit only a few of them) are now using DSS directly (see the discussion on Executive Information Systems in Chapter 5). The Expert Systems' interface would be designed so that the interface would change depending on whether an expert or a naive user is using the system, and on the answers given to questions already asked. There are parallels here to much of present user interface design. This book is being typed using a word processor where three different forms of human-computer interaction can be used: for example, one mode is where instructions are only given on the screen if the user is slow with his keystroking.

The Explanation Program

There is no real equivalent to such a program in DSS. Until recently, it has been one of the roles of the intermediary who has used the DSS to understand it and interpret its output for the decision maker. In this regard, the intermediary was part of the DSS, and it was he who provided the 'explanation program'. When a manager is using a DSS directly, especially when he has designed the system himself or played a large part in its development, he will understand its workings to some extent and explanation and insight will come naturally from its use.

However, the power of current explanation facilities offered by Expert Systems leave a great deal to be desired. The author has not seen any that do more than expose to the user the sequence in which the rules were used. Given the highly constrained format of the Expert Systems programs these so-called explanations are little more than debugging tools that a system designer would use. Exceptionally, Expert System designers program in specific explanations to overcome these restrictions. Interestingly, the financial planning package Javelin has the facility for showing its rules and the path whereby a variable is calculated from the sequence of values obtained by other rules.

The Knowledge Refining Program

It is intended in Expert Systems that the expert uses a knowledge refining program himself to amend and add knowledge to the system. This intention comes from the view that Expert Systems are 'transparent', gaining over some DSS in that the logic used is set out clearly and can be understood by the expert. In the author's experience there are no currently available knowledge refining programs that are good enough to allow a naive user of the program (albeit an expert of his particular domain) to alter an Expert System of size greater than a couple of dozen rules.

In a similar fashion, as DSS are developed, extended and maintained, a means of refining the logic is needed. Normally this is just the language of the standard package used or one of the common general purpose languages such as BASIC and FORTRAN. To use them requires considerable expertise, provided by the system designer/maintainer.

SYSTEMS DEVELOPMENT IN DECISION SUPPORT SYSTEMS AND IN EXPERT SYSTEMS

When confronting the managerial situation at the beginning of the development of the Expert System, the designer will have to determine the variables of importance from discussion with the manager and through his own knowledge. He would be aided in doing this by concentrating on the manager's decision, environmental and output variables.

An Expert System is likely to be dealing with only one part of the overall managerial problem and must be set in the context of a wider framework similar to a scenario, so that the initial phase of developing an Expert System is analogous to that for mathematical models. Expert Systems for decision support must be embedded into the manager's wider perspective. Reasons for keeping a human associated with an Expert System are itemised by Waterman (1986) – in contrast with Expert Systems, humans are creative, adaptive, have sensory experience, have a broad focus and commonsense knowledge.

A 'breadboarding' approach to the development of Expert Systems has been advocated. In the author's experience, this approach is suitable at the beginning of Expert System development, especially for the development of small-scale systems: it is not suitable for larger-scale systems. Here, the system development cycle is more applicable, as would be expected of systems where the goal of the system must be specified before development can begin.

A significant difference in the development of DSS and Expert Systems lies in the ambition of the DSS developer, especially in the development of quantitative DSS. He is concerned with using the power of mathematics to the full, and the full power only becomes available when the model is developed at levels of measurement higher than the nominal and ordinal, i.e. when one moves away from simply ordering quantities by magnitude. Operating with these levels of measurement, the mathematical modeller is further removed conceptually from the client than is the Expert System modeller, who is content to remain at the ordinal level and thus with more transparent models. This smaller conceptual gulf between the modeller's and manager's world is likely to lead to Expert Systems gaining more acceptance than have mathematical models. This would follow the path taken by Data Retrieval Systems vis-a-vis Extrapolatory Systems, where the arithmetical models of Data Retrieval Systems have been more widely accepted (because of the greater transparency) than have the mathematical models of Extrapolatory Systems.

EXPERT SYSTEMS IN THE TYPOLOGY OF DECISION SUPPORT SYSTEMS

Several classifications of Expert Systems have been made (see, for example, Alty and Coombs (1984). In this book, the major classification of DSS has been between MIS and MINTS, and a similar division might be sought for Expert System. However, since Expert Systems work in well structured domains they are firmly on the MIS side of DSS, not MINTS.

Data Retrieval Systems are those operating in a known, or at least knowable world, where the outcomes are all specified, exhaustive and mutually exclusive. Most Expert Systems are of this form. An example is a system to decide whether a claimant is eligible for Social Security benefit. Here there is a 'right' answer.

In contradistinction, the Expert Systems that are of the Extrapolatory System type will be such that outcomes are not exhaustive or mutually exclusive, and where conjecture plays a part. Here there is no 'right' answer. Knowledge is difficult to elicit, little of it will have been documented, some of it will never even have been unambiguously articulated. The Expert System will be providing insights to the user – in a way very similar to that offered to the user of a financial planning system for example. Examples of such Expert Systems are those used in the medical domain where the systems do not take into account all aspects of a patient's condition (for example, the patient's demeanour and attitude).

When using such an Expert System, as with any other Extrapolatory System, the user is not surrendering his judgement, rather he is using the system to enhance his judgement.

Decision Support and Expert System Terminology

One reason why DSS and Expert Systems seem so different is due to the different nomenclature used by the workers in the two fields.

The terms used in both disciplines are summarised and compared in Table 15.2. On balance a common terminology would be advantageous, and it is suggested that the terms 'Relation', 'Domain', 'Knowledge Base' 'Data Base' and 'Knowledge Engineer' be used by both parties.

SUMMARY

Superficially, Expert Systems and DSS appear to have little in common. However, with the exception of granularity and the availability of explanatory programs, the features of the two types of system show substantial overlap. This leads on to the recommendation that DSS designers and the builders of Expert Systems move towards using the same nomenclature.

Although Expert Systems and DSS exhibit many common features, the difference between the two is primarily one of emphasis in the employment of these features: for example, both are likely to include heuristics and both are likely to include mathematical relations, but with many more heuristics in an Expert System and many more mathematical relations in a DSS.

Table 15.2   Nomenclature Used

Decision support systems	Expert systems
Relation	Rule
Range of application of the model	Domain
Logic model	Knowledge base
Data model	Datbase
Modeller	Knowledge engineer
Designer	Designer

Since the goals of Expert Systems are fully specified before substantive development takes place, they are all MIS. In the typology of DSS most current Expert Systems would be classified as Data Retrieval Systems. A few are Extrapolatory Systems.

REFERENCES

Alty J.L. and Coombs M.J., (1984) *Expert Systems-Concepts and Examples*, NCC Publications, Manchester, England.

Bramer M., (1982) *A Survey and Critical Review of Expert Systems Research*, Introductory Readings in Expert Systems, Gordon and Breach.

O'Keefe R.M., Belton V. and Ball T. (1986) *Experiences Using Expert Systems in O.R.*, Journal of the Operational Research Society, Vol.37, pp 657–668.

Simons G.L., (1984) *Introducing Artificial Intelligence*, NCC Publications, Manchester, UK.

Waterman D.A., (1986) *A Guide to Expert Systems*, Addison Wesley.

16 The Future of Decision Support Systems

DECISION SUPPORT SYSTEMS DEVELOPMENTS IN RETROSPECT

In this book DSS have been considered in terms of a set of system types, in which the major contrast has been made between systems that primarily support decision efficiency (MIS) and those that primarily support decision effectiveness (MINTS). Historically, all or almost all the emphasis in DSS has been with MIS, concerned with doing the thing right, rather than with MINTS which are concerned with doing the right thing.

Satisfactory Data Retrieval Systems are established in most organisations today, and Extrapolatory Systems have also been successfully implemented. In the early days, Extrapolatory Systems were overly concerned with optimisation and with so-called objectivity (see Ackoff (1977)). As managers seldom work with optima and subjectivity is present in most decision making, these features of DSS did not fit easily with the way managers thought and operated.

The one area of Extrapolatory Systems that has been a conspicuous success has been that involving spreadsheets, and here, most tellingly, the cognitive coupling between model and user is usually very close. The limitations of the spreadsheet are its great strength – the spreadsheet appears like one of the large pieces of columnar paper beloved of accountants, and what is displayed on the screen is what can be printed off on to a sheet of paper.

A major cognitive difficulty is the problem managers have in coping with inexactitude. Data Retrieval Systems deal with the past and in 'facts': inexactitude does not intrude on this deterministic world. In contrast, Extrapolatory Systems and MINTS are looking into the future, into a world that is most certainly not deterministic. Extrapolatory Systems tend to deal with fairly well defined uncertainty, whereas MINTS are concerned with less well structured situations. Most people cannot cope with risk or uncertainty in any formal fashion, and baulk at trying to do so.

Further reasons why the emphasis has been on MIS arises from a mismatch between the available systems software and the decision making processes in organisations. For many years, computers have had the raw power to help with decision support outside of MIS. It has been the economic and commercial imperatives that have driven and kept the concentration on MIS.

Until very recently, information technology has been concerned solely with processing quantitative material. Decision making, especially at the more strategic levels of an organisation, tends to be qualitative and messy. Both features are little in evidence in conventional computer systems, and consequently computers have had little impact in this area. Another reason why DSS have had little impact outside of MIS is that they have been concerned very much with helping individual managers in their jobs, rather than at helping managers in group decision making. The esoteric nature of many DSS has precluded their use by anyone other than their specialist creators. This emphasis on individuality was evident until recently in MIS, where the systems software was such that information systems had to be implemented for each specific manager. With the widespread use of database management systems, MIS can now be implemented that satisfy many users from the same body of data.

Finally, the emphasis in many DSS has been on analysis – the area where the management scientist excelled – rather than on the need to promote action through involvement and through consensus. Also, the emphasis has been on restructuring a manager's thought processes towards a more scientific. rational direction, rather than accepting his decision approaches and working to support them.

LONG-TERM TRENDS IN INFORMATION TECHNOLOGY

Hall (1983) sees a steady evolutionary development with the use of information technology (IT) in organisations. In the first stage, independent and self-contained Electronic Data Processing Systems supporting routine transaction processing were implemented. The second stage was the linking of Electronic Data Processing Systems and the expansion of such systems to encompass non-transactionary tasks such as capital budgeting. The next stage was the implementation of MIS to provide all organisational units with the information that they needed to perform efficiently. The fourth stage is concerned with supporting ill-structured decisions. We are presently moving into this fourth phase, albeit slowly. In large commercial organisations in the UK, typically 10% of the budget spent on DSS is spent on MINTS, with the remaining 90% spent on MIS. The proportion spent on MINTS is increasing.

This trend is encouraging, but should be seen in the light of other IT developments vying for the same limited resources.

Hall was concerned with trends in the level of organisational use of IT. Additionally, there has been a continuous trend towards end user computing, with much more user-friendly human-computer interfaces, and much more powerful and easy to use software, particularly the widespread availability of packages aimed at particular applications (good examples here are spreadsheets, simulation and project scheduling packages). There has also been the trend for almost all hardware to become ever smaller, cheaper and more widely available.

A more subtle but equally important development has been the move to 'modularise' computer systems. This development has made great advances through the use of database management systems that separate data from the applications in which they are used. This separation of data model from logic model provides considerable flexibility to meet a variety of information needs. As will be seen later when Expert Systems are discussed, this move to modularise systems is being extended to the creation of knowledge bases.

INFORMATION TECHNOLOGY TAKES CENTRE STAGE

Many organisations are now becoming to realise that it is imperative that they develop an IT strategy. The basis for this imperative is that Business is becoming ever more competitive, with tighter margins and with companies needing to become ever more selective in the identification of customers and segments.

The literature contains many examples of the use of IT for competitive advantage. The successes have been analysed and a number of frameworks suggested to help organisations search for strategic applications (*see*, for example, Earl (1989)). The concept though is still relatively new and not fully understood. Vitale's (1986) analysis provided a more sober perspective in recognising that IT initiatives could have unintended, negative, competitive consequences. Johnston and Cararico (1988) have investigated factors that influence strategic IT developments. In his book on expert systems, Chorafas (1987) lists 20 examples whereby organisations have used IT for competitive advantage. Porter and Millar (1985) mentions a further 30 examples.

THE SUSTAINABILITY OF AN INFORMATION TECHNOLOGY ADVANTAGE

The major problem with attempting to obtain competitive advantage through the use of IT is that IT is easily transferable. Consider the early uses of computers for data processing. In a relatively short time, most large organisations introduced computerised systems for order processing, inventory control and the common accounting routines. Any advantage that one organisation had over another quickly evaporated as others followed suit. Additionally, the first organisations into computers often suffered high implementation costs (not suffered by the followers as more expertise was gained). Thus any (tactical) gains of being first in the field seemed to be counterbalanced somewhat by the disadvantages of being a pioneer.

Vitale (1986) discusses specific examples where IT had given an initial advantage, but had not been sustained. An example is the eventual Government intervention to resolve the claims against United and American's airline reservation system. They also discuss an appliance company's initial information systems success changing into competitive failure as a major competitor implemented a similar but more modern and accessible system.

The situation has altered somewhat since the early days, because at that time the only computers available were the expensive mainframes, and these could only be afforded by the large companies (and thus their use by such companies should in theory have increased their advantage over the smaller ones who could not afford them). Now appropriate computer power is available to small and big organisations alike. Also, in the early days organisations had to develop a large portion of the software themselves, putting a premium on the efficient use of skilled computer staff. Today, higher level languages, wider computer literacy and inexpensive packages have brought sophisticated software to most organisations. The transferability of IT has increased, and is likely to go on increasing especially in the era of Open Systems.

This transferability is not restricted to general purpose hardware and software. For example, the Management Science techniques for reducing transportation costs have not stayed with a single company; other Management Science groups have followed suit, and any initial competitive advantage for the pioneer has been lost.

Although IT and its associated techniques are relatively easily transferable, what is much less transferable is the ability of the people within an organisation to use the information that IT makes available. This is especially true of the decision making processes embedded within an organisation. It is within the 'soft' parts of an organisation that sustainable competitive advantage can be found: in the context of IT it is within the decision making processes that competitive advantage might best be sought.

FUTURE DEVELOPMENTS IN DECISION SUPPORT SYSTEMS

Although the technology of DSS is now reasonably well established, there remains a substantial mismatch between the information and intelligence made available, and that necessary for managerial decision making. There is also a mismatch between the means by which information is made available and intelligence is produced. This is especially true at strategic levels, where the need is to be able to handle qualitative, ill-structured and messy information. Most present DSS are only able to handle quantitative, certain and well defined data.

Three general areas can be identified where the future thrusts of DSS lie. These are improvements in current DSS (generally single-user DSS), the inclusion of Expert System methodologies into DSS, and developments in Group DSS. In all cases there will be strong moves into the softer, more qualitative areas.

Improvements in Present Decision Support Systems

Around a decade ago, Carlson (1982) investigated 56 DSS and identified the following problems with DSS current at that time.

1. Existing DSS do not provide decision makers with familiar representations which support conceptualization. In addition, the decision maker is often forced to deal with concepts (e.g. flowcharts) and representations (e.g. printouts) which are unfamiliar and have little to do with the way the decision maker usually conceptualizes the decision.

2. (a) Existing DSS tend to segment Intelligence, Design and Choice activities, whereas decision makers tend to integrate them. For example, Alter's data-oriented systems primarily support Intelligence activities, but not Design or Choice, and the model-oriented systems primarily support Design and Choice and assume Intelligence has been completed. [Author's note: this is using Simon's terminology mentioned in Chapter 2].

    (b) Existing DSS tend to support a single decision making process.

3. (a) Existing DSS provide long-term memory aids (i.e. a data base) but do not provide short-term memory aids. For example, the scratch paper and staff reminders to which a decision maker is accustomed are not available in most DSS.

    (b) Existing DSS impose additional memory requirements, such as learning the names of the data in the DSS, and often the DSS does not provide memory aids to support these requirements.

4. (a) Existing DSS do not provide enough control aids to help the decision maker learn the new skills (e.g. signing on to a computer terminal), styles (e.g. automated support rather than manual), and knowledge base (e.g. learning what the operations do) which a DSS introduces.

    (b) Existing DSS replace direct control with indirect control, where one or more intermediaries interpret the DSS capabilities and outputs for the decision maker. This type of control introduces the well-known communication problem.

It is interesting to see how far these criticism have been met by developments during the 1980s and early 1990s. The cases were investigated towards the end of the 1970s, when microcomputers were in their infancy. Certainly any form of managerial input other than by keyboard was almost unheard of. Outputs were restricted to printouts – often voluminous ones – or to very crude graphics: colour was a rarity. The ability of managers to get quick ad-hoc information was very restricted.

The situation today is very different. Many representations of information are now available (very powerful graphics in full colour for example), as are methods for inputting data and selecting information: this is particularly true in Executive Information Systems with mouse and touch screens available.

Criticism 2 is still valid for most DSS today, although the linking of the logic modelling of Extrapolatory Systems with the database technologies and design methodologies used in Data Retrieval Systems has led to much more powerful decision support, and support that integrates the phases of decision making. It is still rare for a DSS to support more than a single decision making process. However, Decision Conferencing (see Chapter 9) does make several decision support techniques explicitly available. Cognitive Mapping (see Chapter 8) and Soft Systems Methodology are approaches that support almost any type of process through the flexibility of the process of decision support.

Short-term memory aids in the form of diaries and electronic notepads are becoming increasingly available. In this regard criticism 3 is becoming less significant. However, many managers still find the effort of using a DSS to be too great, outweighing the gains that they perceive they will get from its use. This is particularly so for the intermittent user. Managers are happy to let others use systems to provide them with information: by doing so they are failing to utilise the system as a learning aid. To refer back to Earl's somewhat cynical view described in Chapter 4, managers are seeking answers when they should be seeking insights.

Criticism 4 seems somewhat ill-directed even in 1980. The DSS were only replacing direct control with indirect control because the use of sophisticated techniques made this worthwhile. Today, the human-computer interfaces are far more user-friendly, allowing managers to use DSS based on sophisticated DSS techniques. A good example of this is the What'sBest package: with its very user-friendly data entry and sensitivity analysis, it makes available to non-expert users the formally esoteric technique of linear programming.

Integrating Expert Systems and Decision Support Systems

In the last chapter, the notion that Expert Systems are independent, computerised systems that support decision makers was examined. Here a further view is taken, that of Expert Systems as a component of DSS.

There is no doubt that what are sometimes considered uniquely Expert System features are becoming available in DSS (see, for example, Ignizio, 1991). In particular, the 'front-end' capabilities for providing easy-to-use human-computer interaction are available for DSS developments. The use of such natural language interfaces should considerably increase the accessibility of DSS to managers.

Expert Systems are constructed to make decisions, and so tend to replace the decision maker. Whilst DSS has generally emphasised the matching of the system to the personality and abilities of managers, Expert Systems developers have needed to determine the cognitive processes of the expert in order to include them in the system. This is an area where Expert System developments can extend DSS, by encompassing some of the more common heuristics, freeing the decision maker to concentrate on the more nebulous areas. This is similar to the use of discounted cash flow techniques within a DSS aiding an investment appraisal by freeing the decision makers from tedious calculations.

One area of Expert Systems that is currently being strongly researched is knowledge acquisition – how to extract the knowledge held by the expert that is difficult to identify and articulate. This is an area where the results of the research will be of great assistance to the designers of DSS.

Another area in which researchers are showing great interest is that of knowledgebases, whereby the flexibility offered by database management systems to store and access data is parallelled by knowledgebase management systems to store and access knowledge. Almost all DSS have within themselves the logic suitable for their own specific applications, and some of these relations are likely to be used elsewhere in the organisation in other DSS. Database management systems have solved the problems associated with data inconsistency: knowledgebase management systems would aim to do the same for knowledge. With the difficulties found in 'down loading' knowledge from experts, it is important to store this knowledge and be able to retrieve it efficiently once the knowledge has been elicited.

Group Decision Support Systems

Management development takes two forms: development for the individual manager and development of the management of an organisation as a whole – organisational development. Although there is healthy movement towards greater professionalism of the individual manager, there is also a strong pressures towards organisational development. This favours the continued research into Group DSS, and the implementation of systems to aid group decision making processes.

Adequate Decision Room technology is currently available, and with Executive Information Systems well past the prototype stage, there are likely to be many implementations of Decision Rooms over the next few years.

SUMMARY

DSS are barely 15 years old and the advances in them have been startling, both in terms of the techniques on offer and on the user-friendliness that they provide. There is still some way to go however before their use, apart from spreadsheets, becomes part and parcel of a manager's professional life. As information technology further pervades his working environment and the use of a workstation becomes a normal part of everyday working – for electronic mail or some other reason – the barriers to the use of computers generally and to the use of DSS in particular will break down.

DSS developments will be achieved more quickly and with greater user involvement through the use of the fourth generation languages that are now readily available. These tools allow prototyping to be used far more widely than simply the speedy development of input and output formats. Expert system advances, such as those in knowledge elicitation and knowledgebase management systems will find widespread application in the development of DSS.

The enhancement of decision making through the use of DSS and the embedding of new IT-led processes of decision making into an organisation is one of the few ways that competitive advantage through IT can be sustained. With data processing now firmly established in most organisations, the move will be to further enhance MIS and to move forcefully into MINTS.

REFERENCES

Ackoff R.L., *Optimization + Objectivity = Optout*, (1977) European Journal of Operational Research, Vol.1, pp 1–7

Carlson E.D., (1982) *An Approach for Designing Decision Support Systems, Chapter 2 in Building Decision Support Systems*, J.L.Bennett (ed.), Addison-Wesley Series on Decision Support, Addison-Wesley.

Chorafas D.N., (1987) *Applying Expert Systems in Business*, McGraw Hill, New York.

Earl M.J., (1989) *Management Strategies for Information Technology*, Business Information Technology Series, Prentice Hall.

Hall J.A., (1983) *Management Information Systems*, Management Accounting, July, pp 10, 23

Ignizio J.P., (1991) *Introduction to Expert Systems: The Development and Implementation of Rule-based Expert Systems*, McGraw-Hill.

Johnston H.R. and Carrico S.R., (1988) *Developing Capabilities to Use Information Strategically*, MIS Quarterly, Vol.12, No.1, March, pp.37–48.

Porter M.E. and Millar V.E., (1985) *How Information Gives You Competitive Advantage*, Harvard Business Review, July–August, pp.149–160.

Vitale M.R., (1986) *The Growing Risks of Information Systems Success*, MIS Quarterly, Vol.10, No.4, December, pp.327–334.

Appendix A

System Definitions

System   In the context of computer systems, a system will be considered any combination of logic and data models and user interface used to provide information and/or intelligence.

Information   Data that is seen to be relevant or potentially relevant to a manager in his job.

Intelligence   The outcome of the meshing and reconciliation of a set of information carrying inferences.

Decision Support System (DSS)   To support decision making, a system must be capable of doing one or more of the following: help deal with uncertainty: help managers form preferences: enhance the ability of managers to make judgements. For a system to be considered a DSS, it should also involve a significant use of information technology.

Management Information System   A system to provide management with information.

Data Retrieval System   A Management Information System that is limited to the retrieval and analysis of past data.

File Drawer System   A system that provides a simple 'look-up' facility, with no analysis of data.

Data Analysis System   A system that provides predetermined analyses of past data.

Executive Information System   A Management Information System designed for the use of senior management. A feature that tends to distinguish such systems from other Management Information Systems is that information external to the organisation is also provided by the system.

Extrapolatory System A Management Information System that uses past data, or information in the form of cause and effect relationships, to predict possible states in the future.

Definitional System A system whose logic model consists solely of relations that are defined to be as they are.

Causal System A system that predicts future outcomes using cause and effect relations.

Probabilistic System A system that explicitly includes probabilistic features in a quantitative manner within the system.

Management Intelligence System A system that enhances decision making in high or ill-defined uncertainty, by evolving, structuring and evaluating relationships and/or options. Such systems take information as input, reconcile and mesh together these input to form intelligence.

Preference Determination System A system that assists in formulating and exposing the structure of a decision-making situation and evaluates the outcomes.

Decision Tree System A system whereby the consequences of a chronological sequence of decisions can be identified.

Multi-attribute Decision System A system which allows the consequences of judgements about preferences to be exposed and explored.

Scenario Development System A system that allows ideas and concepts to be logically analysed and linked, in order to help form a more appropriate scenario. Often these systems are used in a group context in which scenarios are developed through the integration of managers' perceptions, leading to the agreement of objectives through negotiation and consensus.

Cognitive Mapping System A system that allows the articulated thought processes of managers to be exposed, codified and analysed. The result is a cognitive map that shows the underlying cause and effect relations and other cognitive links between concepts.

Ideas Generation System A system to support the unearthing of novel ways for tackling problems.

Appendix B

Quantitative Scales of Measurement

A QUANTITATIVE measurement is defined as the systematic assignment of numbers to individuals in a group in order to represent one of their attributes. Under this definition measurement can be any of four levels – nominal, ordinal, interval and ratio. Each level has a characteristic not present at a lower level, as shown in Table B.1.

Table B.1   Scales of Measurement

Characteristic	Nominal	Ordinal	Interval	Ratio
Distinctiveness	*	*	*	*
Ordering in Magnitude		*	*	*
Equal Intervals			*	*
Absolute Zero				*

NOMINAL measurement has only the characteristic of distinctiveness. On this level of measurement the different numbers given to individuals in the group only indicate a difference between the individuals. If in a collection of vegetables it is decided to assign the number 0 to cabbages, 1 to beetroots, 2 to peas and so on, the numbers distinguish between the various kinds of vegetable, but in no sense is it implied that peas are any more of a vegetable than are beetroots.

ORDINAL measurements order individuals according to the magnitude of an attribute they possess: the higher the number assigned, the more of the attribute the individual possesses. If the height order of individuals in a group were to be indicated, then a low number (say 1) would be assigned to the smallest individual, a higher number (say 2) to the next smallest and so on. The greater the height the greater the number: but note, there is no implication that an individual with rank 3 say, is 2 units of any meaningful measure higher than the individual with a rank of 1.

Ordinal measures do not say anything about how much more of an attribute one individual has than another; only that he has more or less, or the same. An INTERVAL level of measurement is needed in order to signify the amount of an attribute. What is required is that equal differences between measurements be represented by the same amount of difference of the attribute being measured. Temperature measurements using a Centigrade or Fahrenheit thermometer are examples of an interval scale of measurement. For a given individual, a 3 degree rise in temperature when the individual is cold represents the same amount of change in heat as a 3 degree rise in temperature when the individual is hot.

Lastly there is the RATIO level of measurement. This level occurs when a measurement of zero represents the absence of a property being measured. The ordinary ruler has this property for measuring length: zero length is represented by zero on this scale.

Whilst mathematical manipulation can be performed at any level of measurement, there are great limitations in what can be done if low levels of measurement have to be used. For example, the simple mathematical operations of addition, subtraction, etc, have no meaning when a nominal scale is used. Measurements on an ordinal scale may be manipulated mathematically but the results are not always very meaningful. It is only with interval or ratio levels of measurement that the real power of mathematical modelling can be deployed: and this is only possible when the characteristic of equal intervals is present.

Appendix C
List of Decision Support Software

PACKAGE NAME, CONTACT, ADDDRESS AND TELEPHONE NUMBER

(All addresses in the UK unless otherwise stated)

1,2,3 Forecast!	Distributed in Europe by 4-5-6 World Ltd., Wellington House, Butt Road, Colchester, Essex CO3 3DA, (0206) 44456.
Autobox	Automatic Forecasting Systems Inc., PO Box 563, Hatboro., PA 19040, USA (215) 675-0652.
BrainStorm	BrainStorm Software, Canada House, 272 Field End Road, Eastcote, Middlesex HA4 9NA, (081) 866 4400.
CA-SuperCalc	Computer Associates Ltd., Computer Associates House, 183/187 Bath Road, Slough, Berks. SL1 4AA, (0753) 577733.
CA-SuperProject	Computer Associates Ltd., see above.
Command Center	Pilot Executive Software, Pilot House, Abbey Green, Chertsey, Surrey KT16 8RF, (0932) 569944.
Commander EIS	Comshare, 22, Chelsea Manor Street, London SW3 5RL, (071) 351-4399.
COPE	Professor Colin Eden, Department of Managenment Science, Strathclyde Business School, Livingstone Tower, 26, Richmond Street, Glasgow G1 1XH, (041) 552 4400.
Criterium	Sygenex Inc., 15446 Bel-Red Road, Suite 540, Redmond, WA 98052, USA, (303) 292-2291.

DATA	TreeAge Software Inc., 23rd Floor, One Post Office Square, Boston, Mass 02109, USA, (617) 426-5819.
DataEase	Public Sector Software Ltd., The Maltings, 55 Bath Street, Gravesend, Kent DA11 0AH, (0474) 329932.
DBase	Borland International(UK), 8 Pavilions, Ruscombe Business Park, Twyford, Berks. RG10 9NN, (0734) 320022.
EMPOWER	Metapraxis Ltd., Hanover House, Coombe Road, Kingston upon Thames, Surrey, KT2 7AH, (081) 546 2105: Metapraxix Inc., 900 Third Avenue, 36th Floor, New York, NY 10022, USA, (212) 935 4322.
Epic	Planning Sciences Ltd., Tuition House, St George's Road, Wimbledon, London SW19 4EU (081) 879-3828.
Excel	Microsoft, Excel House, 84 Caversham Road, Reading, Berks. RG1 8LP, (0734) 500741.
Expert Choice	Decision Support Software Inc., 4922 Ellsworth Avenue, Pittsburgh, PA 14213, USA, (412) 682-3844.
Express	Information Resources, Foundation Park, Roxborough Way, Maidenhead, Berks. SL6 3UD, (0628) 411000.
Express/EIS	Information Resources, see above.
FCS-MULTI	Pilot Software Ltd, Pilot House, Abbey Green, Chertsey, Surrey KT16 8RF, (0932) 569944.
FORECALC	Business Forecast Systems Inc., 68, Leonard Street, Belmont, MA 02178, USA, (617) 484-5050.
FORECAST!	Intex Solutions Inc., 35 Highland Circle, Needham, MA 02194, USA, (617) 449-6222.
FORECAST/DSS	Management Editor, John Wiley and Sons Inc., 605 Third Avenue, New York, NY 10158, USA, (800) 225-5495.
Forest & Trees	European Software Publishing Ltd., 36 King Street, Maidenhead, Berkshire, SL6 1EF, (0628) 23453.

GPSS/H	Wolverine Software Corporation, 4115 Annandale Road, Suite 200, Annandale, VA 22003-2500, USA, (703) 750-3910.
GPSS/PC	Minuteman Software, PO Box 171, Stow, MA 01775-0171, USA, (508) 897-5662.
GroupSystems	Ventana, 1430 E. Fort Lowell Road, Suite 301, Tucson, AZ 85719, USA.
HIVIEW	IT Partners Ltd., Beaumont, Burfield Road, Old Windsor, Windsor, Berks SL4 2JP, (0753) 832888.
Holos	Holistic Systems Ltd., Suite C, 2nd Floor, International House, 7 High Street, Ealing, London W5 5DB, (081) 566 2330.
INFORMIX	INFORMIX Software Inc., 4100, Bohammon Drive, Menlo Park, CA 94025, USA, (415) 322-4100.
Ingres	The ASK Group, Ingres Technology Centre, 220 Wharfdale Road, Winnersh Triangle, Wokingham, Berks GR11 5TP, (0734) 496400.
Lightship	Pilot Software Ltd, Pilot House, Abbey Green, Chertsey, Surrey KT16 8RF. (0932) 569944.
Lightyear	Thoughtware Inc., 200 South Biscayne Blvd, Suite 2750, Miami, FL 33131, USA, (305) 854-2318.
LINDO	LINDO Systems Inc., 1415 North Dayton Street, Chicago, Ill 60622, USA, (312) 817 2524.
LINDO/PC	LINDO Systems Inc. – see above.
Lotus 1-2-3	Lotus Development (UK) Ltd., Lotus Park, The Causeway, Staines, Middx. TW18 3AG. (0784) 455445.
Lotus Improv	as above.
Lotus Notes	as above.
Microtab	Minitab Inc., 3081, Enterprise Drive, State College, PA 16801, USA. Distributed in Europe by CLE.COM – see CAPS-ECSL
Minitab	Minitab Inc., 3081, Enterprise Drive, State College, Pa 16801, USA. Distributed in Europe by CLE.COM – see CAPS-ECSL

OptionFinder	Option Technologies Ltd., Toad Hall, Odiham Road, Winchfield, Nr. Basingstoke, Hants RG27 8BU, (0252) 844720.
ORACLE	Oracle Corporation UK Ltd., The Oracle Centre, The Ring, Bracknell, Berkshire RG12 1BW, (0344) 860066.
Paradox	Borland International(UK), 8 Pavilions, Ruscombe Business Park, Twyford, Berks. RG10 9NN, (0734) 320022.
pcExpress	Information Resources – see under Express above.
PC-Model	Simulation Software Systems, 2107, North First Street, Suite 680, San Jose, CA 95131, USA.
PertMaster Advance	People in Technology Ltd., 34, London Wall, London EC2M 5QX, (071) 638 5739.
Predict!	Distributed in the UK by Risk Decisions Ltd., 27, Park End Street, Oxford OX1 1HU, (0865) 727025.
Priorities	Work Sciences Associates, 26 Southwood Lawn Road, Highgate, London N6 5SF, (081) 348 5822.
Project Managers Workbench	Hoskyns Group plc., 95, Wandsworth Road, London SW8 2BR, (071) 735-0800.
ProModelPC	Production Modeling Corporation of Utah, 1834, South State, Orem, Utah 84058, USA (801) 226-6036.
Quattro Pro	Borland International (UK), 8 Pavilions, Ruscombe Business Park, Twyford, Berks. RG10 9NN, (0734) 320022.
Sciconic	EDS-Scicon Ltd., Wavendon Tower, Wavendon, Milton Keynes MK17 8LB.
Simscript	CACI, Coliseum Business Centre, Watchmoor Park, Riverside way, Camberley, Surrey GU15 3YL, (0276) 671671. Also, 3344 N. Torrey Pines Court, La Jolla, CA 92037, USA, (619) 457-9681.
Slam	Pritsker & Associates, PO Box 2413, West Lafayette, IN 47906, USA.

SPSS	SPSS (UK) Ltd., SPSS House, 5 London Street, Chertsey, Surrey KT16 8AP, (0932) 566262.
SPSS-PC	see SPSS
Statgraphics	Cocking & Drury (Software) Ltd., 180, Tottenham Court Road, London W1P 9LE, (071) 436 9481.
STRAD	Stradspan Ltd., Sheffield Science Park, Arundel Street, Sheffield S1 2NS (0742) 724198. Also distributed by CLE.COM Ltd., The Research Park, Vincent Drive, Edgbaston, Birmingham B15 2SQ, (021) 471-4199.
SuperTree	SDG Decision Systems, Dept. 707-1, 3600, Sand Hill Road, Menlo Park, CA 94025, USA.
SystemBuild	SystemBuild Software, High Street, Market Deeping, Peterborough PE6 8ED, (0778) 344388.
System-W	Comshare – see under Commander EIS.
The SAS System	SAS Software Ltd., Wittington House, Henley Road, Medmenham, Marlow, Bucks, SL7 2EB, (0628) 486933.
TeamWorker	Decision Dynamics Ltd., PO Box 142, Parsons Walk, Wigan, Lancs WN1 1RW, (0942) 522030.
Timeserver	Pilot Executive Software, Pilot House, Abbey Green, Chertsey, Surrey KT16 8RF, (0932) 569944.
Trackstar	T & B Computing Ltd., 19, Stratford Place, London W1N 9AF, (071) 493-7546.
VISA	SPV Software Products, 6 Bonaly Steading, Edinburgh, EH13 0HA.
VisionQuest	Collaborative Technologies, 8920 Business Park Drive, Suite 100, Austin TX 78759, USA. distributed in the UK by Lloyd McKenzie & Partners, Hollybush house, Darby Green Lane, Camberley, Surrey GU17 0DL, (0252) 876635.
What's Best!	General Optimization Inc., 2251, North Geneva Terrace, Chicago, Ill. 60614, USA, (312) 248-0465. Distributed in Europe by 4-5-6 World (see 1,2,3 Forecast! above).

Witness

AT&T ISTEL Ltd., Highfield House, Headless Cross Drive, Redditch, Worcs. B97 5EQ, (0527) 550330.

XPRESSMP

Dash Associates Ltd., Blisworth House, Church Lane, Blisworth, Northants NN7 3BX, (0604) 858993.

Index